D1569591

UNDERSTANDING THE TALMUD

A Dialogic Approach

UNDERSTANDING THE TALMUD

A Dialogic Approach

JACOB NEUSNER
Bard College

KTAV PUBLISHING HOUSE, INC.
Jersey city, New Jersey

East Baton Rouge Parish Library
Baton Rouge, Louisiana

© Copyright 2004 Jacob Neusner

Library of Congress Cataloging-in-Publication Data

Neusner, Jacob, 1932-
  Understanding the Talmud : a dialogic approach / Jacob Neusner.
    p. cm.
Includes bibliographical references.
  ISBN 0-88125-736-2 (hc) -- ISBN 0-88125-739-7 (paper)
  1. Talmud--Criticism, interpretation, etc. 2. Talmud--Philosophy. I.
Title.
  BM504 .N444 2002
  296.1'2061--dc21

                          2002022828

                Manufactured in the United States of America

                          Published by
                KTAV Publishing House, Inc.
                      930 Newark Avenue
                    Jersey City, NJ 07306
                  Email: info@ktav.com
                        www.ktav.com
                      (201) 963-9524
                    Fax (201) 963-0102

CONTENTS

ACKNOWLEDGMENTS

Understanding the Talmud: A Dialogic Approach complements the companion work, *The Mishnah: Introduction and Reader, An Anthology*, Philadelphia, 1992: Trinity Press International, Library of Rabbinic Literature. These works are addressed to a broad academic audience. Within the study of Religion, with emphasis on Judaism, I emphasize direct encounter with the accessible data of the faith, which is to say, with the documents that preserve the religious experience and knowledge of the sages of Judaism. That is why I require a reader of Talmudic texts in my own teaching. I prepared this textbook for students in the academic study of Judaism and, more broadly, in the humanities. I hope others will find it useful as well.

Bard College makes much appreciated provision for my research. I thank the administration of Bard College for participating in my work, and my colleagues there for their warm welcome. I am especially fortunate to enjoy the collegiality of stimulating and interesting co-workers at Bard College.

Jacob Neusner
Research Professor of Religion and Theology
Bard College
Annandale-on-Hudson, N.Y.

I

Why the Talmud Matters

The Talmud sets forth, in a single coherent statement, the systematic presentation of the law and theology of the Torah revealed by God through Moses at Sinai to holy Israel.[1] To understand the religion, Judaism, the Talmud is the starting point and the definitive statement. For Judaism is the religion of the Torah, oral and written; the written part everyone knows as the Hebrew Scriptures or "the Old Testament," and the oral part, originally formulated and transmitted in the medium of memory, ultimately was written down in its official form in the Talmud.

It follows that to study Judaism, we open not the Hebrew Scriptures alone but the Talmud, which authoritatively sets forth the Scriptures alongside their oral amplification in a coherent statement. Thus, the Torah, written and oral together, finds its authori-

---

1. I say "holy Israel," meaning, the supernatural people, children of Abraham and Sarah and onward, who are called to worship and serve the one, unique God who is made manifest in the Torah revealed to Moses. That is the "Israel" of which the prayers of Judaism speak. "Israel" in contemporary times also refers to the nation and Land of Israel and its citizens ("Israelis"), as well as to the secular ethnic group, the Jewish people or the People of Israel, wherever they live, whatever the state of their religious convictions, if any. In this book, a religious text is interpreted in the framework of the supernatural society, the holy community of Israel, to which that text is addressed. To avoid confusion, "holy Israel" indicates that reference is made to the consecrated community, children of the patriarchs and matriarchs, whether in the flesh or of the spirit, to whom the Torah is revealed.

1

tative statement in the Talmud, which therefore forms the starting point for all sacred study in the religion, Judaism. The Talmud matters because from its closure, probably at the early seventh century of the Common Era (C.E. = A.D.], that document has defined the world view and the holy way of life of Israel, the holy community. The complete statement of the Torah, the Talmud has mediated to Israel God's will in the form of the law and theology that define the religion the world calls "Judaism" and that calls itself "the Torah." The various Judaic religious systems that flourish in the world today, whether Orthodox or reformist, all turn to the Talmud as authoritative, and for most of holy Israel's faithful, Talmud-study "for its own sake" embodies a sacred act, along with prayer and moral conduct.

If to those that faithfully practice Judaism—in this context meaning, study the Torah—the Talmud sets forth the way to the Godly life, in intellect and in practice, to Jews who do not practice Judaism matters appear otherwise. To those Jews the Talmud represents little more than a famous Jewish book. If they want to know about it, it is because they are told the Talmud defines Judaism. But there is a more important reason to want to study the Talmud. It is one of the great, classical writings of human civilization—enduring, influential, nourishing. The Talmud indeed claims its place among the most successful pieces of writing in the history of humanity, along with the Bible, Plato's *Republic*, Aristotle's *Politics,* the Qur'an, and very few other writings. What those books have in common is the power to demand attention and compel response for many centuries after their original presentation. The Qur'an, for example, is received by Muslims as God's word, as is the Bible by Christians and the Torah—comprised of the Hebrew Scriptures of Old Testament and the oral traditions ultimately preserved in the Talmud—by the faithful of Judaism. For generations beyond memory, the Talmud exercised the power to impart its ideals of virtue, moral and intellectual, and so shaped generations of Israel into a single intellectual model, one of enormous human refinement. Here is what, for the Torah, it means to be a human being, in God's likeness, after God's model.

Among those great and enduring classics of humanity, the Talmud, like the great Hindu classic, the Mahabharata, is distinctive because it is not really a book, but a living tradition, a focus for ongoing participation in age succeeding age. The brilliant anthropologist of Hindu religion, William Sax, states, "The Mahabharata . . . was not a book at all, but rather an oral epic . . . a tradition more than a book . . . not only a book but also a practical model, a bedtime story, a tradition of dance, a dramatic spectacle, and much much more." The same is true of the Talmud. It is not so much a book as an intellectual enterprise for eternity. The Talmud embodies the tradition of Judaism; the modes of thought and analysis set forth in the Talmud form the school house for the intellectual life of Judaism. The Judaic religious systems we know today treat the Talmud as the court of final appeal, receiving Scripture (Tanakh, the written Torah, "the Old Testament") through the mediation of the Talmud's mode of reading and interpretation.

To study the Talmud is to study the Torah, and, when Israel, the holy people, assembles to study the Torah, God is present. So tractate Abot, the sayings of the sages, states in so many words:

> R. Hananiah b. Teradion says, "[If] two sit together and between them do not pass teachings of Torah, lo, this is a seat of the scornful, as it is said, 'Nor sits in the seat of the scornful' (Ps. 1:4). But two who are sitting, and words of Torah do pass between them—the Presence is with them, as it is said, 'Then they that feared the Lord spoke with one another, and the Lord hearkened and heard, and a book of remembrance was written before him, for them that feared the Lord and gave thought to His name' (Mal. 3:16). I know that this applies to two. How do I know that even if a single person sits and works on Torah, the Holy One, blessed be he, sets aside a reward for him? As it is said, 'Let him sit alone and keep silent, because he has laid it upon him' (Lam. 3:28)."
>
> R. Simeon says, "Three who ate at a single table and did not talk about teachings of Torah while at that table are as though they ate from dead sacrifices, as it is said, 'For all tables are full of vomit and filthiness if they are without God' (Ps. 106:28). But three who ate at a single table and did talk about teachings of Torah while at that

table are as if they ate at the table of the Omnipresent, blessed is he, as it is said, 'And he said to me, "This is the table that is before the Lord"' (Ez. 41:22)."

Tractate Abot 3:2–3

In light of these statements, two facts stand at the beginning of our entry into Talmud-study.

The first is the conviction that, in Judaism, we meet God in the Torah. That is where God is made manifest. What is at stake in Talmud-study is knowledge of God in concrete terms: What does God want of me in the here and now? How does God want our sacred community to form its social order through justice and equity? What we know about God we know through the Torah. And the Torah portrays the life of holy Israel, the supernatural community that in the here and now embodies God's image of humanity, through the concrete regulation of the just society, living a holy way of life. Those other acknowledged sources of knowledge of God—nature and history—convey their knowledge only because the Torah identifies nature and history as sources for the knowledge of God: "The heavens declare the glory of God," so nature speaks; "You have seen what I did . . . ," so history testifies. Standing outside of the Torah, by contrast, we learn nature's lessons and history's truths without grasping their full meaning and intent, so Scripture insists.

And, second, when we ask what Judaism means by "the Torah," we find the answer not only in the Hebrew Scriptures, which Judaism knows as "the written part of the Torah," but in the Talmud, which Judaism identifies as the writing down of "the oral part of the Torah." So to study the Talmud, in the setting of faithful Israel, the holy people, is to meet God. In secular language, if we want to know how the religion, Judaism, sets forth the encounter with God and its consequences, we turn not alone to Scripture—none of the heirs of the Hebrew Scriptures deems the Scriptures sufficient, though all insist they are necessary[2]—but to the Torah, written and

---

2. Christianity adds the New Testament to the Old; Islam values Scripture's traditions but regards them as inadequate; and Judaism speaks of the oral, alongside the written, Torah. In more concrete terms still, the Mormons value the Old

oral. And, as a matter of fact, for Judaism through the ages and for most of the Judaic religious systems that flourish today, to study the Torah means to study not only the written, but also the oral Torah.

What, exactly, is the Talmud? The Talmud is made up of [1] a philosophical law code, the Mishnah, completed in ca. 200 C.E. and [2] the gemara, an extensive analysis and commentary upon the law (halakhah) of the Mishnah, which reached closure in ca. 600 C.E., and which encompasses also [3] the aggadah or narrative, mostly on the exemplary actions of sages of the Torah, in ancient Israel and through the times of the Mishnah and gemara as well.

[1] The Mishnah covers all 63 tractates, nearly all of them topically organized; these are set forth in six divisions. These divisions attend to the regulation of the holy society of Israel, its politics, economics, and philosophy, or, in other categories, its theory of the social order and how it is organized and governed, its way of life, both practical and spiritual, and its world-view.

[2] The gemara of the Talmud of Babylonia, which has enjoyed the most attention over time,[3] conducts an acute analysis of the laws and the principles of the laws and contains four of the six divisions in the Mishnah. It is intellectually ambitious but economical and not prolix: a few questions recur throughout. The result is that the Talmud finds it possible to say the same thing about many things and so to demonstrate the coherence of truth. The Mishnah and Gemara attend to the norms of everyday life, practical things.

Testament and the New Testament but have, in addition, the book of Mormon; the Essene community at Qumran not only interpreted Scripture, but also produced holy books of its own; and the same is so for all those who receive as revealed the ancient Israelite writings. The conception that an original, historical meaning dictates the sense and imperative of those Scriptures baffles all the religions that flow out of the written record of ancient Israel's encounter with God.

3. The other Talmud, the Talmud of the Land of Israel, requires attention in its own terms, since, while it sets forth the Mishnah, its gemara has a different theory of what Mishnah-study and amplification require. The two Talmuds scarcely intersect in any important ways. When I am studying the Talmud of Babylonia, I find it the pinnacle of humanity's intellectual achievement and tend to look down on the other Talmud. Then, when I am studying the Talmud of the Land of Israel, I find myself swept away by the classicism and elegance of its statement.

[3] The other principal part of the Talmud, the aggadah, completes the work by restating matters in moral terms. The aggadah sets forth the theology of the law spelled out in exemplary accounts of virtue.

In this book, therefore, we devote ourselves to the study of the Mishnah, the gemara that elucidates the Mishnah, and the aggadah that exemplifies in concrete ways the virtues of the Torah.

That briefly describes the document in formal terms. But that definition hardly explains why we should take steps toward studying the Talmud. The reason is that it misses the key to the document and what makes it open-ended, a writing to which every generation makes its contribution—including ours, including even us. We can join in the discussion, not just acquire knowledge or information, because the Talmud is open-ended and invites us to join in its discussion. The main trait of the Talmud is its contentious character, its argument, back and forth. And that is where we enter in. For once we have not only a proposition, but the reason for it, then we may evaluate the reason, criticize it, or produce a contrary proposition based on a better reason and argument. And since the Talmud shows its hand at every point, its framers indicate that they want us to join in. And we do. And that is why so many generations of learning Jews[4] have found in Talmud-study the substance of a worthwhile life: Talmud study, shaping the perspective of the learning Jew, his or her way of seeing many things in one rational, reasonable manner.

What, exactly, is the dialectical, or moving, argument, one that progresses from point to point rather than setting up a static construct of proposition, argument, evidence? When the Talmud analyzes the Mishnah, it is through a dialectical inquiry made up of questions and answers, yielding propositions and counter-arguments. A closer look still shows that what the Talmud gives us is

4. And, in our time, not only Jews. In my university class room, in Talmud courses, I teach Christians and Muslims, as well as atheists. A document that argues in terms of a common rationality, as do the writings of Plato and Aristotle, on the one side, and the Mishnah and Talmud, on the other, finds a natural hearing in the undifferentiated academy.

not a finished statement, but notes toward the main points of an argument. These notes permit us to reconstruct the issues and the questions, the facts and the use made of those facts, with the result that when we grasp the document, we also enter into its discipline and join in its argument. Few documents invite readers to join the writers, and none with the success of this one. For, through the centuries from the formal closure of the Talmud, in about 600 C.E. [= A.D.], the Talmud formed the single authoritative writing of Judaism, the source of the theology and the law that defined the faith and the community of holy Israel, God's first love, wherever they might be located. Enriched by commentaries, responsa, and law codes over the centuries, the Talmud defined the practical affairs of the community of Judaism. Because of its particular character, as the script for a sustained analytical argument, the Talmud further shaped the minds of those who mastered its modes of thought and, because of its profound sensibility, the document further imparted to those who responded to its teachings a character of intellectual refinement and personal responsibility, an alertness to the meaning of word and deed alike. No wonder, then, that the master of Talmudic learning, the disciple of sages in its native category, has defined the virtuous life for Judaic faithful, down to our own time. Because of its power to impart form and structure to the mind of holy Israel, its capacity to define the good and holy way of life for those who wished to be Israel, God's people, the Talmud enjoyed complete success in that various world to which its compilers or authors entrusted their work. Not many books can compete.

People—both the learned and otherwise—have treated the Talmud as special, private, parochial. The specialists agreed with the ordinary folk. The latter found the writing arcane, inaccessible, impenetrable, unintelligible. And the people who knew something about it did not share, nor did they imagine that outside of their circles the Talmud had a statement to make. They deemed it a closed document, accessible only to adepts, who would utilize the document's authority but not share its intellectual power. Translations were deemed disreputable. Talmud scholarship has concentrated on the meanings of words and phrases, the exegetical task overshadowing questions of meaning and value. A technical vocabulary obscured the traits and meanings of the documents, so that even when scholars wrote in English, they communicated nothing of consequence. In the yeshiva world, people pursued an academic discipline meant to turn out highly skilled jurisprudents, masters of the law and its philosophy; exegesis took as its problem the explanation of one detail of the law in one context with that of another in a different context, all the time in quest of the deeper principle or the more telling distinction. To enter into that world, one was expected to subscribe to its intellectual disciplines, which also defined what was worth knowing about this religious classic. The result was that the many other worlds to which the Talmud could speak scarcely gained access to its messages and meanings. The issue was not one of popularization, it was the very definition of the agenda of learning: what is it that we want to know about this vast, ancient, influential writing, and why do we want to know it?

To answer that question, we have to stand back and ask, how do we make sense out of any great religious classic? The answer must encompass not only what the classic says, but why the document is important, how the document works—broader questions of context and circumstance demand attention. If we only know what a document says, we cannot make a judgment of what it means and why it matters. When we can explain for ourselves how a document holds together, in what way its writers or compilers accomplish their goals, then the message of the document takes on depth and meaning. For we can identify alongside the message also the medium of discussion, paying attention to how people say what they wish to say, insisting that the way in which we speak (our tone of voice) bears heavily on the message that we deliver. How a piece of writing persuades us, compels us, to reach the conclusions its writers or compilers wished us to reach, moves us, makes us laugh or cry—these are not matters that necessarily emerge simply from what a document says. And I would maintain, the most important question about the Talmud concerns not what it says, but how it works, meaning, why the Talmud has exercised the amazing power that it has wielded over the life of holy Israel, God's people, for the whole of its history.

After all, how many documents compare? Here is a piece of writing that faced a particular group of people and from its appearance to our own time defined for that group everything that really mattered: questions of order, questions of truth, questions of meaning, questions of purpose. Individuals devoted their lives to the study of this writing, but more important, the entire society of Judaism—that is, the community formed by the Torah—found in the Talmud those modes of thought and inquiry, those media of order and value, that guided the formation of public affairs and private life as well. The Talmud is a public, political, anonymous, collective, social statement; its compilers intended to define the life of the public polity by forming the kingdom of God in the here and now that the Torah, beginning with the Pentateuch, had recorded as God's will for Israel, the holy people.

That is the context in which we ask what we need to know about a piece of writing—this piece of writing—to explain for ourselves how the writing works, meaning two things: how does it do its work, and why does it work? If the compilers put together two stories, what message have they formulated through making that particular connection? If they have taken as self-evident the coherence of a given set of propositions, what has instructed them on why things fit together so well—and in this way, rather than in that way? That is to say, how people make connections and draw conclusions from those connections is the key to how they see their world, their modes of thought. What people find self-evident defines the source of truth and meaning that governs for them. And the Talmud will express that profound principle of the analysis of a culture in so many words when it perceives an incongruity and says, "Now, who ever mentioned that?" What does subject A have to do with subject X? The upshot will be a point of disharmony that requires attention, and in the harmonization of incongruity much new truth emerges.

And there is a deeper dimension still. A piece of writing holds together because of a logic of coherence, which the writer and the reader share, and which the writer uses to show the reader why one thing follows from another, and how two things hold together. In a composite such as the Talmud, the issue of coherence surfaces everywhere. In following the unfolding of an argument, knowing precisely where we stand, understanding how one thing follows from some other and inexorably leads us onward to a further conclusion—these are precisely the elements that generate the power of the document. If we are ever studying a passage of the Talmud and ask ourselves what one thing has to do with another, we may take comfort in the fact that we have asked the one question that we must ask—and must answer if we are to make sense of things.

It is the fact that the Talmud as a whole is cogent, doing some few things over and over again; it conforms to a few simple rules of rhetoric, including choice of languages for discrete purposes, and that fact attests to the coherent viewpoint of the authorship at the end—the people who put it all together as we have it—because it speaks, over all, in a single way, in a uniform voice. The Talmud is not merely an encyclopaedia of information, but a sustained, remarkably protracted, uniform inquiry into the logical traits of passages of the Mishnah or of Scripture. It is not a chaotic mishmash, it is not disorganized, nor is it over all just a compilation of this, that, and the other thing. Quite to the contrary, I have outlined the Talmud, beginning to end, and have shown through that outline that the Talmud moves from main points to subsidiary ones, follows a coherent program of argument, presents information in a generally coherent way for a clear, propositional purpose, and, in all, can be followed in the same way we follow other writings.

First of all, the outline demonstrates, the Talmud does some few things, and does them over and over again in the same order: first this, then that. Most of the Talmud deals with the exegesis and amplification of the Mishnah's rules or of passages of Scripture. That is to say, every sustained discussion begins with a passage of the Mishnah, which will be read with great sensitivity. The rules of reading the Mishnah are few and strong. Wherever we turn, that labor of exegesis and amplification, without differentiation in topics or tractates, conforms to a small number of rules in inquiry, repeatedly phrased, implicitly or explicitly, in a few simple rhetorical forms or patterns. We will be told the meanings of words and phrases, but more than information, we will be asked to participate in a sustained inquiry into the scriptural foundations, in the written Torah, of the Mishnah's rule, which are received as oral Torah. We further will be told that the implicit governing principle of a rule before us intersects with the inferred governing principle of some other, on a different subject, and these have to be compared, contrasted, harmonized, or differentiated. All of this is exhilarating and empowers us to join in the analysis and argument.

True, the Talmud is made up of diverse materials. Its compilers used ready made writing as well as making up their own compositions. But once we outline some pages, from the very beginning to the very end of the discussion of a given paragraph of the Mishnah, we can see what was essential to the purpose of the Talmud's compilers, and what served a subsidiary purpose, for instance, of just giving us information on a topic at hand. So we will find a proposition, demonstrated at some length, followed by an appendix of topically interesting material, which is not party to the argument but which is useful and illuminating. Once we understand how things are put together and why a given passage is included, we see the document as coherent, purposeful, and quite reasonable in its inclusions and juxtapositions—anything but that mess that people tell us it is.

I have been able to identify the types of compositions and large-scale composites of which the Talmud's framers made use, which allows us systematically to study the classifications of those types, for example, Mishnah-commentary, other-than-Mishnah-commentary, to take the two most obvious classifications of all. Not by a repertoire of examples, but by a complete catalogue of all items, therefore, I can now say precisely what types of materials are used, in what proportions, in what contexts, for what purposes, and the like. Generalizations, accompanied by reasonably accurate statements of the numbers and proportions of exemplary data, take a probative role in all study of the character and definition of the Talmud. My experience with the world of Talmud study to which I have access is positive; I find that people who spend their lives studying the document, as I do, rapidly recognize the validity of my observations, which turn out to conform to their intuitive grasp of matters. But then, the Talmudists, all of us, share the conviction that here we study the record of God's revelation, that is, God's self-manifestation. Here we learn the logic of God, how God thinks, those patterns of reason that govern in the creation of the world. From the wording of the Torah, we work our way back to the processes of thought, the rules of coherent analysis, that yielded that wording. The stakes in our learning are very high indeed.

To state the result in just a few words: the Talmud throughout speaks in a single, uniform voice, and that voice is unique in the context of rabbinic compilations of late antiquity. Now, there can be no further argument on that point; the evidence of the uniformity of discourse is spread out in stupefying detail. Why does it matter, and what is at stake in this-worldly terms? In fact, the difference it makes is fundamental: Is the Talmud, Judaism's foundation-document after Scripture, organized or disorganized, purposive or random, systematic or chaotic? Many accounts of the character of the Talmud as a piece of writing describe the documents as unsystematic. Some describe the document as disorganized, others as exhibiting no well-established program that accounts for why a given passage appears where it does and not somewhere else. The regnant theory of the document, along these lines, holds that it developed through a sedimentary process of agglutination and conglomeration.

These characterizations misrepresent the document. The Talmud is not a mere compilation of this-and-that, the result of centuries of the accumulation, in a haphazard way, of the detritus of various schools or opinions. In fact, when we outline the Talmud beginning to end, as I have done in my eight-part *The Talmud of Babylonia: A Complete Outline*, the results do not indicate a haphazard, episodic, sedimentary process of agglutination and conglomeration. They point, quite to the contrary, to a well-considered and orderly composition, planned from beginning to end and following an outline that is definitive throughout. That outline has told the framers of the passage what comes first—the simplest matters of language, then the more complex matters of analysis of content, then secondary development of analogous principles and cases. The Talmudic compilers always move from simple criticism of language to weighty analysis of parallels. There is a fixed order, and it governs everywhere. The authorship always claims to discuss the Mishnah-paragraph that it cites, and it discusses that Mishnah-pargraph.

Why do many Talmudists describe the document as incoherent? The reason is that in the yeshiva world, which is the sole venue for authentic and sustained learning in this writing, people study words and phrases, concentrating on the exegesis of sentences. They turn from a sentence and its declaration to the topic of the sentence, and so move into the commentaries, which discuss the substance of matters, rather than the cogency of a large-scale Talmudic argument. The nature of jurisprudence requires just this kind of phrase-by-phrase study, but such study hardly will produce on the student the impression of a large-scale, sustained argument.

Any experienced study of the Talmud knows that the real issue of Talmud learning flows from the coherence of the whole. If we can explain the meanings of words and phrases but do not grasp the flow of argument, we know nothing. Devoting my life to this document but emerging from a world to which it was alien, my greatest concern has been, have I followed the argument, have I made sense of the coherence of the whole? It is one thing to stumble over words and phrases; these are matters easily corrected but trivial, since, after all, if we mistranslate wheat as barley, or even misconstrue the name of a rabbi, well, too bad, but a second glance will correct matters. But if the very sense I make of a passage turns out to be nonsense, then I have to concern myself with the real issue.

There is another problem that impedes even the most logical disciple of the Talmud from following its structure and order, and that has to do with a technical limitation that affects all books coming to us from ancient times. To understand the problem, we begin with the present. When I am composing an argument, I will subordinate, in footnotes, bits and pieces of clarification, for example, facts, meanings of words and phrases, that the reader will find useful, but that will greatly impede the exposition if left in the body of the text. So, in the text I make my main point, and in footnotes I add supplementary information, even further thoughts. Not only so, but when I am writing a book, I may wish to take up an entire subject and present it in a systematic way, but I may also find that the subject does not allow for the systematic exposition of an important topic. Now, what do I do? I simply write up the topical exposition and place it into an appendix. In that way the reader benefits from the information, but the progress of exposition flows unimpeded. But the technology of footnotes and appendices and the similar media by which writers in our own place and time protect the cogency of their presentation are the gift of movable type and printing (not to mention, in this glorious age, the miracle of the computer.[5]) Since our sages (like everyone else in antiquity) had to put everything together in interminable columns of undifferentiated words, without punctuation, without paragraphing, without signals of what is primary and what is secondary, what we have demands a labor of differentiation. And, when we do that work, and I have done it for the entirety of the Rabbinic literature, we see (now limiting ourselves to the Talmud) some well-demonstrated and incontrovertible facts.

First, we may speak of a composition, not merely a compilation. That is because, first, the Talmud's authors, or authorship, follow

---

5. *My The Talmud: An Academic Commentary* (Atlanta, 1994–1996: Scholars Press for South Florida Studies in the History of Judaism) is executed mainly through graphics made possible by the computer. I signal my views on the place and role of every unit of thought by a simple medium of spatial organization and variation that before computers would have been exceedingly difficult to execute, but, more likely, beyond my imagination. Now, it is the simplest thing to signal language-variation (Hebrew/Aramaic, and what the difference means); sources as against the use of sources in an argument; what is primary in a composite and what is subordinate; a comment on a prior discussion; a comment on the comment; and onward up one page and down another.

a few rules, which we can easily discern, in order to say everything they wish. So the document is uniform and rhetorically cogent. The highly orderly and systematic character of the Talmud emerges, first of all, in the regularities of language. Second, the Talmud speaks through one voice, that voice of logic that with vast assurance reaches into our own minds and by asking the logical and urgent next question tells us what we should be thinking. So the Talmud's rhetoric seduces us into joining its analytical inquiry, always raising precisely the question that should trouble us (and that would trouble us if we knew all of the pertinent details as well as the Talmud does). The Talmud speaks about the Mishnah in essentially a single voice, about fundamentally few things. Its mode of speech as much as of thought is uniform throughout. Diverse topics produce slight differentiation in modes of analysis. The same sorts of questions phrased in the same rhetoric—a moving, or dialectical, argument, composed of questions and answers—turn out to pertain equally well to every subject and problem. The fact that the Talmud speaks in a single voice supplies striking evidence that the Talmud is a coherent piece of writing. It is not a pastiche of sentences from here, there, and everywhere. It is a coherent statement, to be located at a particular place and time. That work was done toward the end of that long period of Mishnah-reception that began at the end of the second century and came to an end at the conclusion of the seventh century. A handful of remarkable geniuses did it all, taking over a heritage of writing of diverse compositions and forming out of them a coherent composite, capable of saying some few things about many things.

The single governing fact is that in a given unit of discourse, the focus, the organizing principle, the generative interest—these are defined solely by the issue at hand. The argument moves from point to point, directed by the inner logic of argument itself. A single plane of discourse is established. All things are leveled out, so that the line of logic runs straight and true. Accordingly, a single conception of the framing and formation of the unit of discourse stands prior to the spelling out of issues. More fundamental still, what people in general wanted was not to create topical anthologies—to put together instances of what this one said about that issue—but to exhibit the logic of that issue, viewed under the aspect of eternity. Under sustained inquiry we always find a theoretical issue, freed of all temporal considerations and the contingencies of politics and circumstance.

Once these elemental literary and structural facts make their full impression, everything else falls into place as well. Arguments did not unfold over a long period of time, as one generation made its points, to be followed by the additions and revisions of another generation, in a process of gradual increment and agglutination running on for two hundred years. That theory of the formation of literature cannot account for the unity, stunning force, and dynamism, of the Talmud's dialectical arguments. To the contrary, someone (or small group) at the end determined to reconstruct, so as to expose, the naked logic of a problem. For this purpose, oftentimes, it was found useful to cite sayings or positions in hand from earlier times. But these inherited materials underwent a process of reshaping, and, more aptly, refocusing. Whatever the original words—and we need not doubt that at times we have them—the point of everything in hand was defined and determined by the people who made it all up at the end. The whole shows a plan and program. Theirs are the minds behind the whole. In the nature of things, they did their work at the end, not at the outset. There are two possibilities. The first is that our document emerges out of a gradual increment of a sedimentary process. Or it emerges as the creation of single-minded geniuses of applied logic and sustained analytical inquiry. But there is no intermediate possibility.

In this regard, then, the Talmud is like the Mishnah in its fundamental literary traits, therefore, also in its history. The Mishnah was formulated in its rigid, patterned language and carefully organized and enumerated groups of formal-substantive cognitive units, in the very processes in which it also was redacted. Otherwise the correspondences between redactional program and formal and patterned mode of articulation of ideas cannot be explained, short of invoking the notion of a literary miracle. The Talmud, too, underwent a process of redaction, in which fixed and final units of discourse were organized and put together. The probably antecedent work of framing and formulating these units of discourse appears to have gone on at a single period, among a relatively small number of sages working within a uniform set of literary conventions, at roughly the same time, and in approximately the same way. The end-product, the Talmud, like the Mishnah, is uniform and stylistically coherent, generally consistent in modes of thought and speech, wherever we turn. That accounts for the single voice that leads us through the dialectical and argumentative analysis of the Talmud. That voice is ubiquitous and insistent.[6]

The upshot is that we may speak about "the Talmud," its voice, its purposes, its mode of constructing a view of the Israelite world. The reason is that when we claim "the Talmud" speaks, just as in the yeshiva world people have always heard the Talmud speaking, we are right: the Talmud does speak, in a uniform, coherent voice. It does sustain and hold together an on-going conversation, into which we enter, in which we may use our own minds to reconstruct and then to carry forward. The Talmud's power to persuade and compel, to impose its viewpoint everywhere and upon everything, to say some one thing about everything, and to make a statement that in each detail proves consequential and formidable—that power affects us when we follow the Talmudic discourse ("sugya") from beginning to end and make sense of its sequence and flow. Talmudists with vast experience in the pages of the document know instinctively how things work, because the Talmud's writers and compilers teach by example and through detail. And, in the detail, there Israel, God's first love, the holy people whom God called forth to serve and to love, finds God.

---

6. The Bavli also contains large topical composites, comparable to sizable appendices, and these do disrupt the orderly flow of exposition and argument. Once these are properly identified and understood in context, they form part of the plan of the document overall. I have done that work in my *The Bavli's Massive Miscellanies: The Problem of Agglutinative Discourse in the Talmud of Babylonia* (Atlanta, 1992: Scholars Press for South Florida Studies in the History of Judaism). I have further explained their purpose in *Rationality and Structure: The Bavli's Anomalous Juxtapositions* (Atlanta, 1997: Scholars Press for South Florida Studies in the History of Judaism).

II

The Mishnah's Judaism

THE TOPICAL PROGRAM OF MISHNAH

Since the Talmud is the foundation-document of Judaism along with the Hebrew Scriptures of Ancient Israel ("the Old Testament"), and since the Talmud forms a commentary to the Mishnah,[1] we begin with basic questions of religious studies. These lead us to the Talmud by establishing the context of the Talmud within the religion, Judaism.

What is (a) Judaism? A Judaism is a subspecies of the species, Judaism, in the genus, Religion. When we say "Judaism," we may mean a variety of things, some religious, some secular; when we speak of "Israel," we may refer to the Land of Israel, the State of Israel, the People of Israel, and much more. But here, "Judaism" refers to the Judaic religious system that defines the life of the supernatural community formed by the faithful of the Torah, who inherit the blessing of the patriarchs and matriarchs, the "Israel" of whom Scripture speaks. That religious system covers three components: the way of life, the world view, and the definition of what, and who, is the "holy Israel" to whom the Torah is given. In secular categories, a Judaism sets forth the way of life or ethos, the world

---

1. This chapter reviews the issues addressed in *The Mishnah Introduction and Reader: An Anthology* (Philadelphia, 1992: Trinity Press International, Library of Rabbinic Literature).

view or ethics, and the theory of the social order or ethnos, of its particular "Israel," that is, us as against everybody else (whether ethnically Jewish or gentile for that matter). The Mishnah sets forth a fully articulated religious system, a Judaism. When we approach the Talmud and wish to identify its principal statement, we begin with the Mishnah, because it is the religious system of the Mishnah that defines the contents of the Talmud, serving as it does only as an amplification of the Mishnah.

The Mishnah's Judaism, through countless details produced by a broad slice of the life of its "Israel," delivers the message that through order—through the reordering of Israelite life—holy Israel attains that sanctification that inheres in its very being. The purpose of the Torah is to purify the heart of humanity—so a sage says— and the purpose of the laws of the Torah, to which the Mishnah is devoted, is to sanctify the everyday life of holy Israel. To make this statement concrete, let us consider the substance of the document.

The Mishnah is divided into six divisions, covering sixty-three tractates, comprising 531 chapters, the whole encompassing six large topics, by today's standards some secular, some religious, but by the Torah's conception, all of them arenas for the articulation of the holy. Before turning to specific passages, we start with a rapid survey of the several parts of the system, the six divisions and their sixty-two tractates (excluding tractate Abot, The Fathers, which while printed with the Mishnah was composed a generation or two later on).

The Division of Agriculture treats two topics, first, producing crops in accord with the Scriptural rules on the subject, second, paying the required offerings and tithes to the priests, Levites, and poor. The principal point of the Division is that the Land is holy, because God has a claim both on it and upon what it produces. God's claim must be honored by setting aside a portion of the produce for those for whom God has designated it. God's ownership must be acknowledged by observing the rules God has laid down for use of the Land. In sum, the Division is divided along these lines: (1) Rules for producing crops in a state of holiness—tractates *Kilayim, Shebiit, Orlah*; (2) Rules for disposing of crops in accord with the rules of holiness—tractates *Peah, Demai, Terumot, Maaserot, Maaser Sheni, Hallah, Bikkurim, Berakhot.*

The Division of Appointed Times forms a system in which the advent of a holy day, like the Sabbath of creation, sactifies the life of the Israelite village through imposing on the village rules on the model of those of the Temple. The purpose of the system, therefore, is to bring into alignment the moment of sanctification of the village and the life of the home with the moment of sanctification of the Temple on those same occasions of appointed times. The underlying and generative theory of the sytem is that the village is the mirror image of the Temple. If things are done in one way in the Temple, they will be done in the opposite way in the village. Together the village and the Temple on the occasion of the holy day therefore form a single continuum, a completed creation, thus awaiting santification.

The division is made up of two quite distinct sets of materials. First, it addresses what one does in the sacred space of the Temple on the occasion of sacred time, as distinct from what one does in that same sacred space on ordinary, undifferentiated days, which is a subject worked out in Holy Things. Second, the Division defines how for the occasion of the holy day one creates a corresponding space in one's own circumstance, and what one does, within that space, during sacred time. The issue of the Temple and cult on the special occasion of festivals is treated in tractates *Pesahim, Sheqalim, Yoma, Sukkah,* and *Hagigah.* Three further tractates, *Rosh Hashanah, Taanit,* and *Megillah,* are necessary to complete the discussion. The matter of the rigid definition of the outlines in the village, of a sacred space, delineated by the limits within which one may move on the Sabbath and festival, and of the specification of those things which one may not do within that space in sacred time, is in *Shabbat, Erubin, Besah,* and *Moed Qatan.* While the twelve tractates of the Division appear to fall into two distinct groups, joined merely by a common theme, in fact, they relate through a shared, generative metaphor. It is the comparison, in the context of sacred time, of the spatial life of the Temple to the spatial life of the village, with activities and restrictions to be specified for each, upon the common occasion of the Sabbath or festival. The Mishnah's purpose therefore is to correlate the sanctity of the Temple, as defined by the holy day, with the restrictions of space and of action, which make the life of the village different and holy, as defined by the holy day.

The Division of Women defines the women in the social economy of Israel's supernatural and natural reality. Women acquire definition wholly in relationship to men, who impart form to the Israelite social economy. The status of women is effected through both supernatural and natural, this-worldly action. What man and woman do on earth provokes a response in heaven, and the correspondences are perfect. So, women are defined and secured both in heaven and here on earth, and that position is always and invariably relative to men. The principal interest for the Mishnah is the point at which a woman becomes, and ceases to be, holy to a particular man, that is, enters and leaves the marital union. These transfers of women are the dangerous and disorderly points in the relationship of woman to man, therefore, the Mishnah states, to society as well.

The formation of the marriage comes under discussion in *Qiddushin* and *Ketubot*, as well as in *Yebamot*. The rules for the duration of the marriage are scattered throughout, but derive especially from parts of *Ketubot*, *Nedarim*, and *Nazir*, on the one side, and the paramount unit of *Sotah*, on the other. The dissolution of the marriage is dealt with in *Gittin*, as well as in *Yebamot*. We see very clearly, therefore, that important overall are issues of the transfer of property, along with women, covered in *Ketubot* and to some measure in *Qiddushin*, and the proper documentation of the transfer of women and property, treated in *Ketubot* and *Gittin*. The critical issues therefore turn upon legal documents—writs of divorce, for example—and legal recognition of changes in the ownership of property, for example, through the collection of the settlement of a marriage contract by a widow, through the provision of a dowry, and through the disposition of the property of a woman during the period in which she is married. Within this orderly world of documentary and procedural concerns a place is made for the disorderly conception of the marriage not formed by human volition but decreed in heaven, the levirate connection. *Yebamot* states that supernature sactifies a woman to a man (under the condition of the levirate connection). What it says by indirection is that man sanctifies too: Man, like God, can sanctify that relationship between a man and woman, and can also effect the cessation of the sanctity of that same relationship. Five of the seven tractates of the Division of Women are devoted to the formation and dissolution of the marital bond. Of them, three treat what is done by man here on earth, that is, formation of a marital bond through betrothal and marriage contract and dissolution through divorce and its consequences: *Qiddushin*, *Ketubot*, and *Gittin*. One of them is devoted to what is done by woman here on earth: *Sotah*. And *Yebamot*, greatest of the seven in size and in formal and substantive brilliance, deals with the corresponding heavenly intervention into the formation and end of a marriage: the effect of death upon both forming the marital bond and dissolving it through death. The other two tractates, *Nedarim* and *Nazir*, draw into one the two realms of reality, heaven and earth, as they work out the effects of vows, perhaps because vows taken by women and subject to the confirmation or abrogation of the father or husband make a deep impact upon the marital life of the woman who has taken them.

The Division of Damages comprises two subsystems, which fit together in a logical way. One part presents rules for the normal conduct of civil society. These cover commerce, trade, real estate, and other matters of everyday intercourse, as well as mishaps, such as damages by chattels and persons, fraud, overcharge, interest, and the like, in that same context of everyday social life. The other part describes the institutions governing the normal conduct of civil society, that is, courts of administration, and the penalties at the disposal of the government for the enforcement of the law. The two subjects form a single tight and systematic dissertation of the nature of Israelite society and its economic, social, and political relationships, as the Mishnah envisages them.

The main point of the first of the two parts of the Division is expressed in the sustained unfolding of the three *Babas*, *Baba*

Qamma, Baba Mesia, and *Baba Batra.* It is that the task of society is to maintain perfect stasis, to preserve the prevailing situation, and to secure the stability of all relationships. To this end, in the interchanges of buying and selling, giving and taking, borrowing and lending, it is important that there be an essential equality of interchange. No party in the end should have more than what he had at the outset, and none should be the victim of a sizable shift in fortune and circumstance. All parties' rights to, and in, this stable and unchanging economy of society are to be preserved. When the condition of a person is violated, so far as possible, the law will secure the restoration of the antecedent status.

An appropriate appendix to the *Babas* is at *Abodah Zarah,* which deals with the orderly governance of transactions and relationships between Israelite society and the outside world, the realm of idolatry, relationships which are subject to certain special considerations. These are generated by the fact that Israelites may not derive benefit (e.g., through commercial transactions) from anything which has served in the worship of an idol. Consequently, commercial transactions suffer limitations on account of extrinsic considerations of cultic taboos. Although these cover both special occasions, for example, fairs and festivals of idolatry, and general matters, that is, what Israelites may buy and sell, the main practical illustrations of the principles of the matter pertain to wine. The Mishnah supposes that gentiles routinely make use, for a libation, of a drop of any sort of wine to which they have access. It, therefore, is taken for granted that wine over which gentiles have had control is forbidden for Israelite use, and also that such wine is prohibited for Israelites to buy and sell. This other matter—ordinary everyday relationships with the gentile world, with special reference to trade and commerce—concludes what the Mishnah has to say about all those matters of civil and criminal law which together define everyday relationships within the Israelite nation and between that nation and all others in the world also whom, in Palestine as abroad, they lived side by side.

The other part of the Division describes the institutions of Israelite government and politics. This is in two main aspects, first, the description of the institutions and their jurisdiction, with reference to courts, conceived as both judicial and administrative agencies, and, second, the extensive discussion of criminal penalties. The penalties are three: death, banishment, and flogging. There are four ways by which a person convicted of a capital crime may be put to death. The Mishnah organizes a vast amount of information on what sorts of capital crimes are punishable by which of the four modes of execution. That information is alleged to derive from Scripture. But the facts are many, and the relevant verses few. What the Mishnah clearly contributes to this exercise is a first-rate piece of organization and elucidation of available facts. Where the facts come from we do not know. The Mishnah tractate *Sanhedrin* further describes the way in which trials are conducted in both monetary and capital cases and pays attention to the possibilities of perjury. The matter of banishment brings the Mishnah to a rather routine restatement on flogging, and application of that mode of punishment concludes the discussion. Our selection from the Mishnah derives from Mishnah-tractate Sanhedrin, because that is where the reward and punishment involved in eternal life, or life in the world to come, takes its place within the larger category of penalty for violating the law of the Torah.

The character and interests of the Division of Damages present probative evidence of the larger program of the philosophers of the Mishnah. Their intention is to create nothing less than a full-scale Israelite government, subject to the administration of sages. This government is fully supplied with a constitution and by-laws (*Sanhedrin, Makkot*). It makes provision for a court system and procedures (*Shebuot, Sanhedrin, Makkot*), as well as a full set of laws governing civil society (*Baba Qamma, Baba Mesia, Baba Batra*) and criminal justice (*Sanhedrin, Makkot*). This government, moreover, mediates between its own community and the outside ("pagan") world. Through its system of laws it expresses its judgment of the others and at the same time defines, protects, and defends its own society and social frontiers (*Abodah Zarah*). It even makes provision for procedures of remission, to expiate its own errors (*Horayot*).

The Division of Holy Things presents a system of sacrifice and

sanctuary: matters concerning the praxis of the altar and maintenance of the sanctuary. The praxis of the altar, specifically, involves
sacrifice and things set aside for sacrifice and so deemed consecrated. The topic covers these among the eleven tractates of the
present Division: *Zebahim* and part of *Hullin, Menahot, Temurah,
Keritot,* part of *Meilah, Tamid,* and *Qinnim.* The maintenance of the
sanctuary (inclusive of the personnel) is dealt with in *Bekhorot,
Arakhim,* part of *Meilah, Middot,* and part of *Hullin.* Viewed from a
distance, therefore, the Mishnah's tractates divide themselves up
into the following groups (in parentheses are tractates containing
relevant materials): (1) Rules for the altar and the praxis of the
cult—*Zebahim Menahot, Hullin, Keritot, Tamid, Qinnim* (*Bekhorot,
Meilah*); (2) Rules for the altar and the animals set aside for the
cult—*Arakhin, Temurah, Meilah* (*Bekhorot*); and (3) Rules for the altar
and support of the Temple staff and buildings—*Bekhorot, Middot*
(*Hullin, Arakhim, Meilah, Tamid*). In a word, this Division speaks of
the sacrificial cult and the sanctuary in which the cult is conducted.
The law pays special attention to the matter of the status of the
property of the altar and of the sanctuary, both materials to be utilized in the actual sacrificial rites, and property the value of which
supports the cult and sanctuary in general. Both are deemed to be
sanctified, that is: "holy things." The Division of Holy Things centers upon the everyday and rules always applicable to the cult.

The Division of Purities presents a very simple system of three
principal parts: sources of uncleanness, objects and substances susceptible to uncleanness, and modes of purification from uncleanness. So, it tells the story of what makes a given sort of object
unclean and what makes it clean. The tractates on these several
topics are as follows: (1) sources of uncleanness—*Ohalot, Negaim,
Niddah, Makhshirin, Zabim, Tebul Yom;* (2) objects and substances
susceptible to uncleanness—*Kelim, Tohorot, Uqsin;* and (3) modes of
purification—*Parah, Miqvaot, Yadayim.* Viewed as a whole, the Division of Purities treats the interplay of persons, food, and liquids.
Dry inanimate objects or food are not susceptible to uncleanness.
What is wet is susceptible. So liquids activate the system. What is
unclean, moreover, emerges from uncleanness through the opera-

tion of liquids, specifically, through immersion in fit water of requisite volume and in natural condition. Liquids thus deactivate the system. Thus, water in its natural condition is what concludes the process by removing uncleanness. Water in its unnatural condition, that is, deliberately affected by human agency, is what imparts susceptibility to uncleanness to begin with. The uncleanness of persons, furthermore, is signified by body liquids or flux in the case of the menstruating woman (*Niddah*) and the *zab* (*Zabim*). Corpse uncleanness is conceived to be a kind of effluent, a viscous gas, which flows like liquid. Utensils for their part receive uncleanness when they form receptacles able to contain liquid. In sum, we have a system in which the invisible flow of fluidlike substances or powers serve to put food, drink, and receptacles into the status of uncleanness and to remove those things from that status. Whether or not we call the system "metaphysical," it certainly has no material base but is conditioned upon highly abstract notions. Thus, in material terms, the effect of liquid is upon food, drink, utensils, and man. The consequence has to do with who may eat and drink what food and liquid, and what food and drink may be consumed in which pots and pans. These loci are specified by tractates on utensils (*Kelim*) and on food and drink (*Tohorot* and *Uqsin*).

The Mishnah's Vision of Holy Israel's Social Order

The building block of society in the Mishnah's vision is the household, which also is the principal unit of production, and the household is headed by the principal mainstay of the Mishnah's "Israel," and that is "the householder," *baal habbayit*. The encompassing and ubiquitous householder, a technical classification defined presently, is the Mishnah's authorship's most characteristic invention of social thought. Ancient Israelite thinkers of the same order, for example, the priestly authorship of Leviticus, the prophetic schools that produced Isaiah's and Amos's conceptions, discerned within, and as, "Israel" classes identified by their sacerdotal and genealogical traits and functions, in relationship to other classes; or a mixed multitude of poor and rich. We look in vain in the imagination of the Deuteronomist writers in their several layers for a conception of an "Israel" composed of neatly arranged farms run by landowners, of families made up of households, an Israel with each such household arrayed in its hierarchy, from householder on top to slave on bottom. But that is how the authorship of the Mishnah sees things, a vision quite its own in the context of thought on society and economy in all Judaic writings of antiquity. And, in the context of the Mishnah's system and the urgent considerations that lead the framers of the system to locate problems in one order of life rather than some other, that is hardly surprising.

The social foundation of the economy of the Mishnah therefore rested on the household, which in turn formed the foundation of the village, imagined to comprise the community of households, in the charge of small farmers who were free and who owned their land. In fact, the entire economics of the Mishnah's Judaism addresses only the social world formed by this "household." No economics pertained to commercial, professional, manufacturing, trading, let alone laboring persons and classes. Landless workers, teachers, physicians, merchants, shopkeepers, traders, craftsmen, and the like cannot, by definition, constitute a household. The definition of the market and its working, the conception of wealth, viewed within both market- and distributive-economics, sort out affairs only as these pertain to the household. That is to say that the economics of Judaism omitted reference to most of the Jews, on the one side, and the economic activities and concerns of labor and capital alike, on the other. These formidable components of the social entity, "Israel," the system at hand simply treats, from an economic perspective, as null. In passages in which proprietary responsibilities and obligations play no role, for example, matters having to do with the cult, religious observance, the sacred calendar, and the like, by contrast, the Mishnah's authorship speaks not of the householder but of "he who" or "a man," or other neutral building blocks of society, not defined in terms of proprietary status of landholding.

Whether, in fact, all "Israel," that is, the Jews in the land of

Israel, lived in such villages or towns, made up within the neat array of householders and their dependents, we do not know. But, given conditions of a country going through wars and suffering defeats of a catastrophic order, it is difficult to imagine a reality composed of such a neat arrangement of building blocks, and the Mishnah's authorship itself recognizes that the village consisted of more than households and householders, while at the same time recognizing that "household" forms an abstract entity, not a concrete and material social fact, as we shall see in a moment. Not only so, but, even without such passages, we should find it exceedingly difficult to imagine a society made up wholly of smallholders and people assembled in neat array around them, a society or community lacking such other social categories as large holders, landless workers in appreciable numbers, craftsmen laboring for a market independent of the proprietary one of householders, and numerous other categories of production and classifications of persons in relationship to means of production. That makes all the more indicative of the character of the Mishnaic system and its thought the fact that we deal with a single block, a single mold and model. In imagining a society which surely encompassed diverse kinds of person, formed in various molds and in accord with a range of models, the authorship of the Mishnah has made its statement of its vision, and that vision dictates the focus and requirements of analysis.

That "household" as the building block of village, and the two were the fundamental units of Israelite society, forms an abstraction, not a concrete physical or social entity, for example, a house separate from other houses, a family distinct from other families, is easy to demonstrate. It simply is not a concrete description of how people really lived, for instance, of the spatial arrangements of houses, or of the social units made up of distinct household-houses (or, as we shall see in a moment, families as equivalent to households). The supposition of Mishnah-tractate Erubin, for example, is that households are in a village, that people live cheek by jowl in courtyards, and that they go out into the fields from the village. So the notion of the isolated farmstead is absent here. That is important in relating the household to the village, *oikos* to *polis,* and it also shows how abstract is the conception of the household, since it is conceived as a unit, even though, in fact, the households were not abstract and distinct units at all.

The singularity of the household was not in its physical let alone genealogical traits, but in its definition as a distinct unit of economic production. What made a household into a household was its economic definition as a whole and complete unit of production, and the householder was the one who controlled that unit of production; that economic fact made all the difference, and not that all of the household's members were related (that was not the fact at all), or that all of them lived in a single building distinct from other single buildings. What made the household into a social unit was the economic fact that, among its constituents, all of them worked within the same economic unit and also worked in a setting distinct from other equivalent autonomous economic units. In the idiom of the Mishnah, they *ate* at the same table, and eating should be understood as an abstraction, not merely as a reference to the fact that people sat down and broke bread together. That seems to me an interesting point. Nor is the "household" of which courtyards are composed only Jewish. "He who dwells in the same courtyard with a gentile, or with an Israelite who has not conceded the vitality of the *erub* . . . ," so Mishnah-tractate *Erubin* 6:1. This concession of householder-status to the gentile neighbor in a courtyard once more underlines the economic, and functional, definition of the household, rather than its genealogical and cultic meaning. The premise of "the household" as an autonomous unit and building block of society contradicts the realities described by the Mishnah's framers. The social unit of "the courtyard" has numerous cultic affects but it is not an economic unit and is not recognized as such. "The householder" has no counterpart in "the shareholder of a courtyard." The one forms an economic unit, the other does not, for example, M. Erubin 6:3–4, the courtyard is a cultic unit, bearing no economic weight whatsoever. This again shows us the precision in use of the term "household" and "householder"—the precision, but also the utter abstraction of the conception.

The vision of the Mishnah for society emerges in its account of the household, a neat building block for all else, the market, which insures that no one changes in status or in possession, and wealth as land. Once we take full account of the structural components of the Mishnah's economy, the household, defined in terms of command of an ownership of landed domain, however small, composing, with other households, the village; the village constituting the market in which all things hold together in an equal exchange of a stable population in a steady-state economy, we revert to the consequent question: Then what is wealth? And the answer to that question must accommodate the fact that wealth is conceived as unchanging and not subject to increase or decrease, hence, by the way, the notion of true value imputed to commodities. For if we imagine a world in which, ideally, no one rises and no one falls, and in which wealth is essentially stable, then we want to know what people understand by money, on the one hand, and how they identify riches, on the other. The answer is very simple.

For the system of the Mishnah, wealth constitutes that which is of lasting value, and what lasts is real property (in the land of Israel), that alone. Real estate (in the land of Israel) does not increase in volume, it is not subject to the fluctuation of the market (so it was imagined), it was permanent, reliable, and, however small, always useful for something. It was perceived to form the medium of enduring value for a society made up of households engaged in agriculture. Accordingly, the definition of wealth as real and not movable, as real estate (in the land of Israel) and nowhere else, real estate not as other kinds of goods, conformed to the larger systemic givens. A social system composed of units of production, households, engaged in particular in agricultural production, made a decision entirely coherent with its larger conception and character in identifying real estate as the sole measure of wealth.

True enough, we find more spiritual definitions of wealth, for example, Mishnah-tractate Avot 4:2: "Who is rich? He who is happy in what he has." So, too, one can become rich through keeping or studying the Torah, for example, "He who keeps the Torah when poor will in the end keep it in wealth" (M. Avot 4:9). So, too, we find the following, "Keep your business to a minimum and make your business Torah" (M. Avot 4:10). But these sayings have no bearing upon a single passage of the Mishnah in which a concrete transaction in exchanges of material goods takes place, nor does anyone invoke the notion of being satisfied with what one has when it comes to settling scores. None of them, to begin with, occurs in the Mishnah, but only in its later apologetic, produced about a half-century after the closure of the document. No decision in the exegetical literature generated by the Mishnah, for example, the Tosefta, the two Talmuds, ever appealed as grounds for the practical disposition of a case of conflicting interests to the notion that, for example, both parties should forfeit the case and go off and get rich, instead, by studying the Torah. I think we may dismiss as systemically irrelevant, indeed inconsequential, all definitions of wealth outside of the context of how actualities of conflict and exchange are sorted out, and in every such concrete and material setting, ownership of land is the medium of adjudication.

In these principal components of its economics, concerning the definition of ownership of the means of production, the market, and wealth, the Judaism of the Mishnah restated, in its odd and particular idiom, the distributive economics of the paramount, three-thousand-year-old system of the Near East, going back to Sumerian times, to the details of which, for the Mishnah's theoretical economics of the householder, market, and wealth, we now turn. For when we understand the details of the Mishnah's theory of distributive economics, we can explain with little difficulty the reason that the authorship of the Mishnah has appealed to economics for the exposition of its systemic message. But, predictably, God lives in the details, a statement peculiarly congruent to the facts we shall now survey. At the heart of matters is who owns what, when, why, for what purpose, and with what outcome. And these are questions essentially besides the point of market-economics, which deal, after all, with other forces than those that (adventitiously) define ownership, and which care little for the character and definition of what is traded in the market. Before considering the economic vision of the Mishnah further, let us draw the matter into alignment with other fundamental components of the social conception of the same system, beginning with the other critical one, woman. When we can account within a single theory for the disposition of, and policy toward, woman and land, we stand, I think, at the heart of the system. What women and land have in common within the system then tells us about the deepest concerns and preoccupations of the system-builders. Then, all things will fit together into a cogent and well-ordered, neatly composed whole, just as the Mishnah's authorship wanted them to.

WOMEN IN THE HOUSEHOLD OF HOLY ISRAEL

The social vision of the Judaism of the Mishnah says the same thing about everything. Accordingly, knowing the urgent question and the self-evidently valid answer of the system, we can predict what the system has to say about any topic it chooses to treat. The social vision of the Mishnah's Judaism encompasses issues of gender, social structure and construction, wealth and transactions in property, the organization of the castes of society. In all these matters the system seeks the principles of order and proper classification, identifying as problems the occasions for disorder and improper disposition of persons or resources. The fact that we can find our document saying one thing about many things tells us that the document stands for a well-considered view of the whole, and, when we come to the theological and philosophical program of the same writing, that consistent viewpoint will guide us to what matters and what is to be said about what matters.

The principal focus of a social vision framed by men, such as that of the Mishnah, not only encompasses, but focuses upon, woman, who is perceived as the indicative abnormality in a world to which men are normal. But to place into perspective the Mishnah's vision of woman, we have to locate woman within the larger structure defined by the household. That is for two reasons. First of all, as a matter of definition, woman forms the other half of the whole that is the householder. Second, since, as we have already seen, the household forms the building block of the social construction envisioned by the Mishnah's framers, it is in that setting that every other component of the social world of the system must situate itself.

In the conception at hand, which sees Israel as made up, on earth, of households and villages, the economic unit also framed the social one, and the two together composed, in conglomerates, the political one, hence, a political economy (*polis, eokos*), initiated within an economic definition formed out of the elements of production. That explains why women cannot be addressed outside of the framework of the economic unit of production defined by the household. For, throughout, the Mishnah makes a single cogent statement that the organizing unit of society and politics finds its definition in the irreducible unit of economic production. The Mishnah conceives no other economic unit of production than the household, though it recognizes that such existed; its authorship perceived no other social unit of organization than the household and the conglomeration of households, though that limited vision omitted all reference to substantial parts of the population perceived to be present, for example, craftsmen, the unemployed, the landless, and the like. But what about woman in particular?

The framers of the Mishnah, for example, do not imagine a household headed by a woman; a divorced woman is assumed to return to her father's household. The framers make no provision for the economic activity of isolated inviduals, out of synchronic relationship with a household or a village made up of householders. Accordingly, craftsmen and day laborers or other workers, skilled and otherwise, enter the world of social and economic transactions only in relationship to the householder. The upshot, therefore, is that the social world is made up of households, and, since households may be made up of many families, for example, husbands, wives, children, all of them dependents upon the householder, households in no way are to be confused with the family. The indicator of the family is kinship, that of the household, "propinquity or residence." And yet, even residence is not always a criterion for membership in the household unit, since the craftsmen and day laborers are not assumed to live in the household-compound at all. Accordingly, the household forms an economic unit, with secondary criteria deriving from that primary fact.

The Mishnaic law of women defines the position of women in the social economy of Israel's supernatural and natural reality. That position acquires definition in relationship to men, who give form to the Israelite social economy. It is effected through both supernatural and natural, this-worldly, action. What man and woman do on earth provokes a response in Heaven, and the correspondences are perfect. So, the position of women is defined and secured in Heaven and here on earth, and that position, always and invariably relative to men, is what comes into consideration. The principal point of interest on Mishnah's part is the time at which a woman changes hands. That is, she becomes, and ceases to be, holy to a particular man, enters and laves the marital union. These are the dangerous and disorderly points in the relationship of woman to man, therefore, to society.

Five of the seven tractates that pertain to women and family are devoted to the transfer of women, the formation and dissolution of the marital bond. Of them, three treat what by man is done here on earth, that is, formation of a marital bond through betrothal and marriage-contract and dissolution through divorce and its consequences: *Qiddushin, Ketubot,* and *Gittin.* One of them is devoted to what by woman is done here on earth: *Sotah. Yebamot,* greatest of the seven in size and informal and substantive brilliance, deals with the corresponding Heavenly intervention into the formation and dissolution of marriage: the affect of death upon the marital bond, and the dissolution, through death, of that bond. The other two tractates, *Nedarim* and *Nazir,* draw into one the two realms of reality, Heaven and earth, as they work out the effects of vows— generally taken by married women and subject to the confirmation or abrogation of the husband—to Heaven. These vows make a deep impact upon the marital relationship of the woman who has taken such a vow. So, in all, we consider the natural and supernatural character of the woman's relationship to the social economy framed by man: the beginning, end, and middle of that relationship.

Holy Israel's History

The framers of the Mishnah present us with a kind of historical thinking quite different from the one that they, along with all Israel, had inherited in Scripture. The legacy of prophecy, apocalypse, and mythic-history handed on by the writers of the books of the Hebrew Scriptures of ancient Israel, for instance, Jeremiah, Daniel, and Genesis, Exodus, and Deuteronomy, respectively, exhibits a single and quite familiar conception of history. First of all, history refers to events seen whole. Events bear meaning, form a pattern, and, therefore, deliver God's message and judgment. The upshot is that every event, each one seen on its own, must be interpreted in its own terms, not as part of a pattern, but as significant in itself. What happens is singular, therefore, an event to be noted points toward lessons to be drawn for where things are heading and why.

If things do not happen at random, they also do not form indifferent patterns of merely secular, social facts. What happens is important because of the meaning contained therein. That meaning is to be discovered and revealed through the narrative of what has happened. So for all Judaisms until the Mishnah, the writing of history serves as a form or medium of prophecy. Just as prophecy takes up the interpretation of historical events, so historians retell these events in the frame of prophetic theses. And of the two—historiography as a mode of mythic reflection, prophecy as a means of mythic construction—emerges a picture of future history, that is, what is going to happen. That picture, framed in terms of visions and supernatural symbols, in the end focuses, as much as do prophecy and history-writing, upon the here and now.

The upshot is simple. History consists of a sequence of one-time events, each of them singular, all of them meaningful. These events move from a beginning somewhere to an end at a foreordained goal. History moves toward eschatology, the end of history. The teleology of Israel's life finds its definition in eschatological fulfillment. Eschatology therefore constitutes not a choice *within* teleology, but the definition *of* teleology. That is to say, a theory of the goal and purpose of things (teleology) is shaped solely by appeal to the account of the end of times (eschatology). History done in this way then sits enthroned as the queen of theological science. Events do not conform to patterns. They form patterns. What happens matters because events bear meaning, constitute history. Now, as is clear, such a conception of mythic and apocalyptic history comes to realization in the writing of history in the prophetic pattern or in the apocalyptic framework, both of them mythic modes of organizing events. We have every right to expect such a view of matters to lead people to write books of a certain sort, rather than of some other. In the case of Judaism, obviously, we should expect people to write history books that teach lessons or apocalyptic books that through pregnant imagery predict the future and record the direction and end of time. And in antiquity that kind of writing proves commonplace among all kinds of groups and characteristic of all sorts of Judaisms but one. And that is the Judaism of the Mishnah. Here we have a Judaism that does not appeal to history as a sequence of one-time events, each of which bears meaning on its own. What the Mishnah has to say about history is quite different, and, consequently, the Mishnah does not conform in any way to the scriptural pattern of representing, and sorting out, events: history, myth, apocalypse.

The first difference appears right at the surface. The Mishnah contains no sustained narrative whatsoever, a very few tales, and no large-scale conception of history. It organizes its system in non-historical and socially unspecific terms. That is to say, there is no effort at setting into a historical context, for example, a particular time, place, a circumstance defined by important events, any of the laws of the Mishnah. The Mishnah's system is set forth out of all historical framework, as we observed in Chapter One. It is a medium for the presentation of a system that has no precedent in prior systems of Judaism or in prior kinds of Judaic literature. The law codes of Exodus and Deuteronomy, for example, are set forth in a narrative framework, and the priestly code of Leviticus, for its part, appeals to God's revelation to Moses and Aaron, at specific times and places. In the Mishnah we have neither narrative nor setting for the representation of law.

Instead of narrative which, as in Exodus, spills over into case-law, the Mishnah gives description of how things are done in general and universally, that is, descriptive laws. Instead of reflection on the meaning and end of history, it constructs a world in which history plays little part. Instead of narratives full of didactic meaning, the Mishnah's authorship, as we shall see in a moment, provides lists of events so as to expose the traits they share and thus the rules to which they conform. The definitive components of a historical-eschatological system of Judaism—description of events as one-time happenings, analysis of the meaning and end of events, and interpretation of the end and future of singular events—none of these commonplace constituents of all other systems of Judaism (including nascent Christianity) of ancient times finds a place in the Mishnah's system of Judaism. So, the Mishnah finds no precedent in prior Israelite writings for its mode of dealing with things that happen. The Mishnah's way of identifying happenings as consequential and describing them, its way of analyzing those events it chooses as bearing meaning, its interpretation of the future to which significant events point—all those in context were unique. In form the Mishnah represents its system outside of all historical framework.

Yet, to say that the Mishnah's system is ahistorical could not be more wrong. The Mishnah presents a different kind of history. Its authorship revises the inherited conception of history and reshapes that conception to fit into its own system. When we consider the power of the biblical myth, the force of its eschatological and messianic interpretation of history, the effect of apocalypse, we must find astonishing the capacity of the Mishnah's framers to think in a different way about the same things. As teleology constructed outside the eschatological mode of thought in the setting of the biblical world of ancient Israel proves amazing. By "history," as the opening discussion makes clear, I mean not merely events, but how events are so organized and narrated as to teach (for them, theological, for us, religious-historical or social) lessons, reveal patterns, tell us what we must do and why, what will happen to us tomorrow. In that context, some events contain richer lessons than others; the destruction of the Temple of Jerusalem teaches more than a crop failure, being kidnapped into slavery more than stubbing one's toe. Furthermore, lessons taught by events—"history" in the didactic sense—follow a progression from trivial and private to consequential and public.

The framers of the Mishnah explicitly refer to very few events, treating those they do mention within a focus quite separate from what happened—the unfolding of the events themselves. They rarely create or use narratives. More probative still, historical events do not supply organizing categories or taxonomic classifications. We find no tractate devoted to the destruction of the Temple, no complete chapter detailing the events of Bar Kokhba, or even a sustained celebration of the events of the sages' own historical life. When things that have happened are mentioned, it is neither in order to narrate, nor to interpret and draw lessons from the event. It is either to illustrate a point of law or to pose a problem of the law—always *en passent*, never in a pointed way. So, when sages refer to what has happened, this is casual and tangential to the main thrust of discourse. Famous events, of enduring meaning, such as the return to Zion from Babylonia in the time of Ezra and Nehemiah, gain entry into the Mishnah's discourse only because of the genealogical divisions of Israelite society into castes among the immigrants (M. Qiddushin 4:1). Where the Mishnah provides little tales or narratives, moreover, they more often treat how things in the cult are done in general than what, in particular, happened on some one day. It is sufficient to refer casually to well-known incidents. Narrative, in the Mishnah's limited rhetorical repertoire, is reserved for the narrow framework of what priests and others do on recurrent occasions and around the Temple. In all, that staple of history, stories about dramatic events and important deeds, in the minds of the Mishnah's jurisprudents provide little nourishment.

Events, if they appear at all, are treated as trivial. They may be well-known, but are consequential in some way other than is revealed in the detailed account of what actually happened.

Sages' treatment of events determines what in the Mishnah is important about what happens. Since the greatest event in the century and a half, from ca. 50 to ca. 200, in which the Mishnah's materials came into being, was the destruction of the Temple in 70, we must expect the Mishnah's treatment of that incident to illustrate the document's larger theory of history: what is important and unimportant about what happens. The treatment of the destruction occurs in two ways. The destruction of the Temple constitutes a noteworthy fact in the history of the law. Why? Because various laws about rite and cult had to undergo revision on account of the destruction.

THE MESSAGE OF THE MISHNAH TO HUMANITY IN CRISIS: WHAT CAN WE DO?

The human being, in our image, after our likeness, male and female, is counterpart and partner and creation, in that, like God, the human being has power over the status and condition of creation, putting everything in its proper place, calling everything by its rightful name. And that brings us to the meeting of theology and philosophy in the Mishnah's judgment of the nature of the power of the human being in relationship to God. The human being and God are the two beings who possess the active will. The human being is like God in that both God and the human being not only do, but form attitudes and intentions. That theory of the human being, a philosophical issue concerning the nature of will and attitude, meets the theory of God's relationship with humanity, a theological concern concerning the correspondence of God and humanity's inner being. And all of this deep thought is precipitated by the critical issue facing Israel, the Jewish people, defeated on the battlefield and deprived of its millennial means of serving God in the temple in Jerusalem: what, now, can a human being do?

Addressing an age of defeat after the destruction of the Temple in 70 and, in consequence of the permanent closure of the temple in Jerusalem, in 135 an age of despair as well, the Mishnah's framers' principal message, which makes the Judaism of this document and of its social components distinctive and cogent, is that the human being is at the center of creation, the head of all creatures upon earth, corresponding to God in heaven, in whose image the human being is made. The way in which the Mishnah makes this simple and fundamental statement is illustrated on nearly every page of the document. It is to impute the power, effected through an act of sheer human will or intentionality, to the human being to inaugurate and initiate those corresponding processes, sanctification and uncleanness, which play so critical a role in the Mishnah's account of reality. The will of the human being, expressed through the deed of the human being, is the active power in the world. As matters would be phrased in later writings, "Nothing whatsoever impedes the human will." But, of course, looking back on the age at hand, we know that everything did. The "Israel" of the Mishnah never achieved its stated goals, for example, in once more setting up a government of priests and kings, in once more regaining that order and stasis that, in mind at least, people imagined had once prevailed. But, of course, the key is in the "once more," for these were things that, in point of fact, had not been at all. The will for "once more" encompassed nowhere and never.

So, stated briefly, the question taken up by the Mishnah and answered by Judaism is, What can a person do? And the answer laid down by the Mishnah is, the human being, through will and deed, is master of this world, the measure of all things.

But that world of all things of which the human being is the measure is within: in intellect, imagination, sentient reality. Since when the Mishnah thinks of a human being, its authorship means the Israelite, who is the subject and actor of its system, the statement is clear. This is the Judaism that identifies at the center of things Israel, the Israelite person, who can do what he or she wills. In the aftermath of the two wars and defeats of millenial proportions, the message of the Mishnah cannot have proved more pertinent—or poignant and tragic. And yet the power of the message shaped the entire history of holy Israel, and of Judaism, from then to now. Here was the answer to the ineluctable questions of frailty and defeat in society and death for everyone who walked the earth—the self-evident truth that everything that matters depends upon the human will and intention. We are what we think we are, what in mind and imagination and sentiment and heart we hope, believe, insist, we can be; we are because, above all, by act of will we persist in being. The Mishnah sings a sustained hymn of praise to what through an act of will we can make of ourselves: "in our image, after our likeness," like God. How does the Talmud respond to the Mishnah? We turn to the Talmud itself.

III

Studying the Talmud for the First Time

The Talmud, a.k.a., the Gemara, is a protracted, analytical explanation and expansion of the Mishnah. In the framework of the theology of Judaism, the Talmud is part of the "one whole Torah of Moses, our rabbi," because it is attached to, and provides an essential explanation of, the Mishnah. The Talmud is composed of two elements, therefore: a passage of the Mishnah, followed by a long discussion of that Mishnah-passage. Hence, the Talmud is (1) the Mishnah and (2) the Gemara, the Talmudic commentary to, explanation of, the Mishnah. These two components are written in quite distinctive ways, respectively, and we can always distinguish them on the basis of their traits of style as well as the tasks each carries out. In general, the Mishnah is written in declarative and flowing Hebrew, the Gemara or Talmud in allusive, abbreviated, and elliptical Aramaic; the law is given in straight-forward sentences, the analysis of the law in the form of brief notes, by which, with experience and the great commentaries to the Talmud, we reconstruct the analytical thought-problems set forth by the geniuses of the Talmud proper. By their rigorous presentation of demanding thought, the framers of the Talmud—Mishnah and Gemara alike—pay a very high tribute to the reading audience that over eternity they expected to address. And not a single generation of holy Israel

42

from then to now has failed to rise to the challenge, though, admittedly, some generations achieved deeper mastery than others.

How does internal evidence show us that the Talmud is composed of two kinds of writing intertwined with each other? Looking at the Talmud whole, as the selections that follow will show, we notice two totally distinct sorts of materials: statements of law, then discussions of and excursus on those statements. We bring no substantial presuppositions to the text, if we declare these two sorts of materials to be, respectively, primary and constitutive, secondary and derivative. Calling the former, that is, the declaration of laws, "the Mishnah passage," and the latter, the exegesis of these laws, "the Talmud proper," imposes no a priori judgment formed independent of the literary evidence in hand. We might as well call the two "the code" and "the commentary." In fact, as we see everywhere, the Talmud is made up of two elements, each with its own literary traits and program of discussion. Since the Mishnah passage at the head of each set of Talmudic units of discourse defines the limits and determines the theme and, generally, the problematic of the whole, our attention is drawn to the traits of the Mishnah passages as a group.

If we for the first time saw these types of paragraphs of the Mishnah (embedded as they are in the Talmud and separated from one another by several pages of discussion), we should discern that they adhere to a separate and quite distinctive set of literary and conceptual canons from what follows and surrounds them. Hence, at the outset, with no appreciable attention to anything beyond the text, we should distinguish two "layers" of the Talmud and recognize that one "layer" is formed in one way, the other in another way. (I use "layer" for convenience only; it is not an apt metaphor.) If then we were to join together all the Mishnah paragraphs, we should notice that they are stylistically and formally coherent and also different from everything else in the compilation before us. Accordingly, for stylistic reasons alone we are on firm ground in designating the "layer" before us as the base point for all further inquiry. For the Mishnah "layer" has been shown to be uniform, while the Talmud "layer" is not demonstrably so. Hence, itself undifferentiated, the former—the Mishnah "layer"—provides the point of differentiation. The latter—the Talmud "layer"—presents the diverse materials subject to differentiation. In the first stage in the work of making sense of the Talmud and describing it whole, what is the initial criterion through which the Talmud's diverse types of units of discourses are differentiated? It is the varied relationships, to the Mishnah's rule, exhibited by the Talmud's several, diverse units of discourse.

THE TALMUD AND THE MISHNAH

Since the Talmud carries forward and depends upon the Mishnah, to describe the Talmud we have to begin with its relationship to the Mishnah, which is the Talmud's own starting point. While the Mishnah admits to no antecedents and neither alludes to nor cites anything prior to its own materials, a passage of the Talmud is ordinarily incomprehensible without knowledge of the passage of the Mishnah around which the Talmud's discourse centers. The Mishnah permits us at the outset to gain perspective on the character of the Talmud. For the Mishnah does exhibit a remarkable unity of literary and redactional traits. By that standard the Talmud presents none. The Mishnah's sentences are patterned and uniform and set forth in groups of three or five. The Mishnah's sentences use recurrent clichés, fixed expressions to signal the traits of argument at hand, but the Talmud's sentences and paragraphs follow no disciplined protocol of the kind that governs in the Mishnah. Accordingly, while whatever materials reached the framers of the Mishnah—ca. 175–200 were revised by them in line with a single and simple literary and redactional program, the same is not the case for the Talmud, some four centuries later.

How does the Talmud treat the Mishnah? The Talmud invariably does to the Mishnah one of these five things:

1. THE SCRIPTURAL FOUNDATIONS OF THE MISHNAH: The Talmud will systematically identify the basis, in the written Torah, for rules of the oral Torah set forth in the Mishnah.

2. CITATION AND GLOSS OF THE LANGUAGE OF THE MISHNAH
   (MEANING OF A PHRASE OR CONCRETE ILLUSTRATION OF A
   RULE). A unit of discourse of this type will contain a direct
   citation of a sentence of the Mishnah. The word choices or
   phrasing of the Mishnah will be paraphrased or otherwise
   explained through what is essentially a gloss. Or the rule of
   the Mishnah will be explained through an example or a
   restatement of some kind.
3. SPECIFICATION OF THE MEANING OF THE LAW OF THE MISHNAH
   OR THE REASON FOR IT. The discussion tends to allude to the
   Mishnah or to generalize, while remaining wholly within its
   framework.
4. SECONDARY IMPLICATION OR APPLICATION OF THE LAW OF THE
   MISHNAH. The discussion will commonly restate the principle of the rule at hand or raise a question invited by it. Hence,
   if the Mishnah's law settles one question, participants in this
   type of discourse will use that as the foundation for raising a
   second and consequent question.
5. THE MATTER OF AUTHORITIES AND THEIR VIEWS: CASE LAW.
   Here we move on to the state of legal theory spun out of the
   Mishnah's own disputes.

THE FORMAL TRAITS OF THE MISHNAH: In the case of the Mishnah, as is clear, the principal lines of division will be into topical
expositions, that is, tractates devoted to their respective, diverse
subject-matter. What is important is that that fact is shown on the
basis of the internal character of the document, not merely of the
post facto way in which exegetes, copyists, and printers organized
matters. How on the basis of internal evidence are intermediate
divisions ("chapters" of the topical tractates) to be discerned? Having shown that the redactors not only organize their materials topically, but also lay out the discussion of each topic in accord with
its logically sequential parts, I am on firm ground in maintaining
that one criterion for a demarcation will be a shift in topic or
theme. There is, moreover, a second important criterion of delinea-
tion, and that is recurrent grammatical patterns or arrangements of

words. This entails inquiry into the large-scale interplay between theme and form, between what is said and how it is said.

In the chapters of the Mishnah we examined, we took note of the formal traits of the writing, the patterns that governed the way in which matters were expressed. The first thing we notice when we study a Mishnah tractate from its opening sentence onward is that, when the subject changes, the formulary patterns shifts too. A given subtopic of a topical unit—a principal division—will be expressed in a distinctive pattern of syntax. The tight syntactical pattern will govern the layout of words for each concept, thought, or rule devoted to a given subtopic. That is to say, the cognitive unit rarely stands by itself but is grouped together with other such units, devoted to a single principle or theme and exhibiting a single, distinctive syntactical trait or preference. Accordingly, the form-analytical work yields the result that the cognitive unit is shaped within the processes of organization of the intermediate (and principal) divisions of the Mishnah. This means that the work of giving formalized verbal expression to cognitive units and the work of organizing them into groups go together and reciprocally govern one another's results. To state the historical result simply: the Mishnah's formulation and its organization are the result of the work of a single generation of sages—writers, who formulate units of thought, and editors, who organize aggregations of these units. The work follows a few simple rules, and the result holds together in a remarkably cogent structure—strong arguments for the proposition that whatever they inherited, in the end the sages who formulated the Mishnah did the work together in a single, if indeterminate, span of time, not over long centuries and isolated from one another. The Talmud exhibits different traits, which then suggest a different formative history altogether.

THE FORMAL TRAITS OF THE TALMUD: In the case of the Talmud, the principle of organization is provided by the Mishnah itself. Tractates begin and end where the Mishnah does. Accordingly, if all we had were a mass of words, we should know the beginning and end of a tractate of our Talmud precisely as we do in the case of the Mishnah, because the point of demarcation is identical. The

Mishnah forms the trellis, the Talmud, the vine. The Talmud's discussion attached to a given paragraph of the Mishnah runs through two or more completed units of discourse. The principle by which a discussion is inaugurated, worked out, and concluded is different from that of the Mishnah in general. Formal considerations do not come into play in the Talmud before us in so rigid and disciplined a way as they govern the formulation of the Mishnah's ideas. The upshot is that while the framers of the Talmud refer constantly to the Mishnah, they do not see themselves as bound by its patterns of formulation or even of redaction, let alone by its program and problems.

The Contents of the Mishnah's Law and the Talmud's Re-Presentation of that Law;

The Mishnah speaks about uncleanness and holiness, priests and their rations, holy days and appointed times in the Temple, ordinary, everyday rites at the altar. The Mishnah's picture of Israelite government presents a portrait of a king and a high priest in charge of everything. Its conception of civil law aims at preserving the perfect stability of the status quo, all in the name of the sanctification of Israel. The Mishnah's principal concerns are those of priests, not sages. Its focus of interest is in the Temple and its cult, not in the schoolhouse and its ritual learning. Its conception of the civil life rests upon an orderly world in majestic stasis, and does not deal with that disorderly detritus of ordinary life to which, later on, the rabbis address themselves in their small claims court. Above all, the Mishnah provides no place at all for the upheavals of history— public or personal—and the ordering and end to be effected by the Messiah. Rabbinic Judaism, fully exposed, would rest its claim upon its supernatural power to bring the Messiah: do things our way and he will come. So the *persona* of the Mishnah may be described as a priest, facing the destroyed Temple and the now-forbidden city of Jerusalem. The system of The Talmud, ca. A.D. 400, to emerge within two centuries after the closure of the Mish-

nah in A.D. 200, addressed the everyday life of Israel in the towns
and villages of the Holy Land. Its *persona* is a rabbi, walking with
his disciples through the streets and marketplaces of the country
and abroad as well.

What the Mishnah provided, therefore, was not received in a
spirit of humble acceptance. Important choices were made about
what to treat, hence what to ignore. Of the Mishnah's sixty-two
tractates (not counting Abot), the Talmud takes up only thirty-
seven, ignoring two entire divisions, the first, Agriculture (but for
Berakhot), and the Sixth, Purities (but for Niddah). So, as we see,
people really did make up their own minds on what mattered. The
exegetical mode of reception did not have to obscure the main lines
of the Mishnah's system. But it surely did so. The discrete reading
of sentences, or, at most, paragraphs, denying all context, avoiding
all larger generalizations except for those transcending the specific
lines of tractates—this approach need not have involved the utter
reversal of the paramount and definitive elements of the Mishnah's
whole and integrated world view (its "Judaism"). But doing these
things did facilitate the revision of the whole into a quite different
pattern. To use a different metaphor, they shifted the orbit of the
Mishnah from one path to another. The Mishnah centers on
the priesthood and the Temple. The Talmud took over and pushed
the whole into an orbit around the rabbi and his relationship to the
disciple, the rabbi and his activities in the court, the rabbi and his
opinions in the school. The simplest way to overcome gravity is to
reduce the critical mass of the whole. Chopping the Mishnah into
bits and pieces accomplished just that.

In many ways the Mishnah is to Scripture as the Talmud is to the
Mishnah. Just as the framers of the Mishnah received as authoritative the statements of the written Torah but picked and chose the
ones to which they wished to pay close attention, so the framers of
the Talmud treated as valid all sixty-two tractates but subjected to
sustained analysis only some of them. Scripture supplies the Mishnah with a vast wealth of facts. But the Mishnah chooses which of
those facts will shape discourse, and which (accepted as revealed)
will be ignored or left undeveloped. The system of the Mishnah is

prior to the work of identifying what statements of Scripture will be taken up and spun into swatches of the large fabric of the Mishnah itself. When—to pursue the analogy—the spinners of the thread and weavers of the fabric of the Mishnah choose a skein of biblical law, however, they do not reshape or (so to speak) dye it into some color other than the natural one.

Along these same lines, the facts of the Mishnaic law remain facts in the Talmud. They are rarely revised or drastically reshaped into something different from what, to the naked eye, their plain meaning appears to be. I cannot point to a single passage in which, as the goal of their exegetical work, the Talmud's sages seem to wish to set aside a statement of the Mishnah, or otherwise drastically twist it out of its original form and meaning. True, we must concede the possibility that among the many thousand passages of interpretation of the Mishnah in the Talmud, some people may have intended to rewrite the Mishnah's law and may have done so. But the overall impression is the reverse. And that impression is so strong and self-evident (though it may be a flaw in my vision or learning) that I cannot see the need to prove it.

The result is simple. The sages of the Mishnah read the Scripture as closely and as honestly as can be imagined. To be sure, that is not to claim their results always, or even often, coincide with the original intent of the diverse writers and framers of the Scriptural law codes. It is only to allege that the trait of mind of the Mishnaic exegetes of Scripture was no different from our own: to do their best, in an honest and forthright way, to say what the passage meant, and therefore must continue to mean. The sages of the Talmud read the Mishnah in this same way. That simple fact is attested by the whole weight and character of the Talmud. But the framers of the Talmud made choices about which laws of the Mishnah required discussion, and in carrying out these choices, they did to the Mishnah what the Mishnah's sages did to the Scripture: they made it their own.

Then what is Talmudic about the Talmud—not simply an amplification of the Mishnah's rules, but the expression of a distinctive viewpoint on them? The question divides into two. First, when does the Talmud speak for itself, not for the Mishnah? Second, what sorts of units of discourse contain such passages of "Talmudic" in the Talmud? When we collect all units of discourse, or larger parts of such units, in which exegesis of the Mishnah or expansion upon the law of the Mishnah is absent, we find at most four types, which in fact are only two.

1. THEORETICAL QUESTIONS OF LAW NOT ASSOCIATED WITH A PARTICULAR PASSAGE OF THE MISHNAH. There is some tendency to move beyond the legal boundaries set by the Mishnah's rules themselves. More general inquiries are taken up. These, of course, remain within the framework of the topic of one tractate or another, although there are some larger modes of thought characteristic of more than a single tractate.

2. EXEGESIS OF SCRIPTURE SEPARATE FROM THE MISHNAH. It is under this rubric that we find the most important instances in which the Talmud presents materials essentially independent of the Mishnah. These kinds of passages pursue problems or themes through what is said about a biblical figure, expressing ideas and values simply unknown to the Mishnah. Moreover, most of what is said in response to verses of Scripture reveals right on the surface fundamental values of what we may call, for convenience's sake, Rabbinic Judaism.

3. HISTORICAL STATEMENTS. The Talmud contains a fair number of statements that something happened, or narratives about how something happened. While many of these are replete with biblical quotations, in general they do not provide exegesis of Scripture, which serves merely as illustration or reference point.

4. STORIES ABOUT, AND RULES FOR, SAGES AND DISCIPLES, SEPARATE FROM DISCUSSION OF THE MISHNAH. The Mishnah contains a tiny number of tales about rabbis. These serve principally as precedents for, or illustrations of, rules. The Talmud by contrast contains a sizable number of stories about sages and their relationships to other people. Like the items in the second and third lists, these too may be adduced as evi-

dence of the values of the people who stand behind the Talmud, the things they thought important. These tales rarely serve to illustrate a rule or concept of the Mishnah. The main, though not the only, characteristic theme is the power of the rabbi, the honor due to the rabbi, and the tension between the rabbi and others, whether the patriarch, on the one side, the heretic on the second, or the gentile on the third.

Where we do find extensive passages in which the Mishnah is left far behind, they normally are of two kinds: (1) exegesis of narrative or theological passages of Scripture, and (2) fables about heroes. The former speaks of what rabbis said and did, while the latter tells about events on a more generous scale. Accordingly, when the Talmud presents us with ideas or expressions of a world related to, but fundamentally separate from, that of the Mishnah, that is, when the Talmud wishes to say something other than what the Mishnah says and means, it will take up one of two modes of discourse. Either we find exegesis of biblical passages, with the value system of the rabbis read into the Scriptural tales; or we are told stories about holy men and paradigmatic events, once again through tales told in such a way that a didactic purpose is served. In our study of the Talmud, we shall consider an important compilation of such stories.

WHAT IS TALMUDIC ABOUT THE TALMUD?

Distinguishing the Mishnaic from the Talmudic components of the Talmud shows us that the Talmudic sages' reading of the Mishnah takes shape within the wording and contents of the Mishnah. For these set forth the problems to be solved and furthermore guided the exegete to solutions of them. But the entire approach of the Talmud to the Mishnah is itself profoundly and distinctively Talmudic, and this in several fundamental respects.

First, the Mishnah was set forth in 200 by Rabbi Judah the Patriarch, whom we call "Rabbi" par excellence, to whose sponsorship it is credited, whole and complete, a profoundly unified, harmonious document. The Talmud some four centuries later is put together to obliterate the marks of coherence. It treats in bits and pieces what was originally meant to speak whole. That simple fact constitutes what is original, stunningly new, and, by definition, Talmudic.

Second, the Mishnah, also by definition, delivered its message in the way chosen by Rabbi. That is to say, by producing the document as he did, Rabbi left no space for the very enterprises of episodic exegesis undertaken so brilliantly by his immediate continuators and heirs. Insofar as the larger messages and meanings of the document are conveyed in the ways Rabbi chose—through formalization of language, through contrasts, through successive instances of the same, normally unspecified, general proposition, for example—the need for exegesis was surely not generated by Rabbi's own program for the Mishnah. Quite to the contrary, Rabbi chose for the Mishnah a mode of expression and defined for the document a large-scale structure and organization, which, by definition, were meant to stand firm and autonomous. Rabbi's Mishnah speaks clearly and for itself.

For the Mishnah did not merely come to closure. At that moment it also formed a closed system, that is, a whole, complete statement. It does not require facts outside of its language and formulation, so makes no provision for commentary and amplification of brief allusions, as the Talmud's style assuredly does. Taking for granted a vast range of established facts, the Mishnah nonetheless refers to little beyond itself. It promises no information other than what is provided within its limits. It raises no questions for on-going discussion beyond its decisive, final, descriptive statements of enduring realities and fixed relationships. The Talmud's single, decisive, irrevocable judgment is precisely opposite. The Talmud's first initiative is to reopen the Mishnah's closed system, almost at the moment of its completion and perfection. That at the foundations is what is Talmudic about the Talmud: its daring assertion that the concluded and completed demanded clarification and continuation. Once that assertion was made to stick, nothing else mattered very much.

What was to be clarified was obvious. What was to be continued must go forward along an essentially straight line from the starting point. No matter. The message was clear not solely in the character of the whole, still less in its contents—its assertions about the meaning of the Mishnah's laws. At every point, from the simplest gloss to the most far-ranging speculative inquiry, the message was the same. It was conveyed (as we shall learn to perceive) in the very medium of the Talmud: a new language, focused upon a new grid of discourse. The language was what it was: anything but patterned and thus anything but Mishnaic. The grid of discourse lay across, rather than within, the inner boundaries of the Mishnah itself, a profound and fundamental revolution in thought, as I have already stressed. Accordingly, the Talmud's distinctive traits, separate from those defined by the Mishnah for the age beyond the Mishnah's closure, lie not in the depths of what was said, but on the very surface, in the very literary formulation of the Talmud itself.

Yet, the judgment of the Talmud upon the Mishnah—that is, what is Talmudic in the Talmud—is not fully described when we have seen what lies scattered on the surface. When we return to the categories just now found exhaustive, we discover a program of criticism of the Mishnah framed by independent and original minds. Let us bypass the obvious points of independent judgment, the matter of insistence that the very word choices of the Mishnah require clarification, therefore prove faulty. The meanings and amplification of phrases represent the judgment that Rabbi's formulation, while stimulating and provocative, left much to be desired. These indications of independence of judgment among people disposed not merely to memorize but to improve upon the text provided by Rabbi hardly represent judgments of substance. The propositions of the Mishnah cannot stand by themselves but must be located within the larger realm of Scriptural authority. If Rabbi presented his Mishnah without proof texts in the belief that such texts were either self-evident or unnecessary, his continuators and successors rejected his judgment on both counts. So far as the Mishnah was supposed to stand as a law code independent of the revelation of Torah to Moses at Mount Sinai, it was received by people to whom such a supposition was incredible. So far as Rabbi took for granted the Scriptural facticity of the facts of his law code, that was regarded as insufficient. What was implicit (if it was implicit) had to be made explicit.

A second enterprise demands attention, the inclusion, in the Talmud, of formulations of rules in a manner, or in substance, different from the Mishnah's. These indicate that, where sages of the time of the Talmud took up Mishnaic passages, they were not at all limited to the work of gloss and secondary expansion. They recognized and exercised a quite remarkable freedom of initiative. In the Tosefta they undertook to restate in their own words, but imitating the Mishnah's style, the propositions of the Mishnah passage at hand. That is, they both cite what the Mishnah had said and also continue, in imitation of the Mishnah's language, the discourse of the Mishnah passage itself. These complements to the Mishnah are Talmudic in two senses. First, they come to expression in the period after the Mishnah had reached closure, as is clear from the fact that the exact language of the Mishnah is cited prior to the labor of extension, expansion, and revision. So they are the work of the Talmud's age and authority. Second, they self-evidently derive from precisely the same authorities responsible for the formation of the Talmud as a whole. That is the fact, by definition.

Accordingly, both the insistence upon adducing proof texts for passages Rabbi judged not to need, and the persistent revision and expansion of the Mishnah, even in clumsy imitation of the Mishnah's syntax, rhetoric, and word choices, tell us once more that simple truth we saw at the outset. The Talmud is distinctively Talmudic precisely when the Mishnah itself defines the Talmud's labor, dictates its ideas, displays its rhetoric, determines its results. The very shift in usable language, from "the Mishnah" (as a whole) to "the Mishnah passage" or "the Mishnaic law at hand" indicates the true state of affairs. On the surface, in all manner of details, the Talmud is little more than a secondary and derivative document, explaining the Mishnah itself in trivial ways, or expanding it in a casuistic and logic-chopping manner. But viewing that same surface from a different, more distant perspective and angle, we see things quite differently. In detail the Talmud changed nothing. Overall, the Talmud left nothing the same.

In the Talmud we find little to deem Talmudic in particular. But there is much that is Talmudic in general. The particular bits and pieces are Mishnaic. But the Talmud leaves nothing of the Mishnah whole and intact. Its work upon the whole presents an essentially new construction. Through the Mishnah, Rabbi contributed to the Talmud most of the bricks, but little of the mortar, and none of the joists and beams. The design of the whole bore no relationship to Rabbi's plan for the Mishnah. The sages of the Talmud did the rest. They alone imagined, then built, the building. They are the architects, theirs is the vision. The building is a monument to the authority of the sage above all.

What is most strikingly indicative of the Talmudic sages' freedom of imagination has already come before us, the exercise of free choice even among the Mishnah's tractates awaiting exegesis. We do not know why some tractates were chosen for Talmudic expansion and others left fallow. But, it is clear, in accepting authority, in centering discourse upon the ideas of other men in the Mishnah, in patiently listing even the names behind authoritative laws from olden times to their own day, the sages and framers of the Talmud accomplished exactly the opposite of what they apparently wished to do. They made a commentary. But they obliterated the text. They loyally explained the Mishnah. But they turned the Mishnah into something else than what it had been. They patiently hammered out chains of tradition, binding themselves to the authority of the remote and holy past. But it was, in the end, a tradition of their own design and choosing. That is, it was not tradition but a new creation. And so this Talmud of ours, so loyal and subservient to the Mishnah of Rabbi, turns out to be less a reworking of received materials than a work of remarkably independent judgment. The Talmud speaks humbly and subserviently about received truth, always in the name only of Moses and of sages of times past. But in the end it is truth not discovered and demonstrated, but determined and invented and declared.

First Steps in Talmud Study: Halakhah and Aggadah

In the pages that follow, we will learn four passages of the Talmud. These four passages illustrate different sorts of things we find in the Talmud, different kinds of things that the Talmud wants to tell us. For as I have now explained, the Talmud contains a great many more kinds of ideas than only interpretations of what the Mishnah says. It has, first of all, two completely different sorts of passages,

(1) about what we are supposed to do, and

(2) about what we are supposed to think and believe, about our emotions and our attitudes.

Passages about law tell us what we should do. They fall under the title, *halakhah*, from the word *halakh*, "go." The *halakhah* explains the way life should go on, the way we should do things. Passages about beliefs, opinions, attitudes are called *aggadah*, narrative. *Aggadah* spells out the values and ideals that should guide us as we follow the way of the *halakhah*.

In the coming chapters we shall have passages of a purely *halakhic* character, some of a purely *aggadic* sort, and some that mix together both kinds of material. In a given chapter of the Talmud, we are likely to find *halakhic* and *aggadic* discussion (in that order). It is unusual to find only *halakhah* or only *aggadah*. *Halakhah* is closer to the Mishnah's contents—for the Mishnah's literature is a nearly uniform set of laws, a statement of how things should be and are done. But *aggadah*—stories, wise sayings, statements of things we should believe and attitudes we should share and hold—is equally important. In fact, one of the things we should look for is the relationship between *halakhah* and *aggadah*. For the rabbis of the Mishnah and Talmud tell us to do certain things for a reason. And the reason has to do with things we believe. There is, therefore, a relationship between our actions and our attitudes, between what we are supposed to do and how we are supposed to see the world and understand our lives. We are what we do. But we *do* because of what we believe we should do. If we see *halakhah* and *aggadah* as essentially separate, we will make a great error. We will want to know only one part of the Talmud, and not the other. There are Talmud-students who are interested only in the *halakhic* parts. There are others who want to learn only the *aggadic* sections. True, the former are sharper and more compelling. Equally true, the latter are easier to understand. They speak to us more directly. But our work is not so easy. We have to understand the *halakhic* passage and the *aggadic* passage. And then we must ask ourselves how the one and the other are related.

Now we read the words of the Talmud, put together the way the Talmud puts them together. These are not simply abstracts, chosen because they are readily accessible in our terms. They are sustained passages precisely as the framers of the Talmud wrote them. Numerous anthologies of what is in the Talmud provide convenient access to what the Talmud says about various subjects. But presentations of the Talmud's own formulation of its ideas—and that means, the Talmud's mode of argument and analysis—are fewer. Anthologies of sayings and stories tell us part of what is *in* the Talmud. They do not tell us what the Talmud is. For the Talmud is not merely an anthology of this and that. It is a set of carefully worked out discussions, with a plan and a goal. The Talmud does not merely string together wise sayings. It constructs arguments. It does not merely tell stories. It makes points. It does not provide interesting information alone. It conducts serious analysis of ideas and problems.

Now, the Talmud is an extremely varied document. I have selected four sizable passages:

The first passage (Chapter Four) is wholly legal, that is, *halakhic*. It gives us an idea of how the law of the Mishnah is analyzed by the rabbis, that is Talmudic lawyers.

The next passage (Chapter Five) is interesting for two reasons. First of all, it contains discussion of both law (*halakhah*) and theology (*aggadah*). Second, it is complete, not merely an excerpt. Everything in the Babylonian Talmud about the Mishnah-passage will be before our eyes. That will allow we to see how a complete discussion unfolds—beginning, middle, and end.

The third passage (Chapter Six) likewise contains both *halakhic* and *aggadic* materials. It explains the religious life of Judaism as we practice it today and is the most relevant to our own lives as Jews.

The final passage (Chapter Seven) is mainly of an *aggadic* character and deals with issues of religious faith. It teaches us how the great lawyers of the Talmud are also important theologians, people who work out religious beliefs in a systematic and responsible way.

Chapter Eight then presents the Mishnah and the Talmud in the context of Greco-Roman philosophy. By this point we realize that the foundation-documents of the Oral Torah raise human interest, not particular to Judaism at all. So, we must ask about how other philosophers, besides the great Judaic ones, formulated matters and investigate the relationship between the Mishnah and the Talmud as media for analyzing problems of thought and right conduct with the foundation-documents of Western Civilization in Greco-Roman philosophy.

When we have studied these four passages of the Talmud, we will not know much Talmud. But we are empowered to learn more, if we wish, in English translation. For out of this book we should have a clear picture of what the Talmud is and how it works. We may even want to learn more, not only *about* the Talmud but in the Talmud itself. If we do, I should not be surprised. The Talmud has kept the attention of thoughtful intellectuals for hundreds of years and not only because it is a holy book. We can revere a holy book, but we need not study and learn it. The Talmud has fascinated Jews and is coming to engage gentiles as well because it is an interesting book. Yet, the point of interest in the Talmud is not the same as in the Mishnah. When we learn the Mishnah, we find ourselves (not always, but often) in our own world. The Mishnah is open to us. We can get at its ethical and religious issues because it is timeless. It mainly speaks of the ordinary world in which we live and tells us its ideals for and conceptions about that world. So we can move from a paragraph of the Mishnah to a happening in the world.

But while the Mishnah speaks of the world at large, the Talmud speaks of the Mishnah and, only indirectly, about the world in which we live and to which the Mishnah speaks. So we have to ask questions not immediately relevant to our lives. But these questions—the meaning of the Mishnah, the larger ideals of life contained in Scripture, the relationship of the Mishnah to Scripture, for example—also impose upon our minds an experience of asking questions. When we master Talmudic modes of learning, we acquaint our minds with a way of asking questions, a way of analyzing, a way of searching. The Mishnah speaks thoughtfully about the world. Talmud teaches us how to think about the Mishnah and about the world. The Mishnah searches out the reason and the order of the world. Talmud makes explicit the mode of reasonable thinking. The Mishnah is substance, Talmud is method. The Mishnah is what we do and say. The Talmud is *how* we think about what we do and say.

IV

Assigning the Blame

The Talmud to Mishnah Baba Qamma 3:2

What makes the Talmud "Talmudic" is the document's power to see the complicated sides of a simple situation. Indeed, the more Talmud we learn, the more we realize that nothing is so simple as it seems. For instance, if we slip on the ice in front of someone's house, we naturally blame the person who owns the house and is responsible to sand the sidewalk. But what if the owner went to St. Petersburg, Florida, for the winter and hired someone to clean the walk and sand it? Who is responsible now—the owner or the hired hand? And what if the contractor did hire a worker, and the worker did spread what he thought was sand, but the sand did no good—because it was not what it seemed? Then, is not the person who sold the faulty sand—it was granulated teflon—to blame? But he bought the material from someone else, who made it—and so it goes. Nothing is what it appears to be at the outset. The glory of the Talmud is its power to educate us to the realities of life as it really is—an endless tale, with many turnings. And that is what makes fairly assigning blame so tough.

The issue of placing blame is serious because once a person bears the blame or responsibility for something, he or she has to pay for the damages that have been caused. We all want to place the blame on the next person whenever something does go wrong, and chances are we have a considerable job to think through who should have prevented the accident. Where does the accident take place? That is yet another thing to consider. What we do in our own property and what we do in a public park or on a public road are not the same. We may use what is ours. But may we do the same thing in an area that belongs to everyone equally? We may pick our own flowers but not the flowers in a park. We may leave our garage in a mess, but we may not mess up a baseball field. Put these two things together now:

1. We have to fix the blame.
2. What we do in private property we may not do in public property.

That brings us to the problem of our first Mishnah-passage. It presents three separate actions. First, someone puts out into the public road a pile of thorns or glass. Or, second, he or she makes a fence out of thorns or glass. Or, third, he or she builds a fence on his or her own property, but the fence falls into the sidewalk or road. Other people are hurt, stumbling onto the glass, scratching themselves against the fence, of falling over the fence that is in the roadway. The one who has done these things is liable to pay damages to the injured person. Here is the Mishnah-passage that is subject to discussion, Mishnah-tractate Baba Qamma 3:2:

1. He who put away thorns or glass,
2. and he who makes his fence out of thorns,
3. and a fence which fell into the public way—
4. and others were injured by them—
5. he is liable [to pay compensation for] their injury.

Despite the quality of a narrative, the meaning of the Mishnah-passage is not obvious. We have to ask, "What does it tell us? And what are the kinds of questions that it does not answer?" For these kinds of questions are the ones that the Talmud must raise. How far does the Mishnah-passage go in unfolding its problem? And what is left for the Talmud to do? We shall ask these questions each time we (re)learn a Mishnah-passage. Now, the point of No. 1 and No. 3 is clear: a person has taken over the public road for his or her private needs. Someone else is hurt because of what this person has done. But why should a person who builds a fence on his or her own property be liable for damages caused to someone who is scratched by it? After all, the owner of the fence has done no wrong. That seems like a fair question to address to this Mishnah-passage.

Now, there is another sort of thinking we must learn how to do: how to take a principle and apply it to a fresh problem. For example: we know that if a person puts thorns or glass in the public road, he or she has to pay damages to anyone injured thereby. But what if a person tears down the wall not knowing there are thorns and glass in it, and thorns and glass fall into the road? Who is responsible—the owner of the wall? Or the person who put the thorns and glass into the wall? The owner did not put the thorns or glass into the wall. The owner has done nothing to cause damage. But the one who did put the thorns and glass into the wall did *not* tear down the wall and spread the thorns and glass onto the road. So this is a new problem, yet it comes out of the old one. Once we know that the owner is responsible, we must ask about things for which the owner is not *directly* but still is *ultimately* responsible. That matter of ultimate, or second-level, responsibility is not to be missed.

There is still another level of meaning. We have to keep the law. But we want to do more than that. Some people do only what they must. But good people do more. Some people *avoid causing* accidents on their own. Others act in a positive way to prevent accidents. Some people drive too fast and only slow down when they see a police car. Others drive at safe speeds all the time. Obviously, no one is *always* virtuous, and no one is never virtuous. Most of us fall in the middle. But what do the most virtuous people do? That is something we are going to want to know.

Clearly, the work of the explanation of our Mishnah-passage is going to be considerable. We have three areas of concern. First, we want to know why the person referred to in No. 2 is responsible for damage caused by a fence the person built on his or her own property. Second, we want to know about complications in Nos. 1 and 3, when one person does not do the damage, yet is still ultimately responsible for it. Third, we have a question about what we should do—not only what we must not do—to avoid hurting other people.

EXPLAINING THE MISHNAH: If we look again at our passage of the Mishnah, the first thing we notice is the problem in No. 2: Why should someone be liable merely for building a wall of thorns on his or her own property? People do have the right to build on their own land whatever they want. If outsiders stumble onto their land and get hurt, that is not the fault of the land-owner, who did not invite or expect the outsider.

One of the earlier Amoraim in the Land of Israel, Yohanan, who flourished in the third century C.E., will now answer that question. What he will do is simple and daring. He will impose an idea of his own upon the Mishnah. This he does by defining the *case* to which the Mishnah refers. By saying what case the Mishnah treats, he excludes many cases from the rule of the Mishnah. And by limiting the case to which the Mishnah applies, he greatly changes the meaning that the Mishnah had to begin with. The first five lines (A–E) contain Yohanan's comment on the Mishnah-passage. The next three (F–H) have a further explanation of what Yohanan has said. In order to show in a graphic way the relationship of one component of the little construction to the next, I indent what is secondary and derivative.

A. Said R. Yohanan,
B. This Mishnaic ruling refers only
C. [to a case in which thorns] projected.
D. But [in a case in which they were] confined [to private property],
E. there is no liability [he is exempt].
F. Why is he exempt [in this case]?

G. Said R. Aha son of R. Iqa,

H. Because it is not the way of people to rub against walls.

Yohanan asks the obvious question: "Why should the fence I build on my own property cause me to be blamed if someone is injured by it? After all, what's on my land is mine. If you don't want to get hurt, keep off my land." Yohanan takes the Mishnah No. 2 and turns it on its head. He does so by reading into the Mishnah precisely the concern we have spelled out. According to Yohanan, the Mishnaic ruling refers only to a fence of thorns *when the thorns project out onto the public road*. But if the thorns do not project onto the public road, and someone is injured by them, the owner of the fence pays nothing.

That solution proves so compelling that we have to wonder whether it has been manufactured for the occasion, or whether the inner logic of the law demands this and no other conclusion. That is to say, Is Yohanan reading something into our Mishnah-passage? Or has he some basis for what he says in what the Mishnah says for itself? I am inclined to think he is on strong ground. For look at the Mishnah No. 1: He who *puts out* thorns and glass. We took for granted that this means, He who puts out *onto the public road*. No. 3 clinches the matter: a fence that fell into the public way. The context, therefore, says precisely what Yohanan claims phrase No. 2 also says. The whole Mishnah-passage speaks of damage done in the public way. Why should Yohanan not claim that our clause also addresses that same circumstance?

We still must explain why a person would not be liable for damages caused on his or her own property. After all, in general one has to be careful, even at home, not to injure other people. This is the question that Aha, son of Iqa, wants to answer. I might be responsible for what happens on my own land if I could foresee that it might happen. That is, if I have a big hole on my property and someone falls into it, there are circumstances in which I shall be held to blame. But if people in general are not likely to hurt themselves, how could I foresee that this particular person would be injured? This is the view of Aha. If I maintain a nuisance on my own property, I might be liable. But if people do not usually injure themselves in the way in which this person has been injured, there is no way that I could foresee what has happened. I could not, therefore, have prevented this accident. I do not have to pay. People generally do not rub themselves up against walls. How could I know that this person would do what no normal person does? The injured party is to blame. I should not have to pay. And I do not have to pay. Aha completes the statement begun by Yohanan. Yohanan has specified the circumstance in which I am responsible. Aha has explained the circumstance in which I am not responsible.

Have the Amoraim before us, Yohanan and Aha b. R. Iqa, fully explained the Mishnah-passage? The answer to that question depends on us. If we can think of questions they have not asked, or of situations for which they have not made a ruling, then we will have to join in the discussion begun by Yohanan and Aha.

EXPANDING THE MISHNAH'S RULE: Our Mishnah-passage raises its own questions. We know that a person is responsible for what he or she does. If I cause damage and am liable to pay, I pay. That simple fact bears its own complications.

What happens if I do not cause the damage directly? What if someone else starts that chain of events that ends with my doing harm to someone else? Let us take the case begun in our Mishnah-passage. I cannot put away thorns and glass by dumping them into the road. But my neighbor, who is building a fence, can use these materials. Without telling him, I go and pour my garbage—my thorns and glass—into the fence. Then, as the fence is built up, the thorns and glass are covered over. Have I done right? Surely I have, as anyone who has covered over a dump with grass may fairly claim.

Then what happens? The unpredictable! The owner of the fence tears it down because he or she wants to open his field. As a result, glass I hid in the fence is now poured into the public way. Someone is cut on the glass I put in the fence. Am I responsible? Is the owner of the fence responsible? The Mishnah as we know it does not answer this question. Why not? Because Yohanan has only told me that if my glass and thorns are made into a fence on private property, I do not have to pay. Well, I did put them into a fence on private property. Someone else has made them fall into the road. But why should that other person—the owner of the fence—be made to pay? After all, the glass and thorns belong to me.

This is the problem of the following teaching (A–E). Here we come to an important technical signal that the Talmud (among the other halakhic composites) presents very commonly. Section A uses a formula that we will see again, *Our rabbis have taught*. The word for taught, means "repeat." The meaning is that this is a tradition that goes along with the Mishnah's teachings. The language is the same as that of the Mishnah in general. So is the way in which the words are arranged, as we will notice if we compare the sentence-pattern of the passage before us (called a *"baraita"*) with the Mishnah's sentence-pattern. The formula, our rabbis have taught, and similar formulas signal the status of what is to be stated, namely: the rule that follows enjoys the standing and authority of rules that we find in the Mishnah; it has not been included in the Mishnah but it must be brought into relationship with the rules that are in that authoritative document. That is why the rule that follows the formula will conform to the formal protocol governing in the Mishnah; the named authorities, if any, will always occur, also, in the Mishnah; the rule will be formulated in response to the conventions that govern the counterpart rule in the Mishnah. But the substance of this new, external-to-the-Mishnah (hence, *baraita*, external) rule may well conflict with its Mishnah-counterpart, or it may move beyond the limits of its Mishnah-counterpart, raising secondary problems or introducing complicating factors. We notice, too, that when a post-Mishnaic authority appears, his statement is framed as a comment on the available, prior rule, as though that rule had appeared in the Mishnah itself. Once more, I indent what is secondary or contingent.

After A, our *baraita* proceeds to give its rule, and, once more, we have Yohanan's comment on it.

A. Our rabbis have taught:
B. a person who hid thorns and broken glass in the wall of his fellow,

C. and the owner of the wall came and tore down his wall,
D. and it [the thorns or glass] fell into the public road and did damage—
E. the one who hid [them in the wall] is liable.
F. Said R. Yohanan,
G. This teaching refers only to a wobbly wall.
H. But in the case of a solid wall,
I. he who hides [them] away is exempt,
J. but liable is the owner of the wall [who tore it down].

The question of responsibility is answered simply: The person who put the thorns and glass into the wall is responsible when the thorns and the glass pour out of the wall and onto the public road. The one who *ultimately* causes the injury is the one who pays. The owner of the wall owes nothing. Why not? Because he or she did not put the glass and thorns into the wall to begin with. Yohanan (F–J) is not very happy with this one-sided ruling. Why should the owner of the wall bear no responsibility? After all, this owner tore down the wall and caused the carefully placed thorns and glass to scatter onto the public road.

Showing remarkable imagination and independence of spirit, Yohanan's solution is to rewrite the *baraita*, just as he rewrote the Mishnah-passage. He says that the one who hid the thorns and glass in the wall bears full responsibility only when the wall is not a strong one. If it is wobbly and obviously going to collapse, then this is hardly a safe place for the thorns and glass. The one who puts them there has to have the foresight to expect the wall to collapse and the thorns and glass to fall out onto the public road. So what happens is his or her fault.

But if the wall is solid, then the one who hid thorns and glass in its rubble has no reason whatsoever to expect the thorns and glass to end up on the highway. The person did the right thing, in the right way. So, Yohanan maintains, the one who tears down the wall is responsible for whatever happens. Why? Because the owner of the wall must take responsibility for rubble caused by tearing down the (formerly solid) wall. And so he or she must put away the thorns and glass that—after all—helped to build the wall to begin with. Yohanan's distinction between a wobbly wall and a solid wall thus allows him to turn around the sense and meaning of the *baraita*. Now, we cannot turn to the context of the *baraita* to ask whether the person who made it up would concur with Yohanan. But do we think he would? I doubt it because the author of the *baraita* knows no distinctions between one kind of wall and another.

The author of the *baraita* is clear on his view. The person who puts thorns or glass into the wall is responsible for what they do if and when they fall out of the wall. That person has not done his or her job. So we must take careful measures, even beyond the requirements of the law, in order to avoid doing harm to other people. That is the opinion of the pious rabbis of the Talmud whom we shall meet in the next chapter. As I said, Yohanan is a brave man. Living a long time after the completion of the Mishnah, he is willing to take a critical view of the ideas and rules of the Mishnah. He is happy to say what he thinks. He does this by discovering in the Mishnah's words the ideas he holds and the conceptions that he has formed of what is right and just. He then has the courage to insist that the *baraita*, too, claims what he believes Mishnah says. And why not—since if he is right about the Mishnah-passage and its meaning, he must also be correct about the *baraita* and its message.

Here a digression is in order. This attitude of mind, this spirit of autonomous judgment—these do not come naturally; they result from nurture, from an education that stresses the importance of clear, logical, critical thinking. Those many generations of holy Israel that received their education in the pages of the Talmud acquired not only knowledge, but attitudes and modes of thought, such as those for which Yohanan, in the small case at hand, stands out. Holy Israel wants sons and daughters able to think for themselves and make a solid case for their viewpoints.

Now, back to the case at hand: We have spoken thus far only about the specific case of our Mishnah-passage. We have the fence, glass, thorns, and a public road. Are we limited to this case? Or will the principle extend to a variety of other cases? Obviously, no rule can cover all possible situations. We have to be able to articulate the rule and uncover its general principle, then apply that encompassing principle to a variety of cases; otherwise we are stuck with useless facts, historical facts.

If all we talk about is one event or one situation, we have no law at all; each event is treated differently from all others, then there are no useful rules. Where there are no rules, there can be no justice, no equity—no sanctified society. How can things be done fairly if there is one law for me and another for you, one law for this case, another law for that case? Now the expansion of the Mishnah passage accomplished by the *baraita* and by Yohanan calls forth its own explanation and expansion. Rabina, who lived a century or more after Yohanan, gives us a fresh case.

But the case only looks new. In fact, it appears to say something so obvious as not to require articulation. If we know the rule that governs the wall, we shall not need a new case to repeat the established principle. So, the problem of explaining the expansion of the Mishnah-passage is this: We have to make sense of what appears to be not an explanation, but merely a repetition. Why recapitulate? The passage before us begins with the second version of the story of the wall, then we are told the version is obvious, and that brings us to the real purpose, which is to say something new and interesting. What we now take up is one of the glories of the Talmud, its insistence that banality and repetition be condemned, that diverse possibilities be weighed—once more a means of opening minds to fresh possibilities in an on-going speculation on the inner logic of the everyday:

A. Said Rabina,
B. That is to say, he who covers his pit with the cover of his fellow
C. and the owner of the cover came along and took away his cover
D. the owner of the pit is liable [for damage done to someone who falls into the pit]

E. That is obvious!

F. What might we have said [had we not been told the case about the pit]?

G. [We might have said], this ruling [about the wall] applies where [the owner of the wall] did not know [the identity of the one who put thorns or glass into his wall] so as to inform him [that he planned to tear it down].

H. But here [in the case of the pit], where he [the owner of the cover] knew [the identity of the one who had borrowed his cover to cover up the pit], he should have informed him [of his plan to remove the cover] [and therefore the owner of the cover is liable].

I. Thus, the ruling teaches us [that the contrary is the case. That is, the owner of the pit remains responsible under all circumstances].

First comes the case, then the analysis. The case is simple. I have a pit on my land. I need to cover it up. My neighbor has a garbage can with a lid. I take the lid and use it to cover over the hole in my ground. The neighbor comes over and takes the lid back. Then someone walks on my land and falls into the hole. Does my neighbor have to pay? Obviously not! He or she did not dig the hole and was not responsible to cover it. I dug the hole. I did not cover it properly. I am responsible. Now, did I tell anything we did not know? Not if we paid attention to the *baraita* we just studied. For if I put thorns or glass into a wobbly wall, I am responsible for damage that they do. Why? Because I have to suppose the wall may fall down. If I cover a hole with a lid belonging to my neighbor, I am responsible for damages done by the hole. Why? Because I have to realize my neighbor is going to need the lid back. Rabina is not going to say obvious things. Therefore, he must have told this case for a reason. And he also has to know the story of the wobbly wall. So what can be his purpose?

This is the view of E and F. What seems obvious is not, when we realize what we might have imagined! G and H show what is at issue. They read into the *baraita* a problem and a solution just as

Yohanan, when he read the baraita, rephrased its message. This is, as I said, a free and courageous process in which people use their minds and exercise their reason without restraint. The *baraita* tells of a wall owner who is in no way responsible for what the wobbly wall has done. The one who put the glass and thorns in the wall should have had the foresight to realize the wobbly wall would fall. But, if the wall owner told the owner of the glass and thorns what was going to happen, the owner of the glass and thorns would be responsible. If the owner of the wall did not inform the owner of the glass and thorns, who is responsible? Surely not the owner of the glass and thorns! He or she never had a chance to correct the situation. If the owner of the wall had told the person to take away the glass and thorns and the person did not do so, then, *and only then*, will the owner of the thorns and glass bear the blame for damage done by them.

Now, in the case of the pit, the owner of the cover knows who has taken the cover. The owner of the pit knows whose cover it is. What happens? C tells us that the owner of the cover comes along and takes it away. So [D], the owner of the pit is liable. Now this is a case in which the owner of the cover has a serious responsibility. He or she should have informed the man of the plan to take back the cover. So the owner of the pit should not be responsible. Not so, not so! The owner of the pit is responsible under *all* circumstances. And if I did not know the case of the pit and the lid, I would never have been able to reach that necessary conclusion. There is no duty to tell the one who owns the thorns, or the one who owns the pit, that those thorns or that pit will do injury to someone. The owner should know that. In both cases, therefore, the owner of the glass or the owner of the pit will bear full responsibility. The owner cannot shift the blame, or part of the blame, to someone else. We have not gone far from our Mishnah-passage. We started by asking about who gets blamed. And we are still asking about who bears the blame. Only the details and the depth of our discussion have changed. The basic principle is the same; the basic conceptions are the same—and the essential rule is unchanged.

How the Pious People Do Things: How shall I behave so as not to cause injury to other people? The Talmud's discussion of this question must come because we cannot be left only with a rule for the average person. We must know what the careful and conscientious person does. It is not enough, therefore, to be told why and how we will not be liable for damage done by our thorns and glass. We have to be told how to avoid doing damage, whether or not we will be liable. The law is for ordinary folk. But we have to be told how the people who go beyond the strict requirement of the law conduct themselves. And that is the purpose of the *baraita* that follows. It, too, has a little explanation attached. The *baraita* is A–D, and E and F provide two illustrations. Then, to conclude this discussion, we have a reflection on the larger issue: How to learn to do not merely what the law requires, but what truly good people do.

Again, I indent to signal the presence of secondary formations and amplifications of the primary statement, A–D. Thus, E–F provide practical illustrations. G–H then add a generalization that transcends the case at hand. To be authentically pious is to be responsible for the public interest; then what must I know to accomplish that goal. I–J then tell where the principles of personal responsibility are to be learned. Tractate Abot, as we already realize, has given us principles in the form of generalizations. The teachings of Berakhot, which concern expressing attitudes of thanks, provide yet another means for reflection on the well-considered conduct of life. These form alternatives to Judah's view that piety flows from knowledge of one's public, civic responsibility, set forth in the division of Torts, in which our tactate finds a prominent position. Now to the text:

A. Our rabbis have taught
B. the pious men of old would hide away their thorns and pieces of glass in their fields,
C. and bury them three handbreadths deep
D. so that the plough should not be hindered.
E.   R. Sheshet [who was blind] would throw them into the fire.

F.   Raba would throw them into the Tigris.

G.   Said Rab Judah, Whoever wants to be pious

H.   should carry out the teachings of the Division of Torts [avoiding causing damage to other people].

I.   Raba said, [Such a person should observe] the teachings in Abot.

J.   And others say, The teachings of Berakhot.

The best way to avoid causing damage is to bury our thorns and glass away from the public road. They should be buried deep, so that the plough will not turn them up. When the thorns and glass are properly buried, then, but only then, we never have to worry about what will happen to them. That ideal solution (B–D) is credited to the pious men of olden times. But then the Talmud refers to people of its own day, of the third and fourth centuries C.E. It shifts its language, as we might have noticed, from Hebrew, in which the Mishnah teachings and stories are told, to Aramaic, in which the Talmud's own authorities express their ideas. In E and F we have two examples of what living authorities do. Sheshet burns up the thorns and glass as best he can. He is blind and cannot rely on any other means of disposing of them. Raba throws them into the river that flows by his farm. This is a sure way of getting rid of them without danger to other people. We notice, once more, how the Talmud respects the people of its own day. What the old authorities of the Mishnah did is a great example for what pious people should do today. But we shall not ignore the pious people of our own day. Their deeds also are recorded. The attitude here is that we are not inferior to our fathers and mothers or to their fathers and mothers.

This brings us to the sayings that conclude our discussion. They are unusual because they depart from the topic we have discussed and turn, instead, to the ethical principle underlying the topic and its rules. That principle is easy to state: We do not want to hurt other people. Rab Judah says that the purpose of being a religious person is to avoid hurting other people. That is why a person who wants to be truly religious should study the rules of Neziqin, that is, the fourth division of the Mishnah, the division that deals with torts and damages. Our Mishnah-passage is in that division. So what Judah is telling us is to study just what we have been studying.

Raba (I) and other people (J) have different views of what we need to know in order to be truly religious. Raba says a person should study the teachings of tractate Abot. J's message is that to be pious we have to know how to thank God for the good things God does for us. Therefore, we should study the teachings of Berakhot. We are going to study some of those teachings also.

THE TALMUD ALL TOGETHER. BABYLONIAN TALMUD. BABA QAMMA 30A (EXCERPT): Now that we have examined each unit *of* the larger Talmud, we have yet another task. It is to see as a whole the Talmud that serves our Mishnah-passage. And I want us to see the Talmud as it is printed. We will realize that while it looks like a mass of words—lacking all indication of where one sentence ends and another begins, one paragraph stops and another starts—we can, in fact, make out the complete thoughts and units of thought. We just need patience. I suggest that we read the passage out loud and explain it, phrase by phrase. Then read it a second time and explain it paragraph by paragraph. That is, give the main idea or gist of what the Talmud is saying as a single, complete idea. Then read it a third time and try to outline the way in which the Talmud organizes its ideas. The third time around, we should be able to predict what the Talmud is going to want to do when it confronts a particular passage of the Mishnah.

1 He who puts out thorns and glass
2 and he who makes his fence of thorns
3 and a fence which fell into the public way
4 and other people are hurt by
5 he is liable for their injury.

I. A. Said R. Yohanan,
    B. This Mishnaic ruling refers only

C. [to a case in which thorns] projected

D. But [in a case in which they were] confined [to private property],

E. there is no liability [he is exempt].

F. Why is he exempt [in this case]?

G. Said R. Aha son of R Iqa,

H. Because it is not the way of people to rub against the walls.

II. A. Our rabbis have taught:

B. A person who hid thorns and broken glass in the wall of his fellow,

C. and the owner of the wall came and tore down his wall,

D. and it [the thorns or glass] fell into the public road and did damage—

E. the one who hid [them in the wall] is liable.

F. Said R. Yohanan,

G. This teaching refers only to a wobbly wall.

H. But in the case of a solid wall,

I. He who hides [them] away is exempt,

J. but liable is the owner of the wall [who tore it down].

III. A. Said Rabina,

B. That is to say, He who covers his pit with the cover

C. and the owner of the cover came along and took away his cover—

D. the owner of the pit is liable [for damage done to someone who falls into the pit].

E. That is obvious!

F. What might we have said [had we not been told the case about the pit]?

G. [We might have said,] This ruling [about the wall] applies where [the owner of the wall] did not know [the identity of the one who put thorns or glass into his wall] so as to inform him [that he planned to tear it down].

H. But here [in the case of the pit], where he [the owner of

the cover] knew [the identity of the one who had borrowed his cover to cover up the pit], he should have
informed him [of his plan to remove the cover [and
therefore, the owner of the cover is liable].

I.   Thus, the ruling teaches us [that the contrary is the case.
That is, the owner of the pit remains responsible under
all circumstances].

IV. A.   Our rabbis have taught
    B.   the pious men of old would hide away their thorns
         and pieces of glass in their fields,
    C.   and bury them three handbreadths deep,
    D.   so that the plough should not be hindered.
    E.   R. Sheshet [who was blind] would throw them into
            the fire.
    F.   Raba would throw them into the Tigris.
    G.   Said Rab Judah, Whoever wants to be pious
    H.   should carry out the teachings of the Division of
               Torts [avoiding causing damage to other people].
    I.   Raba said, [Such a person should observe] the
                  teachings in Abot.
    J.   And others say, The teachings of Berakhot.

Seeing the Talmud whole shows us how logically and cogently it
is organized. Some present the Talmud as simply a mass of information—sayings, stories—with only minimal traits of organization. But this passage shows us that the Talmud is carefully crafted,
with what is primary set forth first, what is contingent, second. The
sequence—first the Mishnah is explained, then further complications are explored—builds from the simple to the complex. By
carefully composing an unfolding analytical argument, the fram-
er(s) of the passage have turned information into knowledge, facts
into data important in an argument, a whole that is greater than
the sum of the parts.

WHAT IS THE TALMUD? A while ago, we asked ourselves why the
Mishnah needed the Talmud at all and what the Mishnah asks the

Talmud to do. We have now studied an important example of what the Talmud does for the Mishnah. Let us specify these important services to the Mishnah.

1. The Mishnah must be explained. There are various sides to the Mishnah that might require explanation. We may see an unusual word or phrase. We frequently (thought not here) will ask about the Scriptural source for the Mishnah's rule. In our passage Yohanan has been troubled by what he thought to be something unfair in the Mishnah. Rather than spelling matters out in detail, our Talmudic passage has simply given Yohanan's conclusion. For our part, we used our reason to figure out what was bothering him and why he interpreted the Mishnah-passage as he did.

2. The Mishnah's rule must be subjected to further thought. The work of Talmud is not merely to comment on the Mishnah's language and its ideas. It has also to pay attention to the larger ideas that the Mishnah passage implies. The second stage in the Talmud's work on the Mishnah, therefore, is to separate the idea from the Mishnah-passage, which expresses that idea.

3. Once we expand and explain the Mishnah's rule, it is perfectly natural to go on and expand and explain our first expansion and explanation. For sometimes what we think is expansion is simply repetition. And the Talmud does not respect people who merely repeat themselves or say in other words what someone already has clearly said. So if the Talmud contains another version of a saying or a story or a rule, and if it then chooses to cite and quote that other version, the first thing the Talmud will ask is, "Is all this not perfectly obvious? If it is obvious, then why are we telling it to me?"

4. If the Talmud were interested only in ordinary folk, its discussion of the present Mishnah-passage would have come to an end. But the Talmud wants to present us with more than rules for everyday people. The Talmud discusses ideals for which we can and should strive. That is why in the end it tells us what we should do to avoid having to know the rule with which we began. We can arrange if we want, to avoid causing damage, and we are able to

cite the actual practice of religious people in this regard. At that same point in the unfolding of our unit of the Talmud, we have more general reflections. At that point our discussion is brought to a conclusion.

SO WHAT IS THE TALMUD? Is it a commentary—an explanation—of the Mishnah? Of course it is, but it is more than that. How much more? Perhaps the obvious answer is, It is an expansion and extension of the Mishnah's rules. But we already know that the Amoraim of our passage—Yohanan, Iqa, and others—move far beyond the rules of the Mishnah. They will not hesitate to reverse what the Mishnah says, to turn it right on its head. So the Talmud's authorities are remarkably free and independent minds. They are deeply respectful of the Mishnah and its rules. But they are not enslaved by them. They take seriously what the Mishnah has to tell them. But they also take to heart their own ideas. So, the Talmud is both dependent on and independent of the Mishnah. It explains, expands, and spells out what the Mishnah says. But it also says what it wants to say.

TALMUD, TORAH, JUDAISM: Now that we have completed our first exercise in learning Talmud, we should not forget why we began this work. It was because Talmud is part of Torah, and Torah is the native word for the secular term, Judaism. Torah is the word we use at home when to the world outside we use the word Judaism. Just as we ask, "What is Talmud?" it is fair to ask, "What have we learned about Torah, that is, about Judaism?" One small passage of the Talmud obviously does not provide the whole answer. But surely part of a whole answer is to say, "Judaism is a religion about a wobbly wall." Judaism speaks about concrete questions of how to act in ordinary life. One important concern of Judaism is to make us people who accept and carry out our responsibilities to other people. To drive a car so as to endanger the life of someone else is a sin in Judaism. To build a wall that is firm and prevents people from getting hurt is a good deed. The Talmud is important for

Judaism today not because it was important a long time ago, but because it teaches us to think about the world in which we live. We study Talmud to learn not history or culture, but the rules of everyday life as holy Israel has uncovered the logic of equity and justice, the prerequisites of sanctification.

V

A Complete Passage of the Talmud:
I Didn't Really Mean It

The Talmud to Mishnah Nedarim 9:1–2

The Talmud has more to say about the Mishnah-passage that we just studied; we only considered an excerpt. This was helpful in showing us how the Talmud does its business. But it does not give us a clear picture of how the Talmud completely discusses a given Mishnah-passage. For this purpose we turn now to one of the most interesting kinds of Mishnah law, which has to do with the force of the words we say. In the times of the Mishnah and the Talmud, people believed that if they took a vow, they had to keep it. If they did not keep it, they feared that heaven would punish them. For example, someone might say something in a fit of anger. Afterward, he would not dismiss as nothing what he had said. He would be full of remorse. He would do what he said he would do.

This sort of vow might be as follows in our day. We are arguing with our friend. We get so angry at him or her that we say, "I'll never talk to you again." Ten minutes later, we get over the argument. But you've said something. Now, how do we take it back? In olden times, things were not much different. We have a friend who wants us to come to his or her house for dinner. We don't want to go. In order to persuade this person to stop nagging us, we shout,

"Qonam be anything I eat of yours." "Qonam" is a word that imitates the word Qorban, offering or sacrifice. What we have said, therefore, is that as far as we are concerned, any of our friend's food is equivalent to a sacrifice in the Temple. That means we cannot each such food. For we cannot eat the animal-sacrifices that are offered up to God or reserved for the Temple priests. It follows that our friend had better stop nagging us because we are not in a position to eat this food again.

This sort of "vowing" took place among ordinary folk because they would frequently lose their tempers and explode into vows. Since they believed that God hears what human beings say, just as God oversees what human beings do, they knew they had to keep their word. And they most certainly did keep their vows. But that is only part of the story. The sages of the Mishnah and the Talmud understood that circumstances can change.

What happens, however, if matters are not so clear? It is possible that there can be a valid vow, which in the end can be released or untied. We should say untie and "tie up" a vow because a vow ties us up in knots—knots made of words. Sages are able to untie the knots of vows if they can find suitable grounds. They are able to show that the vow we made was never binding; it never did tie us up in knots at all. We thought it did, and we kept it. But a sage can find the grounds to declare otherwise.

The Mishnah-passage before us asks, "What are acceptable grounds for declaring a vow to be null?" Eliezer has an interesting idea. He points out that only gross people take vows. It is a sign that we are not well brought up, that we do not think before we speak, that we do not have our wits about us. So, he says, we should declare as proper grounds for untying a vow the fact that by taking the vow, the person has brought shame to his or her father and mother. People will go around saying, "Mr. and Mrs. So-and-so have raised a loud-mouthed bum." So the sage should ask the fellow, "If you had known that people would go around and speak ill of your parents, would you have taken your vow?" If the man says, "No, I should never have vowed had I known people would make fun of my parents for having me as their son," that is enough. The vow is untied.

Sages reject this opinion. They do not think that is a sufficient reason to untie the vow. Then Sadoq comments rather sarcastically on Eliezer's idea. He points out that vows bring shame not only to one's father and mother. They also bring shame to God. After all, taking such vows is hardly respectful to Heaven. And, he then says, if such were to be suitable grounds for untying the vow, then no vow would be valid. For under all and any circumstances, someone could readily say, "If I had known that by taking this dumb vow, I should bring disgrace to Heaven, I should never have taken that vow." So, Sadoq says, Eliezer's position leads to the absurd result that there never could be a valid vow. Finally, sages concede one thing to Eliezer. They say that if a person took a vow that affects one's relations with one's parents—for example, refusing to visit them ever—then we can untie the vow by saying something about the honor we owe our father and mother. If a daughter, for instance, took a vow not to visit her father and mother, we can say to her, "If you had known that by taking this vow, you could *not* pay respect to your father and mother, would you have *taken* the vow?" If the girl *says*, "No," then we *have* the power to declare the vow untied. This is not granting much to Eliezer, for the girl has taken a vow contrary to what the Torah requires, which is that she honor her father and her mother. Sadoq will not be offended by sages' concession. Why not? Because, so far as he is concerned, this is a minor matter—as opposed to the world-shaking conception that vows may be untied by reference to the honor of God.

Let us now turn to the first part of the Mishnah-passage to which the Talmud we shall study is devoted, Mishnah-tractate Nedarim 9:1–2:

Rabbi Eliezer says: They untie [a vow] for a person on account of the honor of his father and his mother.
And sages prohibit [keep it tied].
Said Rabbi Sadoq: Before they untie [a vow] for him on account of his father and his mother, let them untie it for him on account of the honor of the Omnipresent.

[And] if so, there will be no vows [at all]!
And sages agree with Rabbi Eliezer concerning a matter [about which he vowed] between his father and his mother, that they untie it for him on account of the honor of his father and his mother.

The next part of the Mishnah-passage is much easier to follow because it explains itself. As we will see if we look at the passage rapidly, The additions give examples of the same point as is made. Eliezer's position is that if something happens after we take a vow, we can say, "If I had known that that would happen, I should never have vowed." As a result, our vow is null. Sages declare that what happens after the vow has no effect upon the vow. Why not? Because we take the vow in full knowledge of what we are saying. If we are wrong, it is a vow made in error. We are not bound by such a vow. But if the facts are what we think they are, then there are no grounds to untie the vow. It was valid and remains in force. The right grounds for annulling a vow must be that things were not what we thought they were when we said what we said. Then we can claim there never really was a vow in force.

And furthermore did Rabbi Eliezer say: They untie [a vow] on account of something which happened [later on]. And sages prohibit
How so? [If] he said, Qonam—that I shall not derive benefit from so-and-so and he [so-and-so] became a scribe or was going to marry off his son very soon
and he said, If I had known that he would become a scribe or that he would marry off his son very soon I should not have taken a vow Qonam against this house, that I shall not enter it and it was made into a synagogue [if] he said, If I had known that it would be made into a synagogue, I should not have taken a vow,
Rabbi Eliezer unties [the vow], and sages prohibit [keep it tied].

The cases provide a beautiful explanation for the basic dispute. We have three examples of the same thing. In each of them a person says that if he or she had known what was going to happen later on, he or she would not have taken such a vow. At the end comes the predictable decision. Eliezer declares the vow to be untied. These are suitable grounds because they untie a vow on account of something which happens later on. Sages declare the vow to be tied. These are not suitable grounds. The vow was valid when the person took it. Why should it not be valid now?

EXPLAINING THE MISHNAH: The most interesting statement in the Mishnah-passage we just examined is the claim of Eliezer, there won't be any more vows. Precisely what does he mean? Does he mean that no one will vow any more? Why should that be the case merely because we have made it remarkably easy to untie a vow? Sadoq claims that if we may untie a vow on the grounds that a vow is not respectful to God, there will not be any more vows at all. This is a curious statement. The first task of the Talmud that serves our Mishnah-passage is to explain the meaning of the language. As soon as that work is done, we immediately test the meaning we have assigned to the Mishnah-passage. We have to be sure that we are right. And this we shall do by reading the rest of the Mishnah-passage in the light of the explanations we have given. First, let us examine the meaning of Sadoq's saying as it is analyzed by the great Amoraim, Abbaye and Raba.

A. What is [the meaning of,] "There will be no vows?"
B. Said Abbaye,
C. If so, no vows may be unbound.
D. And Raba said,
E. If so, Vows will not be brought for inquiry [and absolution] to a sage.
F. We have learned:
G. And sages concede to R. Eliezer that in a matter involving himself and his father and mother, they do release him by reason of the honor of his father and his mother.
H. Certainly, this accords with Abbaye, who said, If so, no vows may be unbound;
I. here, if he has been so impudent, he is impudent.

J. But so far as Raba is concerned, who said, If so, vows will not be brought for inquiry [and absolution] to a sage,

K. in this case, why do they unbind [the vow]?

L. I shall tell you:

M. since all vows cannot be [untied] without a sage,

N. here, too, they [sages] will declare the vow unbound.

Abbaye claims (B) that Sadoq means: If we accept the honor of God as a suitable pretext for annulling a vow, then there will be no more proper annulling of vows. Abbaye's thinking is: On what grounds do we ever declare a vow to be untied? It is because of genuine regret, when someone truly repents what he or she has said. If a person does not truly regret his or her vow, it cannot be properly annulled or untied. Now what happens if we say to someone, "Would we have taken such a vow if we had known it was not respectful to God?" Is there anyone in the world who would have the gall—the hutzpah—to say, "Yes, I would have taken that vow!"? Abbaye says, "No one in the world would make such a statement." As a result, however, people will be able to untie vows that they do not sincerely repent taking. Why? Because no one is so impudent as to say otherwise. As a result, vows will no longer be properly revoked. In other words, the grounds for untying the vow, in Sadoq's opinion, are so slight that vows that still should be binding will be untied. That is one way of seeing Sadoq's statement in the Mishnah passage.

Raba's view is close to Abbaye's. But it still differs. Raba says, "We make it so easy to annul a vow that no one will go to a sage. Why not? Because everyone can do it for himself or herself." God's honor applies to all vows. If it is sufficient grounds for annulling the vow, then everyone will carry out the untying without going to a sage. As a result, vows will no longer be supervised by sages. Do Abbaye and Raba disagree? According to what we have just said about their opinions, they certainly do not disagree. In fact, they say almost the same thing, though in slightly different language. Each one is concerned about proper untying of vows. Abbaye is afraid that the wrong motives will be considered effective. Raba is afraid that the wrong people will do the untying. Both see Sadoq as expressing concern about the proper untying of vows by the right people for the right motive.

There is one small problem with Abbaye's and Raba's explanation of the Mishnah-passage. Sadoq is not talking about untying vows. He is talking about vows. He says to Eliezer that there will not be any more vows. He does not talk about proper untying of vows. Yet, Abbaye and Raba have a strong basis for what they read into Sadoq's sentence. It is this: Eliezer has spoken of grounds for absolving, not foundations forsaking, vows. So, if we read what Sadoq has said as a reply to Eliezer, then it must have only one reference. Sadoq, too, must speak of untying vows, not making them. So when he says, "There will be no vows," he must mean, "There will be no untying of vows." If that sentence in Sadoq's saying does not belong there, then it can be seen in a different way. It can mean bluntly and precisely what it says: "If it is so easy to annul vows, then no one will take vows any more, because vows will not be taken seriously. What Sadoq means, viewed from this angle, is simple: If vows are easy to untie, then they will no longer be made: There will no longer be valid vows.

The Talmud proceeds to test what Abbaye and Raba offered as explanations of the Mishnah by placing their explanations up against the Mishnah-passage itself. This brings us to the quotation of No. 3 of the Mishnah-passage itself, which, we see, the Talmud cites word for word (F–G). The Talmud begins by saying, We have learned, which means, "we have learned in a Mishnah-passage." And it goes over the grounds that sages will accept for untying the vow. Sages are willing to say that a vow is untied if a person confesses that he or she would not have taken such a vow had it been known that parents would be shamed. If someone says, "If I had known what this would do to my father and mother, I should never have taken that vow," we can and should believe that person. Why? Because someone possibly would say the contrary. Therefore, only if someone has honestly repented would he or she make such a claim. As far as Abbaye is concerned, therefore, the vow is honestly and sincerely nullified by a statement concerning the honor of one's parents. What about Raba? He worried about people who would not go to a sage at all. If they won't go to a sage when the honor of God is involved, why should they go to a sage when the honor of their parents is involved? Will it follow that Raba cannot explain the concession of sages to Eliezer? No, it will not follow. Why not? Because here, too, one will not be able to untie his or her own vow. Why not? Because Raba makes it impossible for someone to untie a vow without a sage in general. He will make sure that it is general practice to go to a sage. In this case, too, therefore, people will go to a stage.

In other words, Abbaye distinguishes between the shame of parents and the shame of God. Raba holds that if we arrange things properly, then we will not have to worry about the case that sages concede. Shall we than admit to Abbaye and Raba that what is important to them is important to the sages? Is this the decisive consideration? Not likely. For Raba and Abbaye explain the Mishnah-passage along the lines of that original explanation. Is it then possible to explain better than Abbaye and Raba why sages will accept as suitable grounds for untying the vow the person's regret at shaming his or her parents? There certainly is a better reason. Sages really concede nothing to Eliezer; they give up only a small point. They say that if one takes a vow specifically involving a father or mother, and the vow shames the father or mother, one can go to a sage (as Raba wants) and claim that the vow would never have been taken had the person known how the vow would affect the father or mother. That is a far cry from saying "Under all circumstances we can invoke the shame we have caused our family by being a person who takes vows!"

In fact, sages notice only that we can not take a vow that requires us to do something contrary to the law of the Torah. We can not take a vow that will require us to shame our father and our mother because we are all commanded to honor our fathers and our mothers. If we have taken a vow that causes shame to come upon our father and our mother, that vow is null and void. Why? Because it contradicted the law of the Torah—and therefore never was valid, not at the outset, not at the end. So when the sage declares the vow to be untied, he says that it never was a vow. But can we find something even more persuasive? The conversation continues. We can, and should, join in with Raba and Abbaye, Yohanan and Judah, and all the other great Amoraim. To be sure, we can join in only after we have listened to what they have to tell us.

THE SOURCES OF THE MISHNAH: If we have an argument with a friend and say, "I'll never speak to you again," can you take it back? Clearly, in Mishnah and Talmud, there is a tougher question. We make a vow to God. How in the world can we take that back? We turn to the written Torah to find the answer because without its authority we simply have no right to untie what has been tied up in God's name. We also must find out how Eliezer can claim that a person may untie a vow on the basis of something that will happen long after the vow is made. Why should a later happening make any difference? Are there no rules? Is nothing sacred? Eliezer makes an amazing assertion: We can declare a vow to be untied on the basis of something that happens after the vow is made. The position of sages seems reasonable. We declare untied a vow that never really was valid, it was null at the outset. Eliezer's opinion is daring. It also does not stand to reason, the way sages' view does. Therefore the Talmud must ask a basic question. How does Eliezer know? What is the source of his opinion?

The only valid source, of course, is the Torah of Moses at Sinai, and, specifically, the written Torah. When the Talmud asks for a source for what Mishnah holds, it is saying that Mishnah alone is not sufficient. It implies that there is a superior, true source, which is the written Scripture, not the Mishnah. If the question, "What is the source?" or, "What is the reason?" were addressed only to an individual rabbi of the Mishnah, we might come to a false conclusion. We might say that the Talmud asks for reasons and sources because it does not rely upon an individual. But if the Talmud faced an opinion in the name of all the sages—or in no one's name—then it would accept that opinion as Torah. That is not true. The Talmud asks for the sources when the Mishnah speaks in the name of all of its authorities, just as often as when it quotes only one person's name. When the Talmud wants to know the Mishnah's authority, it is not satisfied with the authority of the Mishnah alone. Now, let us consider what will be a sufficient authority for the Mishnah. One ample authority will be a rule or a law given in Scripture in the name of Moses, our rabbi. But in the present case, we have another suitable authority. It is a biblical story, which indicates that the principle we are looking for is accepted and true. Let us consider how the Talmud answers the question, What is Eliezer's reason?

A. R. Eliezer says, They unbind a vow on account of something that happened later on.
B. What is the reason of R. Eliezer?
C. Said R. Hisda,
D. Since Scripture has said,
E. [And the Lord said to Moses in Midian, Go, return to Egypt,] for all the men [who sought to kill you] are dead (Ex. 4:19).
F. Now death was something that happened later on.
G. On this basis [it is ruled] that they unbind a vow on account of something that happened later on.
H.   And as to the rabbis [in opposition to Eliezer's rule]: What is their reason?
I.   They argue: Did these men die?
J.   Now said R. Yohanan in the name of R. Simeon b. Yohai.
K.   Wherever nissim [quarreling] or nissavim [standing] is mentioned, the reference is only to Dathan and Abiram (Ex. 2:13).
L.   But, said Resh Laqish,
M.   They lost their money.

We notice, through my indentations, that the passage is so constructed as to give each party a complete statement of his position. Once more we observe how the Talmud sets forth in a scrupulously fair way the conflicting viewpoints; each side gets its say, so that we gain the benefit of a complete review of not only the positions, but the reasons behind them. The trait of intellectuals, when they live up to their calling, is to dismiss personal interest and focus on the logic and reason of things. In real life, alas, that is not how even the most intelligent people conduct an argument. But the Talmud defines the right way for wise people to pursue truth—the right, the pure, the only way.

Now, to the passage at hand: This is a complicated passage, and we shall have to work our way through it, step by step. First, Eliezer's reasoning. The Talmud here takes for granted that we knew something that it says elsewhere—later on in this same passage, in fact. It says that Jethro was anxious about Moses's safety, since Moses was his son-in-law and friend. Therefore, Jethro made Moses take a vow that he would not go back to Egypt because there were men in Egypt who wanted to kill him. Now in the light of that story, what do we have in Ex. 4:19? God tells Moses in Midian to go back to Egypt. Why? Because the men who wanted to kill him are all dead. But when Moses took the vow these same men were alive. It seems that God has untied the vow of Moses because something that has happened after the vow justified doing so. And that is precisely Eliezer's claim: We may untie a vow on the basis of something that happens after the vow is taken. His reason is that God untied the vow of Moses on the basis of something that happened after Moses took the vow. Death is a new fact. A new fact serves as a good basis.

But the rabbis do not see things the way Eliezer does. They, too, read the same passage of Scripture. But they must read it in some other way since they do not concede that Eliezer is on firm ground. How do they read Scripture's tale? Very simply: They deny the men had died! Moses went back to Egypt because God ordered him to do so, not because God absolved his vow. How do the rabbis prove that these men did not die? They identify the men whom Moses was afraid would kill him. And then they maintain that these same men were not dead when Moses went back to Egypt. How do they know? Because the language used with reference to the men—Ex. 2:13—speaks of two Hebrews who "strove together." The verse is as follows: And when he went out on the second day, behold, two men of the Hebrews fought together (nissim). Again, look at Ex. 5:20: And they met Moses and Aaron who had stood (nissavim) in the way. And compare that verse with Num. 16:27: And Dathan and Abiram came out and stood. The same people who stood in one place, stood in the other: Dathan and Abiram. And they were the ones who had the fight that caused Moses to run away. So they were not dead when Moses returned to Egypt—that is shown by Num. 16:27, which tells of Dathan and Abiram in the rebellion of Korah. It follows that they were still alive, and Moses therefore did not return because of something that happened after he took his vow.

Essentially, what sages do is to explain the proof of Eliezer in such a way that it will no longer prove his point. This is a good mode of argument. But it leaves one small problem. God would appear to tell Moses something that is not true. Dathan and Abiram, we now have shown, were still alive. And God has told Moses, "The men who wanted to kill us have died." What could God have meant? This is the question that Resh Laqish answers. Resh Laqish says: They did not die. But they had lost all their money. And someone who becomes poor is as good as dead.

We shall now go over the proof that a poor death of the man who wanted to kill Moses, Dathan and Abiram, really means they had lost their money. This brings us to the end of this passage (E–J) and to Joshua b. Levi's statement about a group of people—four in all who are as good as dead.

A. Said R. Joshua b. Levi,

B. Any person who does not have children is deemed to be like a dead person,

C. since it is said, Give me children, or else I am dead (Gen. 30:1)

D.   And it has been taught:

E.   Four [types of people] are deemed to be like a dead person:

F.   a poor man, and a person who is a leper; and a blind man, and one who does not have children.

G.   A poor man, as it is written, For all the men [who sought our life] are dead.

H.   A leper, as it is written, [And Aaron looked at Miriam, and behold, she was a leper. And Aaron said to Moses,] Let her not be as one who is dead (Num. 12:10, 12).

I.   A blind person, as it is written, He has set me in dark places, as they that be dead of old (Lam. 3:6).

J.   And one who has no children, as it is said, Give me children or else I am dead (Gen. 30:1).

The proposition is simple. These four sorts of people are as good as dead. The issue is, How shall we prove our point? The answer is that Scripture is proof. The childless person is like a corpse, just as is said in Gen. 30:1. A poor man is like a dead man—on the basis of what God says about Dathan and Abiram. A leper is like a corpse, as Aaron says. A blind person is like a dead person, because Lam. 3:6 is understood to mean, God has put me in dark places, just as the blind, who are accounted as long since dead.

Our passage draws to a close. Yet, it leaves open a question that the Talmud now will want to answer carefully. If God absolved Moses from his vow before Jethro and allowed him to return to Egypt, then what about Jethro? What did he make of all this? Should God or Moses not have told Jethro what was going on? Indeed, that is required. That the Talmud then says without explaining why—if we take a vow in front of someone else, then you must be before that person to untie the vow. This is the basis for understanding the next paragraphs of the Talmud: an important *halakhah*, then a relevant *aggadic* story. And in a moment we shall see that very consideration—untying a vow in the presence of the person who originally witnessed or heard it—led the person who put our Talmud together to go on to just this matter. He will tell us so explicitly.

EXPANDING THE EXPLANATION: Moses's vow not to go back to Egypt was absolved. But Jethro knew nothing about it. That hardly makes sense. Moses will go along and has violated his vow. Jethro will assume that Moses was disrespectful to God, and this is not the right way to act. The Talmudic discussion, therefore, must turn to this question and explain under what circumstances a vow is to be untied. If we looked at the Mishnah-passage, we surely would not have predicted that the discussion would move in this direction. Yet, because of what we have just said, we now realize that it is absolutely necessary to raise just this topic, at just this time. We will raise the general question first—untying a vow in the very presence of the person who witnessed it to begin with—and then link our observation to the discussion we have just concluded, about Moses in Midian.

A further important trait of what follows is that we move from a *halakhic* to an *aggadic* passage. First, we treat what one should or should not do. We engage in an important discussion of rules and laws, of how things are done and the way things should be done halakhah. Yet, without warning, we turn to an *aggadic* tale about Nebuchadnezzar, the king of the Babylonians who destroyed the first Temple and Jerusalem in 586 B.C.E., and Zedekiah, the King of the Jews, who was conquered and taken away into exile. For a brief moment, we might imagine that this *aggadic* tale is simply throw in without any purpose. But, of course, the Talmud is a carefully organized discussion, and we should be able to explain without difficulty why the story is introduced. The story tells us why we should keep the law we have just discussed. It takes the law and spells out its importance.

Let us first read the concluding unit of our complete passage of the Talmud and then return to these two questions.

IV. A. It was taught:
   B. a person who took a vow [against] benefiting from his fellow
   C. they unbind him [from his vow] only in his [the neighbor's] presence.
   D. What is the source of this teaching?
   E. Said R. Nahman,
   F. Since it is written, And the Lord said to Moses in Midian,

Go, return into Egypt, for all the men who sought out life are dead.

G. He said to him, In Midian we took a vow

H. Go and have our vow unbound in Midian.

I. [How do we know that Moses vowed in Midian?]

J. Since it is said, And Moses was content [to dwell with the man]

K. Now *alah* means only "an oath"

L. since it is written, And he has taken an (*alah*) oath of him (Ezek. 17:13).

V. A. And also against King Nebuchadnezzar he rebelled, who had made him take an oath by God (II Chron. 36:13).

B. What was the character of his rebellion?

C. Zedekiah found [Nebuchadnezzar],

D. that he was eating a live rabbit.

E. He [Nebuchadnezzar] said to him, Take an oath to me that you will not tell on me,

F. and that a word [on this] will not get out.

G. He took an oath.

H. Later on, Zedekiah was pained.

I. He made inquiry for his vow [and had it unbound not in the king's presence],

J. and he said [what he had seen Nebuchadnezzar eating].

K. Nebuchadnezzar heard that they were making fun of him.

L. He sent and summoned the Sanhedrin and Zedekiah

M. He said to them, Have you seen what Zedekiah did?

N. Did he not take an oath by the name of Heaven that he would not tell on me?

O. They said to him, He was absolved of his oath

P. He said to them, Are people absolved of oaths?

Q. They said to him, Yes.

R. He said to them, In his presence, or even not in his presence?

S. They said to him, [Only] in his presence.
T. He said to them, And you people—what have you done?
U. Why did you not say so to Zedekiah?
V. Forthwith, The elders of the daughter of Zion sit upon the ground and keep silence (Lam. 2:10).
W. Said R. Isaac,
X. That they removed the pillows from under them.

Let us first analyze the story (A–V), and then try to find its relevance to the larger discussion that it concludes. The story begins with the citation of a verse of Scripture If we understand why the story-teller made up the story the verse has two significant elements:

(1) the rebellion of Zedekiah (not named, but look up the verse and you will see him), and
(2) the matter of the oath.

Nebuchadnezzar imposed the oath. The cited verse makes that clear, "who had made him take an oath." What was the cause of the oath? The fact that Nebuchadnezzar was doing something he did not want anyone to know about. The worst thing the story-teller can imagine is eating a live rabbit. A rabbit is not kosher food for Jews. Moreover, the story-teller is disgusted by the idea of eating any live animal. So the Babylonian king Nebuchadnezzar made Zedekiah take an oath not to tell anyone that the king ate a live rabbit. The first part of the story ends with the oath (G). The narrator then adds that Zedekiah regretted his oath, had himself absolved from it, and reported what he had seen. Nebuchadnezzar was rightly angry. He thought Zedekiah had violated his oath (K–N). He did not know that the sages had released the oath (Q). Then Nebuchadnezzar shows the wisdom of the law. One may untie an oath only in the presence of the person who witnessed the oath to begin with. The sages had made a gross error. It was, moreover, an injustice. So, the story ends, the sages (V) had to keep quiet. They had no answer to the Babylonian king. W–X add that the sages were unworthy and were deposed. The story underlines the value and wisdom of the law. A sage must deal with a vow in the presence of the person who is affected by the vow, not only in the presence of the person who took the vow.

Now, let us ask ourselves, if we want to make a general rule about the relationships between *halakhah* and *aggadah*, what would be the rule? The answer I hope readers give is, the *aggadah* states in narrative and readily accessible terms what the *halakhah* sets forth in normative and general, abstract, terms. For if that is how readers see matters, then the great theological task of our times will become relevant and urgent: to show the meaning, in human terms, of the numerous rules that define the Torah in theological and supernatural terms. Our task is to see the human meaning of the holy way of life that the Torah sets forth. We are, therefore, helped by *aggadah* to grasp the deeper, inner significance of the *halakhah*. Then, and only then, the Torah's commandments attain their full significance: not just rules and regulations of this and that, but imperatives that shape the human condition in accord with God's vision of us: "in our image, after our likeness." This claim about the exact correspondence of *halakhah* and *aggadah* simply carries forward the written Torah's own presentation of matters: The aggadah about the creation of the world culminating on the Sabbath day (Genesis 1:1–2.4) matches the *halakhah* about the Sabbath that we find in the Ten Commandments and elsewhere in the books of Exodus and Leviticus. Now, to the case at hand:

Does *aggadah*—as we see it here—simply tell a nice story? Is it thrown in merely to entertain us? Or does the *aggadah* make a point? And is it an important point? I think the answer is self-evident. The *aggadah* is more than an amusing story. It is a serious tale and makes an important point. The point is precisely the same as the purpose of the halakhah. And both are important, equally and reciprocally. *Aggadah* and halakhah, when properly brought together and made into neighbors, talk to each other. Both say the same thing. But one says its truth as an abstract rule—a statement of how things are done in general. The other says its truth in a concrete way. *Aggadah* tells a tale about specific people at one point and in one place. To be sure, the people are not ordinary. They are important folk—men and women worth remembering and imitating. As we learn other passages of the Talmud, we will want to discover the relationship between a law and a story, between *halakhah* and *aggadah*. The Talmud's arrangers and writers present the two together, and it should be possible to make some sense of the two as they march down the page in single file.

Now let us turn back to the *halakhic* discussion [IV A–L], which is easier. We notice that the passage begins with a general rule (A–C). If a person takes a vow not to make use of anything belonging to someone else, the vow can be untied only in the presence of that other person. We know why this rule has to be introduced at this point. Moses left Midian, we remember, in what would seem to be a violation of the vow he took for Jethro. And the Talmud immediately reminds us of just that fact. The Talmud asks (D), "How do we know that this rule is so?" We, of course, know the answer—Scripture is the source of all rules. So (E) Nahman cites a verse (Ex. 4:19). Notice that Nahman reads the verse in an odd way. We should expect, "And the Lord said to Moses in Midian, 'Go, return to Egypt.'" But Nahman reads, "And the Lord said to Moses, 'In Midian go—then return to Egypt.'" His sense of the verse is, "God back to Midian." And why? "To have our vow annulled. For we took our vow in Midian and, therefore, we have to untie the vow in the presence of the people before whom we took it."

In order to make sense of the passage, we have to supply the question, How do we know that there was a vow? At the outset of our discussion, we introduced the fact that Moses had taken a vow to Jethro. The Talmudic discussion took this fact for granted but did not spell it out. Remember that we explained Eliezer's ruling, "A new fact will serve as a pretext for untying a vow," in terms of God's releasing Moses from the vow he had taken in Midian. But at that point we had no knowledge of such a vow. Here is the proof, then, that there was such a vow, and, further, this same proof is just as relevant at the earlier passage—Hisda's contribution—as it is now. The proof is based on a play on words. Scripture says, And Moses was content (*va-yo'el*) to dwell with the man (Ex.

2:21). The word *va-yo'el* comes from the root *alah,* which means to take an oath. This is proved by the use of the word in Ezek. 17:13, And has taken an oath *(alah).* So Ex. 2:21 is to be read, And Moses took an oath to dwell with the man (Jethro).

Is this far-fetched? The answer is not obvious. On the one hand, the context of Ex. 2:21 surely demands that we read, "And Moses was content to dwell with the man" Yet, the word *content* has another meaning, *take an oath.* And we are able to show that this other meaning is sensible. So it is at least possible to read the verse the way our passage wants us to read it. We must notice one thing: The process of explaining the verse to prove that Moses took an oath to Jethro is a process of discovery. That is, the person who made up this proof wants to find the meaning of a word. He discovers what it means in one passage and introduces the meaning to the passage he is trying to interpret.

Is this what we do in a biology lab or in math? Is this a fair duplication of the processes of discovery that we use in our studies of modern science or history? The methods have similarities and differences. How do we know that Moses vowed in Midian? The question tells the story. We start out to prove a specific proposition. We, therefore, look for a use of the word in question that conforms to what we want the word to mean. Our purpose is not to test or to discover knowledge. It is, rather, to confirm and prove what we already think. We should call this deductive, not inductive, reasoning, since the proof depends upon what we wish to prove. The data for inductive reasoning are what guide us to the propositions we wish to uncover—so matters are generally set forth. So, this is not a process of discovery entirely like what we may have observed in science or in history. It is a different and distinct way of thinking. That does not mean we should reject it. Rather, we have to understand the world of the Talmud, the way in which the Talmud's authorities think, in a different way. Indeed, one of the things worth learning from a book such as the Talmud is a completely different way of thinking from our own.

THE TALMUD ALL TOGETHER. BABYLONIAN TALMUD NEDARIM 64A–65A: Once more we want to see the entire passage of the Talmud as a single unit. But now our purpose is more precise. Not only do we want to see all the elements together—we also want to explain the purpose of the person who put the present passage together. For we are looking for the first time at a complete discussion of the Talmud, beginning with the citation of a given passage of the Mishnah and ending with the conclusion of that discussion. What follows in the Talmud is the citation of another passage of the Mishnah. So, here it is not only all together, but it is also complete. We, therefore, have a better opportunity than we did before to make sense of the Talmud as a whole.

First, we read the passage from beginning to end, with the English translation. Notice the points at which the Talmud is in Aramaic, and those at which it expresses its ideas in Hebrew. The Aramaic is signaled by italics. The Mishnah is in bold face type. See whether we can tell when Hebrew will be used and when we are going to find Aramaic. Does it make sense to offer this theory? When the Talmud wants to cite the Mishnah or to give teachings that belong in the Mishnah, it uses the language of the Mishnah, which is Hebrew. When the Talmud speaks in the voice of its own authorities—the rabbis of its own day—it speaks in Aramaic, which is the language they used. Now, let us proceed to read the complete passage but with the sentences divided.

1. **Rabbi Eliezer says**
   They untie [a vow] for a person on account of the honor of his father and his mother.
   And sages prohibit [keep it tied].
2. **Said Rabbi Sadoq:**
   Before they untie [a vow] for a person on account of father or mother, let them untie it for that person on account of the honor of the Omnipresent.
   [And] if so, there will be no vows [at all]!
3. **And sages agree with Rabbi [Eliezer concerning a matter between father and mother, that they untie it for the person on account of the honor of father and mother.**
4. **And furthermore did Rabbi Eliezer say:**

They untie [a vow] on account of something that happened
[later on]
And sages prohibit

5. How so?
[If] he said, Qonam—that I shall not derive benefit from so-
and-so
and he [so-and-so] became a scribe or was going to marry
off his son very soon

6. and he said, If I had known that he would become a scribe
or that he would marry off his son very soon
I should not have taken a vow

7. Qonam against this house, that I shall not enter it and it
was made into a synagogue
[if] he said, If I had known that it would be made into a
synagogue, I should not have taken a Vow

8. Rabbi Eliezer unties [the vow]
And sages prohibit [keep it tied].

I. A. *What is the meaning of* "There will be no vows"?
    B. Said Abbaye,
    C. If so, no vows may be unbound.
    D. And Raba said,
    E. If so, Vows will not be brought for inquiry [and absolu-
        tion] to a sage.
    F. *We have learned*
    G. And sages concede to R. Eliezer that in a matter
        involving himself and his father and mother, they do
        release him by reason of the honor of his father and
        his mother.
    H. *Certainly, this accords with Abbaye, who said,* If so, no
        vows may be unbound;
    I. here, if he has been so impudent, he is impudent.
    J. But so far as Raba is concerned, who said, If so,
        inquiry [and absolution] to a sage,
    K. in this case, why do they unbind [the vow]?
    L. I shall tell you;

M. since all vows cannot be [declared not binding] without a sage,

N. here, too, they [sages] Will declare the vow unbound

II. A. **R. Eliezer says, They unbind a vow on account of something that happened later on.**

B. *What is the reason of R. Eliezer?*

C. Said R. Hisda,

D. Since Scripture has said,

E. [And the Lord said to Moses in Midian, Go, return to Egypt,] for all the men [who sought to kill you] are dead (Ex. 4:19).

F. Now death was something that happened later on.

G. On this basis [it is ruled] that they unbind a vow on account of something that happened later on.

H. *And as to the rabbis [in opposition to Eliezer's rule] what is their reason?*

I. They argue: Did these men die?

J. Now, said R. Yohanan in the name of R. Simeon b. Yohai, Wherever nissim [quarreling] or nissavim [standing] is mentioned, the reference is only to Dathan and Abiram (Ex. 2:13).

L. But, said Resh Laqish,

M. They lost their money.

III. A. Said R. Joshua b. Levi,

B. Any person who does not have children is deemed to be like a dead person,

C. since it is said, Give me children, or else I am dead (Gen. 30:1).

D. *And it has been taught:*

E. Four [types of people] are deemed to be like a dead person:

F. a poor man, and a person who is a leper, and a blind man, and one who does not have children.

G.   A poor man, as it is written, For all the men [who sought our life] are dead.

H.   A leper, as it is written, [And Aaron looked at Miriam, and behold, she was a leper. And Aaron said to Moses,] Let her not be as one who is dead (Num. 12:10–12).

I.   A blind person, as it is written, He has set me in dark places, as they that be dead of old (Lam. 3:6).

J.   And one who has no children, as it is said, Give me children or else I am dead (Gen. 30:1).

IV. A. *It was taught:*

B.   a person who took a vow [against] benefiting from his fellow

C.   they unbind him [from his vow] only in his [the neighbor's] presence.

D.   *What is the source of this?*

E.   Said R. Nahman,

F.   Since it is written, And the Lord said to Moses in Midian

Go, return to Egypt, for all the men who sought our life are dead.

G.   He said to him, "In Midian we took a vow.

H.   Go and have our vow unbound in Midian.

I.   [How do we know that Moses vowed in Midian?]

J.   Since it is said, And Moses was content [to dwell With the man] (Ex. 2:21).

K.   Now alah means only "an oath,"

L.   since it is written, And he has taken an (alah) oath of him (Ezek. 17:13).

V. A. And also against King Nebuchadnezzar he rebelled, who had made him take an oath by God (II Chron. 36: 13).

B.   What was the character of his rebellion?

C.   Zedekiah found [Nebuchadnezzar],

D. that he was eating a live rabbit.

E. He [Nebuchadnezzar] said to him, Take an oath to me that you will not tell on me,

F. and that a word [on this] will not get out.

G. He took an oath.

H. Later on, Zedekiah was pained.

I. He made inquiry for his vow [and had it rebound],

J. and he said [what he had seen Nebuchadnezzar eating].

K. Nebuchadnezzar heard that they were making fun of him.

L. He sent and summoned the Sanhedrin and Zedekiah.

M. He said to them, Have you seen what Zedekiah did?

N. Did he not take an oath by the name of Heaven that he would not tell on me?

O. They said to him, He was absolved of his oath.

P. He said to them, Are people absolved of oaths?

Q. They said to him, Yes.

R. He said to them, "In his presence, or even not in his presence?"

S. They said to him, [Only] in his presence.

T. He said to them, And you people—what have you done.

U. Why did you not say so to Zedekiah?

V. Forthwith. The elders of the daughter of Zion sit upon the ground and keep silence (Lam. 2:10).

W. Said R. Issac,

X. That they removed the pillows from under them.

Now that we have seen the passage as a whole, we should be able to understand why I divided it to present it as I have. Go back over these divisions and decide whether or not readers may agree with my guess as to what the divisions should be.

A second exercise will not surprise us. Can we explain why the person arranged the passage of the Talmud this way? To answer the question, try to make an outline of the passage. See where the chief headings lie. It may help us to use my chapter-divisions. Now, with such an outline in hand, I want to consider a statement many people make about the Talmud. They say it is disorganized. Many people who know the Talmud in some measure and have studied it for awhile claim that the Talmud is not put together coherently. We just jump from this to that, then to another. Perhaps that is so, perhaps not. On the basis of this sample, what do we think? Do we see the Talmud as disorganized and merely a jumble of materials? Or does it appear to be carefully constructed? We should be able to back up our opinion with arguments based upon our outline. Can we explain to someone precisely why the person who puts things together has done things this way—and not in some other?

Let me offer a specific criterion: let us consider other ways of ordering the units of thought, besides the one that governs here. If the compiler of the composite had put the units of thought in a different order, would he have accomplished his goals? Would the passage have made any coherent sense at all, such as, we must agree, it does. So, here are the questions to consider: What are the choices the editor had? What are the different ways that the material might have been presented? Can we discern why the editor decided to do things this particular way? Or is there no apparent reason? I ask these questions here because we have a whole passage of the Talmud before us: the Mishnah together with everything the Talmud chooses to tell us about that Mishnah. If we cannot make sense of the way in which the person who made up this passage has done the work, then we should conclude two things:

1. The Talmud is just a collection of things but not put together as a work worth our attention.
2. The Talmud is an anthology, not a piece of writing on which someone has spent time and had thought.

But if we can isolate the materials that the person who made up our passage had in hand, and if we can then explain why that person put things together the way it was done, then what do we know? We know the secret of the Talmud: what is Talmudic about the Talmud. Let us explore that big if.

1. What are the basic elements, the sayings and stories, the citations and explanations, that make up our passage?
2. If we copy each one of these down on a card and lay it out on a table, which one would we choose first to begin a Talmud that we make up?

I am inclined to think that, after the Mishnah, the first thing we must do is explain what the Mishnah says. We have to answer the obvious and pressing questions that the Mishnah leaves open. Then what must follow? Once we explain the Mishnah, we will have to explain—and expand—our explanation. And once we have done that, have we not used all our cards? As I said at the outset of this little exercise, "What are the choices? What are the possibilities? And how has the person who arranged our Talmud ('made it up') decided things?"

Have the framers of the Talmud done a good job? We need to entertain the possibility that we have in hand the best of all possible Talmuds. A set of questions shows us where, were we making the Talmud, we should have gone. One question that is not answered is, Who says we may untie vows at all? Another question is, What are other suitable grounds for the untieing of a vow? A third question is, What is the meaning of "a new fact"? A fourth question is, Why do I need three examples of new facts? Why should Eliezer's position be spelled out at such length? A fifth question is, What do we mean by a scribe? What is the meaning of the word Qonam, and how shall we define other words used in this passage? These questions are not like one another. Some of them are trivial, others are basic. Some of them would add mere details. But if we dealt with others of them, we should have produced a different Talmudic passage from the one that we have studied.

The main thing to remember in this exercise is this: We must always use our own imagination. We must figure out the things a person might have done, so we can understand the things he or she actually has done. What are the possibilities? What are the choices among which the person actually has made a selection? Only then shall we understand the purpose and the achievement that are before us. Only when we realize what might have been will we truly understand what is. The greatness of the Talmud is its unfinished quality, its character as a set of notes, out of wich we may reconstruct a large and rigorous argument about important matters. The framers of the Talmud speak elliptically and in abbreviated language, unlike the authors of the Mishnah. Now we see the effect of that rather odd style of theirs: it leaves the Talmud open, an unending conversation, in which we too may participate. That I think is the key to its power to endure and shape those endless generations that would follow the closure and conclusion of the main work, down to us, this very day. As I said in the opening chapter, not many pieces of writing of any civilization have exercised the enduring influence, over just that sector of humanity that the writers wished to shape, as has the Talmud. The fact that readers take up this textbook presents the ultimate proof of the success of the Talmud's writers.

WHAT IS THE TAMUD? This discussion of the choices someone has made allows us to ask our basic question in a new way. For the Talmud is not simply "given"—that is, the way things had to be. It represents a series of careful and deliberate choices, among many possibilities, of how someone wanted things to be. That is to say, once we deal with Mishnah, we have certain jobs to do with Talmud. These are done in a particular way—and not in some other—in the Talmud before us. So when we ask, "What is the Talmud," we have a second basic question: What is the Talmud's conception of how the Mishnah should be explained and understood? If we say, "In part, the Talmud is an explanation of the Mishnah," we have not said a lot. For we also have to say what we mean by "explanation of the Mishnah." I think we now can do this on the basis of the two Talmudic passages we have learned. We will notice that the Talmud begins its work on Mishnah by attention to the Mishnah itself. That means the Talmud regards explanation as something that must be precise, direct, and relevant to the Mishnah. It begins not with examples or generalizations, not with stories, expansions of the law of Mishnah, or sermons about keeping that law. It begins with careful attention to precisely what Mishnah says, its concrete and specific words. Generalization comes much later and in different way.

1. So what the Talmud means by "an explanation of the Mishnah" is this: to spell out the meanings of the words, the phrases, the sentences of the Mishnah. To explain the Mishnah, we ask about its sources. We interpret the meanings of unclear phrases. We ask obvious and compelling questions of concrete meaning. But the Talmud is more things as well.

2. It explains the implications of the Mishnah's rule. The Talmud will want to take Mishnah's specific rule and turn it into something more general. The Mishnah may speak in concrete terms. The Talmud may tell us what those terms imply. The Mishnah may speak of a single case. The Talmud will want to tell us how to rule governing that case which applies to other cases. In this regard, the three examples of Eliezer's opinion are suggestive. They show us how the Talmud will work (even though they are in the Mishnah) to make concrete and specific something general in Mishnah, or to make general and applicable to many things something concrete and specific in Mishnah. In a way, we might say that what the Talmud will do is what Mishnah leaves undone.

3. And the Talmud goes on, beyond the frontiers laid out by the Mishnah's treatment of a law, to explore important new ideas about that same law. The Talmud is given a topic or a theme by the Mishnah. The Talmud will work its way out to the limits of the theme as the Mishnah treats that theme. Then the Talmud will go beyond those limits. It will treat the theme in new ways, in ways unimagined by the Mishnah. So there is a discipline, and there is a kind of freedom. The discipline is to explore fully what is said. The freedom is to use the imagination to treat the topic or theme in entirely new ways. The dis-

cipline of the Talmud requires spelling out the meaning of, "There are no vows." The discipline further requires that we test our theory of what the Mishnah means against other things the Mishnah says, for instance, what Abbaye and Raba say against what the Mishnah says. The discipline demands that we state the sources of the Mishnah, if we can think what they might be.

4. But the Talmud is free, too. It is free to expand upon a subject. It has the right, when treating the topic of the Mishnah—namely, untieing vows—to go on to a related matter. This second notion is that if one takes a vow not to derive benefit from someone, the vow, when untied, must be untied in the presence of the same person. That is an idea relevant to our Mishnah-passage. But it is not in our Mishnah-passage. Our Mishnah passage does not require it. We should have fully and completely understood what Mishnah wants to tell us without knowing that fact. It follows that the Talmud has freedom to move beyond the limits of the Mishnah's treatment of the Mishnah's theme.

It exercises other sorts of freedom as well. The *aggadic* tale about Zedekiah and Nebuchadnezzar surely exists on its own, as a condemnation of faithless sages, and not merely to serve our Talmudic discussion, let along our Mishnah. So the Talmud draws together many things in presenting what its author conceives to be the proper approach to the Mishnah. So, we no longer can say merely, "explanation of the Mishnah."

TALMUD, TORAH, JUDAISM: From the Talmud, what have we learned about Judaism. The answer is, Judaism is a religion about keeping our word because it speaks about ordinary, everyday circumstances, moments when we say something we later regret. The Torah wants to find a middle path between the holiness of our word and the reality of our life. One important concern of Judaism is to make us people who keep our word to God and to our fellow human beings. Another important interest is our own self-respect and self-esteem. A third is how we keep these two values in balance. The reason that the Talmud is important for Judaism today is that it teaches us how to think about problems that we create for ourselves through our power to express ourselves.

VI

The Talmud Speaks to Us About Deeds and Beliefs: Saying Thank You

The Talmud to Mishnah Berakhot 6:1

In our first two passages of the Talmud, Chapters Four and Five, our attention was drawn to the traits of the Talmud itself: what to expect when we open the Talmud, how it explains and expands the Mishnah. For that purpose, we studied topics not familiar in our everyday religious life as holy Israel. We wanted to concentrate on the Talmud, rather than on what we learn from the Talmud for our own lives. I even claimed that the Talmud is not directly relevant to our everyday life, so that we could study the Talmud in the right spirit: to ask *its* questions—which are not necessarily ours—and to learn what it wants to say, not especially what we wanted to hear. That gave us a chance to see the Talmud as talmud and to ask about its traits and its character. Now, we will reverse ourselves and, both in this chapter and in the next, turning to passages in the Talmud that directly speak to us and our religious situation. How does the Talmud lay out things that we as Israel already say and do? What is its mode of thinking and analyzing religious practices with which we are entirely familiar? Finally, what do we learn from the Talmud about things we already know? This is now the work of a new and ambitious passage. But, as we will see, the passage is not difficult.

We study Mishnah-tractate Berakhot, and the topic of the Talmud is the blessings that we say over food. Most Jews know that we say a blessing before we eat a piece of bread or drink a cup of wine. Indeed, one of the things nearly everyone learns in religious education is to say such a blessing. So the topic before us is familiar: blessings for food. But what will the Talmud want to know about that topic? That is the really suggestive question: Given a subject—any subject—what will the framers of the Talmud want to know about that subject? Given the range of possibilities when we come to the matter of reciting blessings over food and other acts of divine generosity, we realize that the Talmud's writers made choices, this and not that. So we come with the question: What will they want to tell us that we do not know? Above all, we may suppose at the very outset, we want to know what it means that we recite such blessings, to ask, what does it say about us and about our attitude toward the world and toward God? What conclusion should we reach?

Here is the main point that we shall gain in this discussion: We are what we do. But we do what we believe. So how shall we learn, from what we do, what we believe? The road to a proper understanding of the theology of Judaism—in religious language, the truths of the Torah—opens before us when we ask, from the things we do, what do we learn about our inner convictions? And how shall we describe what we are on the basis of what we believe and what we do? If we wanted to explore the meaning of life within the Torah—that is, if we wanted to measure our convictions against the truths of the Torah and so form a theology in dialogue with the Torah—here we should find our starting point.

These are deep questions and so inevitably they move our minds from our status as holy Israel to our situation as human beings. They touch the foundations of our humanness, of what it means to us to be created "in our image, after our likeness." The Mishnah is going to surprise us because it is rather bland and merely tells us facts. It raises no problems. It is simply a repertoire of rules: What blessing we say for one thing, what blessing we say for some other thing. We have a question in No. 1. Then we are given three different things: (1) fruit of a tree [No. 2]—except wine [Nos. 3–4]; (2) fruit of the ground [No. 5], except for bread [Nos. 6–7]; and (3) vegetables [No. 8]. We have a triplet: fruit of a tree, fruit of the ground, and vegetables. Before proceeding, let us review the Mishnah carefully. As before, we try to understand how it is put together and why the person who put it together did it in this particular way (Mishnah-tractate Berakhot 6:1):

1   How do they say a blessing over fruit
2   Over fruit of a tree, a person says
    [Blessed are you, Lord, our God, ruler of the world, who] creates fruit of the tree
3   Except for wine, for
4   over wine, a person says [Blessed are you, Lord, our God, ruler of the world, who] creates fruit of the vine.
5   And over the fruit of the ground a person says
    [Blessed are you, Lord, our God, ruler of the world, who] creates fruit of the ground.
6   Except for bread, for
7   Over bread, a person says,
    [Blessed are you, Lord, Our God, ruler of the world who] brings bread out of the earth.
8   And over vegetables, a person says
    [Blessed are you, Lord, our God, ruler of the world, who] creates fruit of the ground.
9   Rabbi Judah says, [A person says, Blessed are you, Lord, our God, ruler of the world, who] creates different kinds of seeds.

The Mishnah-passage is remarkably easy to follow. It simply lists three different things people consume—fruit of a tree, fruit of the ground, and vegetables. In the time of the Mishnah, these were the things people ate daily. So it was natural for the author of the Mishnah to construct a poem in a triplet to give the blessing for these three things. Notice the author takes for granted that we are acquainted with the proper formula for a blessing, which is:

Blessed are you, Lord, our God, ruler of the world, who . . . . So the person who makes up our Mishnah takes for granted we know in advance what he is telling us. (1) We know what a blessing is. We ask, How do they say a blessing? (2) We know the basic formula for a blessing. We start, ". . . who."

We must therefore ask ourselves, what is the real purpose of the person who made up this little poem? What does he want us to learn? Could it be the exceptions of wine, then bread? Could it be the disagreement of Judah in No. 9? Is it not strange that the same blessing—"fruit of the ground"—applies to fruit of the ground and vegetables, things that grow in the ground and not on trees? Why does the Mishnah treat the two separately? Why indeed, if not to allow Judah to give his quite different opinion? The only striking statement in the triplet is the one that breaks free of what has already been said, and that is No. 9. This kind of questioning is interesting, but it does not bring us any closer to the Talmud.

The Talmud for its part is going to be struck by something else entirely. It is going to have its own problem. That problem is in no way related to the simple explanations of the phrasing and wording of Mishnah that my questions are meant to call to our mind. Yet even now, I think we can predict what the Talmud will want to know about our Mishnah-passage: What is the source of this Mishnah? But what will be explained is not the source of the formulas for the several different blessings. The Talmud will take for granted that that is not the most important question it can ask. The Talmud wants to know what everyone would have already known: Why do we have to say blessings at all? Perhaps in our own time, when we are aware of the importance of nature and ecological balance, we do not find blessings so surprising. For what blessings say in a framework of holiness is what we try to do when we protect and watch over the natural environment—we revere the world God made and we want to protect it. We are grateful for what we have.

EXPLAINING THE MISHNAH: The first thing to know is, What is the source of this rule? To understand what the Talmud thinks we should know, we must remember that meals conclude with the

Blessing for Food, Birkat hammazon. What troubles the Talmud is this: Since we have to say a blessing after we eat, why do we—in addition—have to say a blessing before we eat? When the Talmud asks, "What is the source of this rule?" it means the source of the rule that, before eating, we say a blessing over fruit of trees, fruit of the ground, and vegetables. This is not quite to the point of a Mishnah which asks, "What do we say?" But it is relevant.

A. *What is the source of this rule?*
B. *As our rabbis have taught:*
C. [The fruit thereof will be] holy, for giving praise to the Lord (Lev. 19:24).
D. This teaches that they [pieces of produce] require a blessing before them and after them.
E. On this basis did R. Aqiba say,
F. It is prohibited for a person to taste anything before he has said a blessing.

What is the nature of the proof? Not surprisingly, it is a citation of Scripture, Lev. 19:24. That verse refers to fruit of an orchard four years after the trees were planted. That "fruit of the fourth year" may not be eaten at all. The verse says that one must give praise to the Lord. Notice that the word for giving praise, *hillulim*, is plural. It means that there are two acts of giving praise to the Lord. (1) One comes after we eat. (2) The other comes before we eat. It follows that we have to say a blessing before and after we eat these different sorts of produce. It is exceedingly important that Aqiba's saying (E–F) is attached to the proof. For everything that follows in the Talmudic elaboration and discussion of our Mishnah-passage will develop Aqiba's basic idea. It is simple. One must say a blessing before he or she eats anything. Aqiba says this in the negative. One is forbidden to taste anything before saying a blessing over it.

Have we explained the Mishnah-passage? In a way, we have filled it out rather than explained it. The Talmud finds most striking not how we bless these kinds of produce, but that we must bless the food. And not that alone, but that the blessing is required in advance of eating that fruit, and not merely afterward (as everyone knows). We wonder whether the Talmud is not explaining something that hardly requires explanation. The people who made up this passage know full well that we say the Blessing for Food, Grace after meals. They also know that we say the blessings listed in the Mishnah-passage. In fact, they want to know why we say blessings at all. It would, therefore, appear that the Talmud really wants to talk about, in this halakhic passage, a matter of religious conviction: the recitation of blessings and the religious attitude required for saying them. And that is precisely why Aqiba's saying, and not Mishnah at all, will be subjected to extension and amplification. In point of fact, the Mishnah-passage will be forgotten in the Talmud that follows.

EXPANDING THE EXPLANATION: After some discussion that we shall bypass, the Talmud that serves our Mishnah-passage returns to this weighty saying of Aqiba: We cannot enjoy anything of this world without saying a blessing. In expanding our explanation of the Mishnah, we will say some deep things about ourselves as human beings and our relationship to God. The Talmud will now do with Aqiba's saying in explanation of the Mishnah what we have seen the Talmud do with a Mishnah-passage itself. The Talmud will slowly and patiently unpack all the layers of meaning contained in that saying. It will consider each and every implication of what Aqiba has told us. The first thing it will do is repeat the saying and then spell it out. Why, the Talmud will ask, should we not derive enjoyment from this world without saying a blessing over what gives us pleasure of benefit? Because what we are taking does not belong to us. We must at least admit and acknowledge that fact and express our thanks for what is given to us. That is the main point of the Talmudic passage before us.

A. *Our rabbis have taught*
B. It is prohibited for a person to derive enjoyment from this world without a blessing.

C. And all who derive enjoyment from this world without a blessing commit sacrilege.

D. *What is the remedy for such a person?*

E. *Let him go to a sage.*

F. *Let him go to a sage?*

G. *What will he do for him?*

H. *Lo, he [already] has committed a violation.*

I. But said Raba,

J. Let him go to a sage in the first place

K. and he [the sage] will teach the person blessings,

L. so that he may not come into the grip of sacrilege.

M. Said Rab Judah said Samuel,

N. Whosoever derives enjoyment from this world without a blessing is as if he derives benefit from Holy Things that belong to Heaven,

O. since it is said, The earth is the Lord's and the fullness thereof (Psalm 24:1).

P. *R. Levi contrasted [two verses of Scripture]:*

Q. It is written, The earth is the Lord's and the fullness thereof (Psalm 24:1).

R. And it is written, The heavens belong to the Lord, but the earth did he give to people. (Psalm 115:16).

S. There is no contradiction.

T. The former verse applies before [one has said] a blessing; the latter verse applies after [one has said] a blessing.

A–C begins in Hebrew. If I gain benefit from anything in this world, I must say a blessing. Why? Because the fruits and vegetables of the world are the fruits of creation. God made, and continues to make, the world in such a way as to give me everything I need. God creates the world and all its blessings. Therefore, these things belong to God. I cannot enjoy God's belongings without thanks, and if I do, I misappropriate what is holy. That is (C), I commit sacrilege. The analysis of the foregoing passage now shifts to Aramaic. It will comment on what has gone before. What should a person who actually eats an apple without a blessing do? The answer to the question in D is E: Go to a sage. Why? Will the sage make up the blessing the person has not said? No, the Talmud hastens to add. That is not the meaning of D–E. The Talmud does not speak in absurd statements, but it does want to work out its ideas slowly and in a clear way. Go to a sage (F–H) for what purpose? Because, Raba says, a sage will teach us what to say (J–L). The point of it all is to return to our Mishnah. The sage will teach us the blessings we require. That is, the sage will teach us Mishnah-passages such as the one we learned at the outset.

What the Talmud has accomplished is not quite what we had expected. The Talmud began with Aqiba's saying that we cannot enjoy anything without saying a blessing. Now this led us far from the substance of our Mishnah-passage. We learn (1) blessings in the Mishnah-passage. The Talmud then ignores what the Mishnah passage has told us and turns to what the Mishnah-passage has not told us: (2) the purpose of blessings. This troubled the person who developed A–C by adding D–L. And what that person did is clever. He has turned Aqiba's saying back upon itself and forced us to return to the substance of what Mishnah actually tells us. So the Talmudic writer has taken what seemed (quite rightly, I think) a rather irrelevant approach to the explanation of Mishnah and turned it around so that it leads us back to the very lesson Mishnah wishes us to learn—the various blessings we recite. This is impressive and artful, since on the face of it, all we have is a sequence of loosely related thoughts.

What follows are two further relevant expansions of this expansion of the explanation of Mishnah, M–O and P–T. There will be more beyond. Judah's point in the name of Samuel is precisely what we already have said in C and again in K–L. Samuel raises the issue of sacrilege—deriving benefit from Holy Things, which belong to Heaven, that is, to God. What Samuel does is very simple: He provides a proof-text for that fundamental viewpoint. The proof text is good; it says that the whole earth belongs to God. That is the reason we say a blessing before deriving benefit from anything of this world. Notice that the discussion is not quite what we should have expected after A–L. Samuel speaks of enjoying anything, while the principal interest up to now has been food or other sorts of natural produce. But the point is the same.

The second expansion of our expansion (P–T) takes up the preceding one. It is a sign of how carefully and sensibly our passage has been put together. Once we have heard Samuel's proof-text, relevant as it is to what has gone before, we proceed to develop further ideas about that proof-text. Levi takes two verses that contradict one another. One says the earth belongs to God. The other says the earth belongs to the human race (Q and R). S declares there is no contradiction. And T makes the necessary point. The earth belongs to the Lord—until we say a blessing. Once we have said a blessing, God gives the earth to the human race. This shows the main point in a different and engaging way. It is the reason we must say a blessing before we eat a piece of fruit as well as afterward. The same points will now be repeated in yet other ways, as the Talmud runs its course.

EXPANDING THE EXPANSION: The author of the passage we just learned was struck by the contrast between two scriptural passages that seem to say opposite things. He solves that problem by showing that the opposition is not a contradiction, but refers to different points in time or different circumstances. One verse refers to the time before one has said a blessing. Then, the earth is the Lord's. Another verse refers to the time after one has said a blessing, when God has given earth to humanity. This mode of thought naturally invites other sorts of contrasts between two or more Scriptural verses. The supposed contradiction may be solved by reference to different times or different situations.

Once we have introduced a mode of thinking about a given problem, we can apply that mode to other problems. The problem of the importance of saying blessings leads to the view that we must say blessings when we derive benefit from any natural advantage. We contrast verses to underline the importance of saying blessings. Now what do we do? We contrast other verses and make points not directly relevant to the particular problem we have been discussing—saying blessings. Yet, as we shall see, what is said is relevant in general, if not in particular. We never fully abandon the line of thought we began so long ago. We just move along its path, not bound by its own direction, exploring its highways and byways.

A. Said R. Hanina bar Papa,
B. Whoever derives enjoyment from this world without a blessing
C. is as if he steals from the Holy One, blessed be he, and from the community of Israel.
D. since it is said, Whoever robs his father or his mother and says, It is no transgression—that person is a companion of a destroyer (Prov. 28:24).
E. And "his father" refers only to the Holy One, blessed be he, as it is said,
F. Is not he our father, who has begotten us (Deut. 32:6).
G. And mother refers only to the community of Israel,
H. since it is said, Here my son, the instruction of our father, and do not forsake the teaching of our mother (Prov. 1:8).
I. What [is the meaning of the phrase], That person is a companion of a destroyer?
J. Said R. Hanina b. Papa,
K. he is a companion of Jeroboam, the son of Nabat,
L. who destroyed Israel for their Father in heaven.

A–C repeat the earlier main point. Deriving enjoyment from something of this world without saying a blessing is like stealing from God. But, Hanina adds, it is also like stealing from the community of Israel. Now Hanina offers a sequence of proof-texts. Robbing one's father (D) is the first. E then proves that "father" means God, and F is an appropriate proof. Then we come to the community of Israel. G–H explain how Scripture proves that "mother" means Community of Israel. The verse cited in D refers to a companion of a destroyer, and we should explain that odd phrase. So I raises the question. That is, we have a second-level explanation of a first-level explanation of our original proposition. To put matters graphically:

Our original proposition is A–C. Then, this is worked out and explained by D–H. Then, elements of D–H have to be explained, and that is completed by I–L. Our passage is *midrash aggadah*. It is *aggadah* because it deals with beliefs, rather than concrete practices. It is *Midrash* because it involves a search (from the root darash) of Scripture. *Midrash aggadah* is the explanation of *aggadic* passages of Scripture. There is a second kind of *midrash, midrash halakhah,* which explains *halakhic* passages of Scripture, such as the laws we find in Exodus, Leviticus, Numbers, and Deuteronomy.

At this point, the expansion of the Talmud's expansion of its explanation of Mishnah is complete. We turn, then, to an essay expanding the expansion.

> M. R. Hanina b. Papa contrasted [two Scriptual verses]:
> N. It is written, Therefore, will I take back my grain in the time thereof (Hosea 2:11).
> O. And it is written, And we shall gather in our grain (Deut. 11:14).
> P. There is no contradiction
> Q. The latter verse refers to the time in which Israel does the will of the Omnipresent.
> R. The former verse refers to the time in which Israel does not carry out the will of the Omnipresent.

Each verse, in its own context, makes sense, but when they are put together, they contradict one another. Hanina, however, makes an interesting contrast between times of plenty and times of need. We know from the second paragraph of the Shema', that when the Jewish people obey God's commandments, things go well; and when they do not, things go badly. If we will earnestly heed the commandments I give you this day, to love the Lord our God and to serve Him with all your heart and soul, then I will favor your land with rain at the proper season . . . and you will have an ample harvest of grain and wine and oil. . . . Take care lest you be tempted to forsake God and turn to false gods in worship. For then the wrath of the Lord will be directed against you. He will close the

heavens and hold back the rain. The earth will not yield its produce. Hanina makes the same point in striking language: When
Israel, the Jewish people, does the will of God, then you shall
gather in corn. When Israel, the Jewish people, does not carry out
the will of God, then "I will take back my grain." We have not
strayed far from our original point—that we must say blessings.
Saying a blessing is a way of expressing our thanks to God. Then
God gives us what belongs to God. If we do not say a blessing, God
does not give us what is not ours. When Israel does God's will, the
grain belongs to Israel. When Israel does not do God's will, the
grain remains God's.

We now return to "gathering in grain," which has yet another
meaning. "Gathering grain" is something we do by working for a
living. So when we speak of "gathering in grain," we also may
mean work and earn a living, support ourselves (and our family).
The rabbis of the Mishnah and the Talmud considered working for
a living as something one did instead of studying and teaching
Torah. They were not paid for their work as rabbis, as disciples and
teachers of Torah. They made a living as farmers or craftsmen.
Does Scripture tell people to gather in grain, work for a living,
rather than study Torah? That would be an amazing message, and
it is the subject of the next section of our Talmud.

A. *Our rabbis have taught:*
B. And we will gather in our grain.
C. What does Scripture teach?
D. Since it is said, This book of the law will not depart from
   our mouth (Joshua 1:8),
E. one might have thought that these things are to be just
   as they are written.
F. Scripture therefore says, You will gather in your grain.
G. [This means] combine with them a worldly occupation,
H. the words of R. Ishmael
I. R. Simeon b. Yohai says,
J. Is it possible for a person to plough in the time of
   ploughing,

K. sow in the time of sowing,

L. harvest in the time of harvesting,

M. thresh in the time of threshing,

N. winnow in the time of the winnowing

O. [if so]—as to the Torah, what ever will become of it?

P. But when Israel does the will of the Omnipresent,

Q. their work is done by others,

R. since it is said, And strangers shall stand and feed your flocks (Isaiah 61:5).

S. And when Israel does not do the will of the Omnipresent,

T. their work is done by their own hands,

U. as it is said, And you will gather in your grain.

V. and not only so, but

W. the work of other people is done by them [as well],

X. as it is said, And you will serve your enemy (Deut.

V. A. Said Abbaye,

B. Many did things in accord with R. Ishmael,

C. and it worked out for them.

D. [Others did things] in accord with R. Simeon b. Yohai,

E. and it did not work out for them.

F. Said Raba to rabbis,

G. By your leave,

H. in the days of Nisan and the days of Tishré

I. do not appear before me,

J. so that we may not be anxious about your food

K. for the entire year.

If we are told to gather in grain, why does Scripture also say to spend time in Torah study (D)? We might have the notion that we should do nothing but study Torah. Therefore, F says, we have to be told to gather in grain as well. R. Ishmael's view is that one should both work for a living and study Torah. Simeon b. Yohai asks a disturbing question (I–O). If we work for a living, when will we ever find time to study Torah? His answer is that doing God's will is the important thing. Simeon b. Yohai's reading, of course, brings us back to the verse with which we began (U). He carries to its logical extreme the simple claim that the earth belongs to God, but if we say a blessing, God gives it to us.

Simeon maintains that if God really owns the earth, and if we do what God wants, then God will take care of us. Simeon sees that promise in a concrete way. We shall not even have to work. This is an extreme interpretation of the belief that God blesses us—for instance, with rain—when we do God's will. The Shema' says that. It is a radical claim that when we do God's will, "You will gather in grain." Ishmael takes a more even-handed position. But Simeon, moving out to the extremes of the world-view of the Talmud, teaches us something still more important. Simeon believes that when we set one foot into a system, we can never stop until we have walked through all the highways and byways of that system.

Perhaps this mode of thinking seems far-fetched to us. We probably don't know anyone who wonders about finding a balance between work and play, between learning and doing. Yet, there is balance in our lives. Part of the time we play, part of the time we study, and there are other things we do with our life. You take a certain amount of time off and use it to study Torah, just as the rabbis say. In these ways, we seek a balance among the many different things we want and are expected to do. That is why Abbaye says that people who did what Ishmael says, balance earning a living with studying Torah, did all right. People who took the extreme, idealistic advice of Simeon and only studied and kept the teachings of the Torah did not do well. Abbaye's point is that, in the end, we have a right to test the advice of the great masters of the Torah against the practical results of their teachings.

The passage ends with an example of how Raba, like Abbaye, agrees with Ishmael. He told his students to go home during the planting and harvest seasons so that they could provide food for themselves and their families. During those months, they should earn their living. Then, they will study Torah the rest of the year. So, Abbaye and Raba deny that if one only studies Torah, then other people will support the Jewish people and do their work for them. This is a kind of teaching, Abbaye says, that we can test against the realities of the world. And when we do test it, we find it is wrong.

That is one viewpoint. Now let us hear the other. Along comes someone who agrees with Simeon b. Yohai and who criticizes Abbaye and Raba.

II. A. Said Rabbah b. Bar Hana, said R. Yohanan, in the name of R. Judah b. R. Ilai,
   B. Come and see
   C. Not like the olden generations are the new generations.
   D. In the olden generations, they made their study of Torah their fixed concern,
   E. and their vocation their hobby,
   F. both this and that worked out for them.
   G. But the newer generations,
   H. who made their vocation their fixed concern,
   I. and their study of Torah their hobby—
   J. neither one nor the other worked out for them.

Rabbah b. Bar Hana cites a saying that goes back to Judah b R. Ilai, who lived at the same time as Simeon b. Yohai. And Judah says almost the same thing as Simeon. In olden days, people studied most of the time and worked for a living part-time. They became good Torah students and made a proper living. In the new generation, people worked to support themselves and their families most of the time and made Torah study a hobby. They did not make a good living, and didn't learn much. The person who attached Judah b. R. Ilai's saying to Abbaye's and Raba's approval of Ishmael's advice certainly has something in mind, too. If people do what Raba and Abbaye say, things will not work out well. So the issue stands.

The passage at hand takes on deeper significance when we consider how the issue is framed: study Torah as against make a living. Why not both? The issue now is the definition of wealth. In the following story, which clarifies the teachings before us, Tarfon thought wealth took the form of land, while Aquiba explained to him that wealth takes the form of Torah-learning. That the sense is material and concrete is explicit: land for Torah, Torah for land:

Leviticus Rabbah XXXIV:XVI

1. B. R. Tarfon gave to R. Aquiba six silver centenarii, saying to him, "Go, buy us a piece of land, so we can get a living from it and labor in the study of Torah together."
   C. He took the money and handed it over to scribes, Mishnah-teachers, and those who study Torah.
   D. After some time R. Tarfon met him and said to him, "Did you buy the land that I mentioned to you?"
   E. He said to him, "Yes."
   F. He said to him, "Is it any good?"
   G. He said to him, "Yes."
   H. He said to him, "And do you not want to show it to me?"
   I. He took him and showed him the scribes, Mishnah teachers, and people who were studying Torah, and the Torah that they had acquired.
   J. He said to him, "Is there anyone who works for nothing? Where is the deed covering the field?"
   K. He said to him, "It is with King David, concerning whom it is written, 'He has scattered, he has given to the poor, his righteousness endures forever' (Ps. 112:9)."

What is "of value" conventionally is what provides a life of comfort and sustenance and material position. Here we witness what we may call the transvaluation of value. By that I mean that the material and concrete things of worth were redefined. Ownership of land, even in the Land of Israel, contrasts with wealth in another form all together, and the contrast that was drawn was material and concrete, not merely symbolic and spiritual. It was material and tangible and palpable because it produced this-worldly gains, for example, a life of security, comfort, ease, as these, too, found definition in the systemic context of the here and the now. Owning land involved control of the means of production, and so did knowing the Torah. But—more to the point—from land people derived a living, and from Torah people derived a living in *precisely* the same sense—that is to say, in the material and concrete sense—in which from land they could do so. That is alleged time and again, and at stake then is not the mere denigration of wealth, but the transvaluation of value. Then the transvaluation consisted in [1] the disenlandisement of value—that is, the divorce between the conception of value and the concrete capital represented by real estate, and [2] the transvaluation of (knowing or studying) the Torah, the imputation to Torah of the value formerly associated with land. And that is why it is value to claim for Torah the status of a counterpart-category: the system's economics, its theory of the way of life of the community and account of the rational disposition of those scarce resources that made everyday material existence possible and even pleasant: an economics of wealth, but of wealth differently defined, although similarly valued and utilized. So the stakes here are very high indeed.

THE TALMUD ALL TOGETHER. BABYLONIAN TALMUD BERAKHOT 35A–B (EXCERPT): We now review the pieces of the Talmud together as a whole. What do we want to see? Our problem is different from before. The Talmud we now study is more wide-ranging. Its path has twists and turns. The Talmud's explanation of the Mishnah is, in this case, not its principal concern. Rather, the Talmud takes a winding road, and our job is to find out whether or not it is a single road. Earlier, I argued that the Talmud is carefully put together. Someone gave much thought about how to organize the materials logically and in an interesting way. Now we have every right to challenge that opinion on the basis of what we have reviewed. We must wonder about the validity of two opinions:

1. The Talmud explains the Mishnah.
2. The Talmud is a single, whole essay.

We have every right to conclude that the Talmud really is not interested in the Mishnah, and that the Talmud is just a strung-together mass of separate and distinct bits of thought—sayings, stories, *midrash aggadah, midrash-halakhah*. As we reread the Talmudic passage we have studied (excerpts of the materials on Babylonian Talmud Berakhot 35a–b), see whether we can understand the logic of the person who put these things together. Do we see a purpose in the sequence of ideas and topics? More important, do we see a connection between one idea and the next, and is there a coherence of the whole? These are the critical questions for the next exercise. First, we review the whole as we have seen it—phrase by phrase—but now complete.

1. **How do they say a blessing over fruit?**
2. **Over fruit of a tree, a person says [Blessed are you, Lord, our God, ruler of the world, who] creates fruit of the tree.**
3. **Except for wine, for**
4. **over wine, a person says [Blessed are you, Lord, our God, ruler of the world, who] creates fruit of the vine.**
5. **And over fruit of the ground a person says [Blessed are you, Lord, our God, ruler of the world, who] creates fruit of the ground.**
6. **Except for bread, for**
7. **Over bread, a person says, [Blessed are you, Lord, our God, ruler of the world who] brings bread out of the earth.**
8. **And over vegetables, a person says [Blessed are you, Lord, our God, ruler of the world, who] creates fruit of the ground.**
9. **Rabbi Judah says, [A person says, Blessed are you, Lord, our God, ruler of the world, who] creates different kinds of seeds.**

I. A. What is the source of this rule?
   B. As our rabbis have taught:
   C. [The fruit thereof will be] holy, for giving praise to the Lord (Lev. 19:24).

D. This teaches that they [pieces of produce] require a blessing before them and after them.

E. On this basis did R'Aqiba say,

F. It is prohibited for a person to taste anything before he has said a blessing

II. A. Our rabbis have taught:

B. It is prohibited for a person to derive enjoyment from this world without a blessing

C. And all who derive enjoyment from this world without a blessing commit sacrilege.

D. *What is the remedy [for such a person]?*

E. *Let him go to a sage*

F. *Let him go to a sage?*

G. *What will he do for him?*

H. *Lo, he [already] has committed a violation.*

I. But said Raba,

J. Let him go to a sage in the first place,

K. and he [the sage] will teach the person blessings,

L. so that he may not come into the grip of sacrilege.

M. Said Rab Judah said Samuel,

N. Whoever derives enjoyment from this world without a blessing is as if he derives benefit from Holy Things that belong to Heaven,

O. since it is said, The earth is the Lord's and the fullness thereof (Psalm 24:1).

P. R. Levi contrasted [two verses of Scripture]:

Q. It is written, The earth is the Lord's and the fullness thereof (Psalm 24:1).

R. And it is written, The heavens belong to the Lord, but the earth did he give to people. (Psalm 115:16).

S. There is no contradiction.

T. The former verse applies before [one has said] a blessing, the latter verse applies after [one has said] a blessing.

III. A. Said R. Hanina bar Papa,

B. Whoever derives enjoyment from this world without a blessing

C. is as if he steals from the Holy One, blessed be he, and from the community of Israel,

D. since it is said, Whoever robs his father or his mother and says, It is no transgression—that person is a companion of a destroyer (Prov. 28:24).

E. And "his father" refers only to the Holy One, blessed be he, as it is said,

F. Is not he our father, who has begotten us (Deut. 32:6).

G. And mother refers only to the community of Israel,

H. since it is said, Hear my son, the instruction of your father, and do not forsake the teaching of your mother (Prov. 1:8).

I. What [is the meaning of the phrase], That person is a companion of a destroyer?

J. Said R. Hanina b. Papa,

K. he is a companion of Jeroboam, the son of Nabat,

L. who destroyed Israel for their Father in heaven.

M. R. Hanina b. Papa contrasted [two Scriptural verses]:

N. It is written, Therefore, will I take back my grain in the time thereof (Hosea 2:11).

O. And it is written, And we shall gather in our corn . . . (Deut. 11:14).

P. There is no contradiction.

Q. The latter verse refers to the time in which Israel does the will of the Omnipresent.

R. The former verse refers to the time in which Israel does not carry out the will of the Omnipresent.

IV. A. Our rabbis have taught:

B. And you will gather in your grain.

C. What does Scripture teach?

D. Since it is said, This book of the law will not depart from your mouth (Joshua 1:8),

E. one might have thought that these things are to be just as they are written.

F. Scripture therefore says, You will gather in your grain

G. [This means] combine with them a worldly occupation,

H. the words of R. Ishmael.

I. R. Simeon b. Yohai says,

J. Is it possible for a person to plough in the time of ploughing,

K. sow in the time of sowing,

L. harvest in the time of harvesting,

M. thresh in the time of threshing,

N. winnow in the time of the wind—

O. [if so]—as to the Torah, what ever will become of it?

P. But when Israel does the will of the Omnipresent,

Q. their work is done by others,

R. since it is said, And strangers shall stand and feed our flocks (Isaiah 61:5).

S. And when Israel does not do the will of the Omnipresent,

T. their work is done by their own hands,

U. as it is said, And we will gather in our grain.

V. and not only so, but

W. the work of other people is done by them [as well],

X. as it is said, And we will serve our enemy (Deut. 28:48).

V. A. Said Abbaye

B. Many did things in accord with R. Ishmael,

C. and it worked out for them.

D. [Others did things] in accord with R. Simeon b. Yohai,

E. and it did not work out for them.

F. Said Raba to rabbis,

G. By your leave,

H. in the days of Nisan and in the days of Tishré

I. do not appear before me,

J. so that you may not be anxious about your food
K. for the entire year.

VI. A. Said Rabbah b. Bar Hana, said R. Yohanan, in the name of R. Judah b. R. Ilai,
   B. Come and see
   C. Not like the olden generations are the newer generations.
   D. In the olden generations, they made their study of Torah their fixed concern,
   E. and their vocation their hobby,
   F. both this and that worked out for them.
   G. But the newer generations,
   H. who made their vocation their fixed concern,
   I. and their study of Torah their hobby
   J. neither one nor the other worked out for them.

Let us rapidly review the sequence of units.

1. Mishnah: How do we bless?
2. Talmud: How do we know (that we say a blessing before we eat fruit, as well as after).
3. It is prohibited to enjoy anything of this world without saying a blessing.
4. Whoever enjoys anything of this world without saying a blessing is as if he or she steals from God.
   Concluding: We will gather in our grain.
5. Should one work at a worldly occupation or only study Torah?

If we see things this way, at what point do we have a problem? It appears that the person who constructed our Talmud left us a problem in No. 5: What is the connection between 1–4, which is fairly coherent, and the issue of working for a living rather than always studying Torah? Indeed, Torah study is not even mentioned previously. Why is Torah study relevant to (1) saying blessings and (2) expressing our thanks for God's blessings to us?

Once more, we must be struck by the strange intrusion of whether we should spend all our time studying Torah. From our point of view, it simply is not a natural problem. But the person who put together this discussion saw the question as a routine turning. The connection is formed by the reference to gathering in grain. The same verse of Scripture occurs in the two sequential discussions. Therefore, having brought up the subject of gathering grain, we are "naturally" going to talk about that subject. The Talmud is concerned with a life of holiness, but we live in a world uninterested in what is holy. The Talmud wants to talk about serving God, but people we know rarely think about such matters. The Talmud literally believes everything that Scripture says. That is the first and most important truth we have learned in this book. Scripture says if we serve God, we will have blessings, and if we do not serve God, we will have misfortune. And the rabbis of the Talmud believe that we serve God by studying Torah.

Our context, we remember, is how we say blessings for natural benefits. The reason, we recall, is that we say a blessing because the world belongs to God. Only when we say a blessing do we have a right to take what belongs to God and make it our own. And is not learning Torah a way to gain the right to make what is in the world our own? If this is our worldly perspective, then it is natural to ask whether it is better both to work and to study Torah or only to study Torah. To the Talmudic rabbis who were devoted to Torah study this was a real and urgent question. For they also had to make a living for themselves and their families. The issue is our enjoyment of worldly benefits and the way in which we gain that right. What could be a more natural and obvious question than how to live the good life in the good world that God made for us? And since, for the rabbis, the good life is one of studying Torah, what could be more routine than to contrast the good life against the life of making a living?

A paradox exists. The world belongs to God, but we must work to gain the benefits that should come freely if we serve God. This is what troubles both Ishmael and Simeon b. Yohai according to the later Amoraim. Ishmael takes a reasonable position, but—as I explained by invoking the passage from Leviticus Rabbah—it is not logical within the Talmudic system. Simeon takes an unreasonable position, but within the system it makes good sense. When we first saw what they had to say, it seemed just the opposite. But now we turn matters around. Simeon believes that God owns the world. He knows that if we do what the Torah requires, then we shall enjoy without struggle benefits of the world. So why should we not devote our lives to the study of Torah, so that God will bless us with what, after all, belongs to God? In the system we have laid out—as that system is revealed in the Shema' in the words of the prophets, and in the teachings of the rabbis themselves—Simeon's position is completely sensible. Ishmael has one foot in and one foot outside the system. True, he is more practical. True, he deals with the world as it is, not with the world as the Torah describes it. True, many have followed his way and have lived good lives. But Simeon must object, "Is this really the good life?"

To see whether or not we have a single unit, we have to find the meanings of the individual components. Only then are we able to tell whether each unit is connected to the one before and leads directly to the one that follows. I think that we have a natural and orderly presentation of ideas. But these are matters of taste and judgment. We have every right to form our own opinion once we have read the text with care and thought about what it says. Once more we must ask whether the Talmud did a good job explaining the Mishnah-passage. It has not done so in the passages we have considered. However, in some of the materials I did not present the Talmud makes important points about the Mishnah. But we have a right to ask, "Has the Talmud said important things about the Mishnah? Has it made the Mishnah more important?"

I think the answer must be, Yes. For the Talmud has taken what is a routine matter—mumbling this blessing or that blessing—and shown us what is deep and important about it. The Talmud has said something striking about deeds that we perform. It has explained that these deeds bear profound meanings for us, for our view of who we are, and for our understanding of our relationship to the world and to God. So when the Talmud speaks about deeds, it talks of faith, of matters of belief. What is its message? Nothing is to be taken for granted because everything is granted by God. We do not own the world by right. God who made the world owns it: "The earth is the Lord's, and the fullness thereof." Yet, we are here and have needs, and God fills those needs. We should not act as if we own what is a gift, what is in our hands for only a little while. We have to revere the natural world and treat with respect those things that God has made. We have to be grateful for the gifts of nature and treat with high regard and thankfulness what is given to us.

And yet, how great are we, for whom all these things have been done! Who are we to deserve it all? And why is it all coming to us? The answers to these questions will be coming in the next unit of the Talmud. We really do not deserve all that we get. God gives us what we do not deserve and have not earned. The important point is that when we speak about things we are supposed to do—about halakhah—we find we cannot be silent about things we are supposed to believe—about aggadah. When the Mishnah tells us about deeds, the Talmud tells us about beliefs. Later, we shall see the opposite. When the Mishnah tells us about beliefs, the Talmud speaks about deeds: prayers we say at this time, prayers we say at that time. But the deeds are the deeds of faith, and the faith is a faith of deeds. There is no Mishnah without Talmud, there is no halakhah without aggadah, and there is no aggadah without halakhah.

We conclude by asking one more time: "What are the choices among which the person who made up our Talmud has made? What are the things that might have been mentioned? Only when we realize what might have been shall we truly understand what is. That applies to the Talmud. It also applies to the world in which we live.

WHAT IS THE TALMUD? There can be only one answer to that question on the basis of the Talmud we have just learned. It is: The Talmud is a sustained and demanding essay about our religious life.

It takes off from the Mishnah, but it flies off into the skies of its own discovery. When the Mishnah tells us what to do, the Talmud asks why we should do it. And the Talmud's answer explores the deep questions, Who are we? Where are we? What do we owe to God? What do we owe to one another? The Talmud's conception of the Mishnah is that these questions have yet to be answered. That means the Talmud is a criticism of the Mishnah. The Talmud says what the Mishnah has not said. It not only serves to explain the Mishnah's language and ideas. It not only wants to tell us about the sources of the Mishnah's rules. It has an independent view of the Mishnah. It is not only the servant of the Mishnah. It is also the critic of the Mishnah. Its response to a given Mishnah-passage tells us what the Talmud does not find in the Mishnah at all, as well as what the Talmud finds unclear or incomplete in the Mishnah. What the Talmud asks about "how we say blessings" is why we say blessings at all. And that means that the Talmud is dissatisfied with the Mishnah.

The Talmud is a long and serious criticism of the Mishnah. It judges what the Mishnah says, and it offers an opinion on what the Mishnah does not say. That is not to suggest that the Talmud rejects the Mishnah. The Talmud respects the Mishnah. But the Talmud, in some measure, is independent of the Mishnah. It goes its own way. It asks its own questions. It raises its own issues for analysis. That is why when the Mishnah speaks of blessing fruit, vegetables, wine, and bread, the Talmud talks of Torah and its study.

Here the Talmud has done much more than explain the implications of Mishnah's rule. No one can claim that Mishnah speaks of Torah when it mentions apples and loaves of bread. Here the Talmud has also done more than go beyond the frontiers laid out by the Mishnah's treatment of a law. The Talmud gives us more than important new ideas about that same law that Mishnah lays forth in some other aspect or detail. The Talmud now shows us what it can do when it leaves the Mishnah behind entirely and proposes to talk about its own topics and interests. And what it can and does do is striking. The Mishnah is left behind in order to bring forward the Mishnah's own, deepest meaning.

VII

The Talmud Speaks to Us About Beliefs and Deeds: Saying You're Sorry

The Talmud to Mishnah Yoma 8:9

Just as the law of the Talmud expresses beliefs we hold about what it means to be a human being and what we must do to live a holy life, so the beliefs that we hold create Talmudic law governing proper behavior. That is, *halakhah* makes concrete what *aggadah* says in general terms. *Halakhah* brings down to everyday life what *aggadah* leaves up in heaven. And the opposite is also true. If we hold a belief, which is expressed through *aggadah*, then *halakhah* comes into being to give form and concreteness to that belief. There cannot be a belief without an action to express that belief. We are what we do. Our beliefs define what we are, and our deeds express what we are.

To see how beliefs make laws necessary, we look at a Mishnah-passage about the Day of Atonement and sin. In a religious system such as ours, in which there are so many things we are supposed to do or supposed not to do, it is inevitable that we shall do something wrong. We are human. It is not natural for us to keep all the laws. Some of the ritual ones may be inconvenient. Much more important: Some of the rules about right action to our fellow human beings conflict with our deep needs to be selfish and to hurt

136

other people. So we do sin, and when we do, it is more commonly against other people than it is against God.

We know that the Day of Atonement brings forgiveness and reconciliation between us and God. But what about forgiveness for what we have done alone against other people? For that purpose, we have to rely upon our own efforts. The Day of Atonement will not do for us what we do not do for ourselves. The Mishnah and the Talmud are able to work out general rules to tell us what to do in ordinary circumstances. This is hardly as easy as it sounds. Since the Mishnah and the Talmud go back nearly two thousand years, it is amazing that they are still interesting to us. We live in a completely different age and in a totally different world. How is it possible for us to want to hear what the Mishnah and the Talmud have to tell us about our relationships with other people? The reason is in two parts.

First, because human relationships do remain constant. There are just so many things people can do to and for each other, bad things and good things.

Second, because the Mishnah and the Talmud, for their part, are careful to avoid talking about things in a too concrete and specific way. If they are too specific, people will eventually no longer listen to what they have to say.

The Mishnah, as we shall see once again, speaks about fundamental and enduring truths, things that last from age to age and go on from place to place. It talks about sin and saying you're sorry ("repentence"), about relying on the Day of Atonement to do what we can and should do for ourselves. The Mishnah speaks of winning the friendship of people whom we have offended. It is surely relevant to us. We have friends whom we have offended. It certainly speaks to our world and about our problems. It is no accident. The conception of the Mishnah and the Talmud is that we can discover rules that will apply everywhere and to all the Jewish people. That is why the Mishnah and the Talmud claim to be Torah. They speak eternal truths—which God reveals and which we accept as Torah—even though they were written down long after Moses received the Torah at Mount Sinai. The power of Mishnah and Talmud lies in their ability to talk to us. But we are the one who gives the Mishnah and the Talmud their power and influence.

Once more we want to know, therefore, how the Mishnah and the accompanying Talmud arrange things that Jews already say and do. Clearly, the fundamental principle that governs is, since we form a holy community, the community has to define its norms for proper conduct. That means we do not treat as random, personal, and private matters that, within the Torah, form concerns of a public, communal, and social character. That is because we form Israel, holy Israel, and all together bear responsibility for the character of our community, each one in his or her conscience expected to respond to the norms of the community as a whole. Judaism is called "a legalistic religion," meaning, it is a religion that teaches norms of behavior and belief. And so it is—and so is every religion that regards the community as critical, the conduct of life together as consequential. Only religions that people invent for themselves, one by one, as modes of entirely private and personal conviction, may describe themselves as not legalistic. But then, the activities of a person that are wholly idiosyncratic and personal may well shade over into the subjective and irrelevant, and if it is anything, the Torah sets itself up as God's will for the whole community of holy Israel. So we should not find surprising the Torah's provision for rules for activities that people might carry out any which way.

We want to examine, in particular, the Talmud's mode of thinking and analyzing practices. Finally, we hope to see what we may learn from the Talmud about things with which we already are familiar.

The Mishnah-paragraph before us, Mishnah Yoma 8:9, is a set of four sentences, each separate and distinct from the others.

1. He who says I shall sin and repent, sin and repent, they do not give him sufficient power to make repentance
   [He who says], I shall sin, and the Day of Atonement will atone, the Day of Atonement does not atone
2. Sins that are between man and the Omnipresent the Day of Atonement atones for. Sins that are between man and his fel-

low the Day of Atonement does not atone for, until one will win the good will of his fellow [once more].

3. This is what Rabbi Eleazar ben Azariah expounded:
   From all our sins shall we be clean before the Lord (Lev. 16:3)
   Sins that are between man and the Omnipresent the Day of Atonement atones for.
   Sins that are between man and his fellow the Day of Atonement does not atone for until one will win the good will of his fellow.

4. Said Rabbi Aqiba, Happy are you, Oh Israel! Before whom are you purified?
   Who purifies you?
   Your father who is in heaven.
   As it is said, And I will sprinkle clean water on you and you will be clean (Ezek. 36:25).
   And it says, The hope of Israel is the Lord (Jer. 17:13).
   Just as the immersion-pool cleans the unclean people,
   So the Holy One, blessed be he, cleans Israel.

The Mishnah-passage repeats its one idea four times, each time in a somewhat different way. The main point is that the Day of Atonement will do us no good if we do not do our share of the work of repentance. We must say that we're sorry for what we have done wrong. The first point is that we cannot sin and take for granted that the Day of Atonement will make up for us. There is nothing magical, nothing that works without regard to what we do and believe in our hearts. The second point is that the Day of Atonement serves only to atone for those sins that we have done against God. But sins that we have done against other people must be atoned for by going to the person whom we have injured and seeking forgiveness. Our Mishnah is going to demand some amplification here. What sort of "mission" to the one whom we have hurt is required? What if the person will not grant us forgiveness? There are questions of belief, but they are going to demand statements of behavior—rules on what we are expected to do.

The third and the fourth points say what the first two points already have said. Eleazar b. Azariah's lesson is precisely what No. 2 already has told us. The Day of Atonement will do us good only if we first seek the forgiveness of the one we have injured. Before we proceed to the Talmud, let us see whether we are able to list some of the questions we shall want the Talmud to answer.

First, we shall want to know the source of the Mishnah-passage's rule. That source, we need hardly note, is Scripture. So we shall ask, "What is the source of this rule about seeking forgiveness from our friend?"

We shall ask the Talmud to tell us whether we must persist, if the friend will not forgive, and if so, to what extent.

What if the person whom we have hurt moves away, or dies, before we have a chance to gain forgiveness? What do we do then?

These are some of the things we shall not expect the Talmud to tell us, when the Talmud comes before us in its role as an explanation for the Mishnah. What the Talmud will tell us when it proceeds to expand and explain its explanation we can now hardly predict.

EXPLAINING THE MISHNAH: By this time in our learning of Talmud, we surely can predict that the first thing the Talmud will ask about this Mishnah-passage is, what is the source of this law? Sometimes the question is asked directly. Other times, the question is answered without being asked. In the first Talmud-selection, we find the answer without the question. Naturally, the answer is that we learn the rule in Scripture. This time the relevant book of the Bible is Proverbs, and we shall observe that Proverbs says almost exactly what the Mishnah says. But it says the same thing in a different circumstance and for a different purpose. So the contribution of the Amora, Isaac, is to see the relevance of what Scripture says to what Mishnah wants us to do. This we shall see in A–J.

We already know to expect that when we have a statement of an ideal of how we should behave, the Talmud will turn that statement into rules about things we must actually do. We therefore shall not be surprised to find that an important explanation of our Mishnah-passage will be a concrete instruction on precisely how to make friends with someone we have offended. The rule will be spun out of a relevant verse of Scripture since, we remember, the Amoraim do not regard Mishnah as an adequate and complete source of truth. They insist on turning, also and especially, to the written Torah, to the Scriptures. Two Amoraim, Hisda (K–O) and Yosé b. R. Hanina (P–Z), supply us with rules based upon verses of the Scripture.

A. Said R. Isaac,
B. Whoever offends his fellow,
C. even [merely] through words,
D. has to make peace with him,
E. since it is said,
F. My son, if you have become a surety for your neighbor, if you have struck your hands for a stranger, you are snared by the words of your mouth.
   Do this now, my son, and deliver yourself, since you have come into the hand of your neighbor. Go, humble yourself, and urge your neighbor (Prov. 6:1–3).
G. If you are wealthy
H. open the palm of your hand to him.
I. And if not
J. send many friends to him.
K. Said R. Hisda,
L. And he needs to make peace with him through three groups of three people,
M. since it is said,
N. He comes before men and says,
O. I have sinned, and I have perverted that which was right, and it did me no profit (Job 33:27).
P. Said R. Yosé b. R. Hanina,
Q. Whoever seeks pardon of his fellow
R. should not seek it from him more than three times,
S. since it is said, Forgive, I pray you now, and now we pray you (Gen. 50:17).
T. But if he dies,

U. one brings ten men,

V. and sets them up at his grave,

W. and says,

Y. "I have sinned against the Lord, the God of Israel,

Z. "and against Mr. So and So, whom I have injured."

Isaac's rule is not quite the same as Mishnah's, since the Mishnah-passage speaks of the setting of the Day of Atonement. So why has the Talmudic editor introduced this rule at just this point? For the obvious reason that the Mishnah-passage speaks about harm done by a person to another person. It says that the Day of Atonement does not atone in such a case. We must apologize and win the other person's forgiveness. So Isaac's saying A–J is quite appropriate for this setting, even though it is not exactly to the point of the Mishnah-passage. In fact, what he says is rather straight-forward, even self-evident. If we offend our fellow, even by something we have said, we have to make peace.

The proof-text then becomes the main element. Proverbs 6:1–3 contains precisely the advice that Isaac wants to give. If someone has a claim of money against you, pay him off. If it is some other sort of complaint, send many friends to him: "Urge your neighbor." Hisda's point is equally clear. The work of making friends should not go on indefinitely. We try our best. But if the other person cannot be pacified, then let it be. Three times, with three people each time, would be ample. We notice that the verse in Job contains three clauses. The person says, "I have sinned," and then, "I have perverted," and finally, "and it did me no profit." So we find three little "confessions," a fair indication of what is required of you as well. Yosé b. R. Hanina then draws out the implications of Hisda's saying. We do it three times—and no more than three times. This is derived not from what Hisda has said, but from yet another verse of Scripture, cited at S. Here, too, we see a group of three clauses and each represents a request for pardon and forgiveness.

Finally, we have the rule to cover the special case of someone's dying before you can make up. The Talmud's answer is to go to the grave and to state there the confession of what one has done, together with a prayer for forgiveness. It is the best we can do. We should not misunderstand the point of going to the grave. It is to help the person who seeks forgiveness to locate and focus upon the one who has been injured. Going to the grave is for the sake of the one who is alive, not for the sake of the one whose bones are deposited in the ground.

It is time to ask whether—if we were commenting on and explaining this Mishnah-passage—we would add to what the Talmud contributes. Can we make up a Talmud to go along with the one given to us by the Amoraim of Babylonia of the third, fourth, and fifth centuries of the Common Era? This is a good opportunity since the teachings of the Amoraim are expressed fairly simply and they address an issue that we know well. How would we make up—continue—the Talmud? We might add some stories of specific incidents we have witnessed such as occasions on which someone we know has tried to make friends with a person he or she has made angry or offended. Or we might amplify Yosé's case about someone who dies. We might add that if someone moves away, we write letters or make phone calls.

The concluding unit of our Talmudic passage shows us how the person who put the Talmud together added to these rather straightforward rules and made the Talmudic passage more concrete. This was done by adding a series of three stories about what happened to great rabbis of the Talmudic age.

II. A. R. Jeremiah had something against R. Abba
    B. He went and sat down at the door of R. Abba.
    C. As the maid was throwing out water,
    D. a few drops of water touched his head.
    E. He said, They have made me into a dung-heap.
    F. He cited the following verse about himself:
    G. He raises up the poor out of the dust (I Samuel 2:8).
    H. R. Abba heard.
    I. And he came to him.
    J. He said to him,
    K. Now I must make peace with you

     L. For it is written,

     M. Go, humble yourself and urge your neighbor (Prov. 6:3).

The story's purpose is to give the law life. The law takes on new and human meaning when we are told how a particular sage acted. That is why the editor of the Talmud placed this and two other stories alongside the Talmud's explanation and expansion of our Mishnah-passage. But the stories also have their own purposes. They make their own points. It is only later on that the person who put the Talmud together as we have it brought them before us and set them out as illustrations of the Talmud's explanation of the Mishnah-passage.

Jeremiah's behavior is interesting. Jeremiah had injured Abba. So Jeremiah went straight to the other party and sat down at his door. What was the importance of such a deed? It was to make sure that Abba knew that Jeremiah was aware something had gone wrong. Why? Because Jeremiah understood that the worst thing Abba could do is bear a grudge. If we are angry and we express it, the ball is in the other person's court. We do not keep things in. We say what we think. If the other party wants to make amends, well and good. But we are not going to hate that other person. The way to avoid hating him or her is to say what we think. Then why be angry any longer?

So Jeremiah went and sat down at Abba's door. It was a simple, silent, and eloquent gesture. Let Abba say what was on his mind. What happened? The maid threw out some water, and Jeremiah got slightly wet. Just a few drops touched him. But to him this was too much. So he pitied himself. This is not so impressive. But it had a good result. Jeremiah quoted a verse from Scripture, with the notion that the verse spoke about Jeremiah in particular: "He raises up the poor out of the dust." Now Abba heard that Jeremiah was at his door. He came out and realized what was happening. Then he, too, found an appropriate verse in Scripture—that same verse with which we began our account, cited by Isaac to explain and support the teaching of the Mishnah-passage. So we can see that whatever really happened, the story is worked out to remind us of where we are, which is in the Talmudic discussion. This is artful, since in the story itself, the cited verse of Scripture plays an important role as well. Now another story:

A. R. Zeira, when he had something against some one,
B. would go back and forth before him,
C. and make himself available to the other,
D. so that the other would come out
E. and make peace with him.

The story-teller reports something Zeira did under ordinary circumstances, a general rule of behavior, rather than a specific and concrete incident. When someone hurt Zeira, he would go to the other party and say nothing. He simply made himself available. The other person could then see him and do what had to be done. Why has the editor told this story at this point? For the obvious reason that Zeira is said here to have done in general what Jeremiah did in particular. So the story is not told at random or without purpose. It is part of a careful discussion of the notion that if we have a grievance, don't keep it in. Go to the other party. But we don't have to say a thing. All we have to do is remind the other party by our presence that there is some unfinished business.

The third story then proceeds to illustrate the same thing. But it makes another point as well.

A. Rab [Rab Abba] had something against a certain butcher.
B. He [the butcher] did not come to him [Rab].
C. On the eve of the Day of Atonement, he [Rab] said, I shall go to make peace with him.
D. R. Huna met him.
E. He said to him, Where is the master going?
F. He said to him, To make peace with so and so.
G. He said, Abba is going to kill someone.
H. He [Rab] went and stood before him.
I. He [the butcher] was sitting and chopping an [animal's] head.

J. He [the butcher] raised his eyes and saw him.

K. He said to him, You are Abba! Get out. I have nothing to do with you.

L. While he was chopping the head,

M. a bone flew off,

N. and stuck his throat,

O. and killed him.

The story about Rab goes over the same ground as the stories we already have heard. That is, we have to make ourselves available to the party against whom we have a grievance. We don't sit on our high horse. We go to the other person. That is what Rab did. But our opening Talmudic passage has made a second point. If the editor is not to lose that other point, we have to be reminded of it. What if the other party will not then seek to reconcile with us. This is not quite the point of Isaac and Hisda and Yosé, which is that we make an effort to appease the other party. But the important and new idea is precisely this: What happens if we go to the other party, and that person will not atone for the harm he or she has done to us? What do we do then? So the new and final notion of this carefully constructed set completes the whole. Review the points:

1. If we offend our friend, we have to try to appease him or her (Isaac).

2. We send three groups of people, in succession (Hisda).

3. If the friend will not be appeased, we owe no more (Yosé b. Hanina).

4. If our friend has a grievance against us, we make ourselves available (Jeremiah, thus illustrating the general position of Isaac and Hisda).

5. If we have a grievance against our friend, we make ourselves available (Zeira).

6. If we have a grievance against our friend, we make ourselves available. But if the friend will not then try to make amends, that is not our problem.

In No. 6 we conclude the line of thought begun by Isaac and Hisda. Now the story about Rab is rather curious. It invokes something we have not seen often in our passages of the Talmud—supernatural power. When Rab is mistreated by the man, the man accidentally dies. The story-teller does not have to tell us that it is not an accident, but he does so when he has Huna make his prophetic comment. The story-teller wants us to know that the butcher's accidental death is not accidental. So we are warned in advance, through Huna's baleful comment, the Rab, in all innocence, is protected by Heaven.

Rab behaved correctly. Indeed, the story about Rab is the first point in this sequence that reminds us where we began, the Day of Atonement. Until this story, the subject has never been mentioned! So it is the Day of Atonement. In conformity with the Mishnah's teaching, we should have expected the butcher to come to Rab, as Jeremiah did. But the butcher did not come. So, like Zeira, Rab makes himself available to the butcher. Huna intervenes early to warn us of the story's real meaning. Then, the story resumes (H). If we did not have D–G, the story would flow smoothly. But it also would not make its point. That is why I think the clause is integral and not inserted as a gloss.

Rab goes to the butcher and stands up before him—a respectful gesture indeed, since it is Rab who has the complaint against the butcher. I underlines Rab's strange and deliberate behavior. It reminds us that the butcher remains sitting. And, lest we miss the point and think the butcher did stand up, we are told that he merely raised his eyes and saw Rab (J). The butcher remained seated in the presence of one of the great sages of the time. It is a sage, moreover, whom the butcher offended, and it is the eve of the Day of Atonement. All the elements are present for some smashing conclusion. And it is not long in coming. The butcher speaks his own death-sentence in K. "You are Abba—get out!" The world is on its head. The person who is injured is injured again. And all of this is done with great brutality—the butcher continues to chop the animal head (L). The rest follows.

The butcher chops the head—the symbol of death—and a bone

flies off and sticks in the butcher's throat. He is injured by his own actions, and the bone stabs him in the organ that he has used to injure and offend Rab. The butcher died because he killed himself. The irony of Huna's saying now is clear. Abba (that is, Rab) killed no one. The butcher did not really kill himself. It was an accident. But Huna has already told us the meaning of the accident.

Now, why has the one who put the Talmud together told this story here? We notice that there are three halakhic sayings, Isaac's, Hisda's, and Yosé b. R. Hanina's. Then we have three stories that illustrate halakhah where we started—The Day of Atonement, appeasing our friend. We end at precisely the unanswered question: What happens if we do not appease our friend, whom we have injured, by the eve of the Day of Atonement? True, it is an extreme and unusual case. What happens with Rab here happens because, after all, Rab is a holy man and a great sage of Torah. Still the story in its own context is not making the point that Rab is a holy man and that we should not be mean to rabbis. It makes the point that Rab was the injured party and he went to the one who had hurt him (as Zeira did) in order to give the other party a chance to deal with his complaint (as Abba did). And this he did on the eve of the Day of Atonement just as the Mishnah says we must do. So the concluding story, which brings us back to the Mishnah-passage, also has a powerful effect in answering the question the Mishnah has left open.

What happens if we do not do what the Mishnah says? The answer is, God oversees all things. God seals our judgment on the Day of Atonement. If, therefore, on the eve of the Day of Atonement, we do not do what is expected of us, there will be serious results. This artful construction, therefore, has never lost sight of the Mishnah-passage it is meant to explain even though, as we ourselves have seen, it is sometimes difficult to keep our eyes on our starting point. In the end, we can rely on the one who put things together. We never are let down. We will recall that once before we asked ourselves, "Is the Talmud carefully constructed, or is it just one interesting saying or story after another?" We once more observe that the Talmud, as exemplified by this passage, is put together with amazing care. We see there is close attention to form and formality. Three of one thing, then a matching triplet: three teachings, three stories. We see that acute care is paid to the substance as each saying, then each story, carries forward what has been set in the preceding one. And, at the end, we see a remarkable climax—the invocation of God's role in making sense of the whole thing. And at the end, we return to the beginning. We show the relevance to the Mishnah-passage of all that the Talmud has said by way of explaining the Mishnah-passage.

EXPANDING THE EXPLANATION: The Talmud's next important passage goes on to fresh ideas. It deals with the Confession, the recital of sins that we say on the Day of Atonement. The Day of Atonement atones for our sins, so we must list those sins before God in order to seek forgiveness. The Talmud's discussion carries forward, in a general way, its treatment of our Mishnah-passage. The Mishnah-passage provides the theme of forgiveness of sins of the Day of Atonement. But the specific treatment of the theme is another matter. The Talmud has two questions about the confession of sins. First, when are we supposed to confess our sins? Second, precisely what prayer do we say to confess our sins? Before we proceed, let us look at the prayer that nowadays we say in the synagogue as the confession of sins on the Day of Atonement. It is known as the *Vidui*, or Confession, and appears in the Mahzor, the prayer book for the New Year and the Day of Atonement, as follows (in the translation of Rabbi Jules Harlow):

> We abuse, we betray, we are cruel. We destroy, we embitter, we falsify. We gossip, we hate, we insult. We jeer, we kill, we lie. We mock, we neglect, we oppress. We pervert, we quarrel, we rebel. We steal, we transgress, we are unkind. We are violent, we are wicked, we are xenophobic. We yield to evil, we are zealots for bad causes.
>
> We have ignored Your commandments and statutes, and it has not profited us. You are just, we have stumbled. You have acted faithfully, we have been unrighteous.
>
> We have sinned, we have transgressed. Therefore we have not

been saved. Endow us with the will to forsake evil; save us soon. Thus Your prophet Isaiah declared: Let the wicked forsake his path, and the unrighteous man his plotting. Let him return to the Lord who shall forgive, and to the God of our fathers, forgive and pardon our sins, this transgressions from Your sight. Subdue our impulse to evil; submit us to Your service, that we may return to us. Renew our will to observe Your precepts. Soften our hardened hearts so that we may love and revere You, as it is written in Your Torah: And the Lord our God will soften our heart and the hearts of our children, so that we will love the Lord our God with all our heart and with all our being that we may live.

You know our sins, whether deliberate or not, whether committed willingly or under compulsion, whether in public or in private. What are we? What is our piety? What is our righteousness, our attainment, our power, our might? What can we say Lord our God and God of our fathers? Compared to You, all the mighty are nothing, the famous are non-existent, the wise lack wisdom, the clever lack reason. For most of their actions are meaninglessness, the days of their lives emptiness. Man's superiority to the beast is an illusion. All life is a fleeting breath.

What can we say to us, what can we tell You? You know all things, secret and revealed.

You always forgive transgressions. Hear the cry of our prayers. Pass over the transgressions of a people who turn away from transgression. Blot out our sins from Your sight.

You know the mysteries of the universe, the secrets of everyone alive. You probe our innermost depths. You examine our thoughts and desires. Nothing escapes You, nothing is hidden from You.

May it therefore be Your will, Lord our God and God of our fathers, to forgive us all our sins, to pardon all our iniquities, to grant us atonement for all our transgressions.
We have sinned against you unwillingly and willingly.
And we have sinned against you by misusing our minds.
We have sinned against you by immoral sexual acts.
And we have sinned against you knowingly and deceitfully.
And we have sinned against you by supporting immorality.
We have sinned against you by deriding parents and teachers.

We have sinned against you by using bad language,

And we have sinned against you by being foul mouthed against you by not resisting the impulse to evil.

For all these sins, forgiving God, forgive us, pardon us grant us atonement.

We have sinned against you by fraud and by falsehood.

And we have sinned against you by scoffing.

We have sinned against you by dishonesty in business.

And we have sinned against you by taking usurious interest.

We have sinned against you by idle chatter.

And we have sinned against you by haughtiness.

We have sinned against you by rejecting responsibility.

And we have sinned against you by plotting against others.

We have sinned against you by irreverence.

And we have sinned against you by rushing to do evil.

We have sinned against you by taking vain oaths.

And we have sinned against you by breach of trust.

For all these sins, forgiving God, forgive us, pardon us, grant us atonement.

We shall see in a moment that some of the rabbis of the Talmud refer to parts of what now serves as our Confession of sins for the Day of Atonement. Part of their work is to select among different versions of prayers already available the ones they think should be said in the synagogue. Another task is to make up prayers for people to say. Since the rabbis of the Talmud are both learned and holy, they have special gifts for creating prayers. Still, Jews of all later periods in the history of the Jewish people have joined in this neverending work. The first of the two units of the Talmud deals with the time at which we are supposed to say the confession.

B. The religious duty [to say] the confession [applies] on the eve of the Day of Atonement, at dusk.

C. But said sages

D. Let one say the confession before he eats and drinks,

E. Lest one be upset during the meal.

F. And even though he said the confession before he ate and drank,

G. he should say the confession after he eats and drinks,

H. Lest some mishap took place during the meal.

I. And even though he said the confession in the evening service,

J. Let him say the confession in the morning service;

K. in the morning service, let him say the confession in the additional service;

L. in the additional service, let him say the confession in the afternoon service;

M. in the afternoon service, let him say it in the closing service

N. And where [in the service] does he say it?

O. An individual [praying by himself or herself [says it] after the [silent] Prayer.

P. And the agent of the congregation says it in the repetition.

The *baraita,* stated in simple, tight clauses, has its own rhythm. Can we see it? Read the passage out loud, and we should be able to hear it. The baraita is arranged in matching clauses, which we can pick out (I–J, K–L, etc.). In fact, the *baraita* is divided into three parts. We can tell one from the other in two ways. First, the subjects of the two are different. Second, the two parts are phrased differently. These go together, hand in hand: what is said and the way it is said. The three parts are A–H, I–M, and N–P. The first two parts are so neatly stated that we pass from the one to the other without any real break. Then the third part is set off by a question (N). But the whole is a single, coherent statement: When do we say the Confession? How often do we say the Confession? At what point in the service do we say the Confession?

The main point (A–H) is that one should say the confession prior to eating the final meal before sunset on the eve of the Day of Atonement. That way we may be sure that we have said the Confession correctly. We might have too much to drink at supper. Then, at the Kol Nidré service, we might miss something or make a mistake. That good advice leaves the impression that we say the Confession only once. So, I–M hastens to tell us that we say it at each and every service for the Day of Atonement: Evening (which we call *Kol Nidré*), Morning (*Shaharit*), Additional (*Musaf*), Afternoon (*Minhah*), and Closing Service (*Neilah*)—five times in all.

The final question is where in the service one says the Confession. We recall that the service is said both by an individual and by a leader of the congregation in behalf of the whole community. So the silent prayer is said twice, once by ourselves, the second time by the agent of the congregation. When we say it by ourselves (O), we say it at the end of the silent Prayer. The agent of the congregation says it in the middle of the Prayer. And precisely what is this Confession? (Now we shall see something quite surprising. The rabbis of the Talmud have a number of different versions of the Confession. The discussion we just reviewed tells us that the service already had achieved a basic and unchangeable form, a normal structure, that might then be ornamented and embellished. But the basic order of prayer including the Shema' and the silent Prayer was fixed.

Q. What does one say?

R. Said Rab, "We know the secrets of eternity"

S. And Samuel said, "From the depths of the heart, Torah, it is said . . ."

U. R. Yohanan said, "The Lord of all worlds . . ."

V. R. Judah said, "Our iniquities are too many to count, and our sins too numerous to be counted."

W. Rab Hamnuna said, "My God, before I was formed, I was of no worth. And now that I have been formed, it is as if I have not been formed. I am dust in my own life, how much more in my death. Behold, I am before you, like a dish full of shame and reproach. May it be your will that I sin no more, and what I have sinned, wipe away in our mercy, but not through suffering."

X. And this is the confession of Rabbah, during the entire year,

Y. and of Rab Hamnuna the Lesser, on the Day of Atonement.

I count five proposals for the text of the Confession: Rab (R), Samuel (S), Levi (T), Yohanan (U), Judah (V), and Hamnuna (W) Then, at the conclusion, we are told what some people actually said as the confession (X and Y). Rab refers us to the prayer, "You know the mysteries of the universe." This is the one translated by Rabbi Harlow. Samuel's appears to be the same prayer, except that Samuel knows the introductory words as "You know the depths of the heart." Levi's prayer appears to correspond to the prayer we say in the silent Prayer of the Day of Atonement, in Rabbi Harlow's translation:

> Our God and God of our fathers, forgive our sins on this Day of Atonement. Blot out and disregard our transgressions, as Isaiah declared in Your name, "I alone blot out your transgressions, for My sake your sins I shall not recall. I have swept away our transgressions like a cloud, your sins like mist. Return to Me, for I have redeemed you." And the Torah promises, For on this day atonement shall be made for us, to cleanse you; of all your sins before the Lord shall you be cleansed.

We may readily see why this prayer would be relevant to the Mishnah with which we began so long ago. As we notice, precisely the same biblical verse is important to both the Mishnah and the prayer of Confession as Levi cites it. This brings us to Yohanan's prayer of Confession. It occurs, in fact, in every Morning Service of the year, again in Rabbi Harlow's translation:

> Lord of all worlds! Not upon our merit do we rely in supplication, but upon Your boundless compassion. What are we? What is our piety? What is our righteousness? What is our attainment, our power, our might? What can we say, Lord our God and God of our fathers? Compared to you, all the mighty are northing, the famous are non-existent, the wise lack wisdom, the clever lack reason. For most of their actions are meaninglessness, the days of their lives emptiness. Man's superiority to the beast is an illusion. All life is a fleeting breath.

If we look back at the Confession now in our *Mahzor*, we will see that Yohanan's opinion is certainly taken into account. For the Confession to which he refers is included in the paragraph beginning, You *know our sins*. Judah's sentence would not seem to occur in our Confession. Hamnuna spells out the prayer as he wants it to be said. This prayer now occurs at the end of the silent Prayer of the Day of Atonement, at the conclusion of the Confession. It appears that the several proposals before us in the Talmud have made their way into the *Mahzor* as we know it.

If we now look back at our Mishnah-passage, we see that the Talmud has essentially gone its own way. We have seen this before. While the Mishnah provides the point of departure, it does not indicate the only road to be followed. As we know, the rabbis of the Talmud do not hesitate to explore issues, ideas, or problems important to them but which are not raised in the Mishnah-passage on which they are working. This is another sign of the essential independence and freedom of the rabbis who created the Talmud. They are deeply royal to the Mishnah. They are eager to clarify it. They want to be sure that every one of its words is defined. They make certain that any questions left open in the Mishnah-passage under discussion will be answered thoroughly and that the answers themselves will be fully explained. But they do go their own way. They ask their own questions. Obviously, at this point in their treatment of our Mishnah-passage they have not strayed far from the basic theme, which is the Day of Atonement and the forgiveness of sins. But we see that they also introduce the subjects important in their own day, not only in the time in which the Mishnah was made up. That is why they can ask about what Confession we say on the Day of Atonement and which of the available versions we are supposed to say.

Yet, if we look at the *Mahzor* as we know it, we will see that other people have been just as independent of the Talmudic rabbis as those rabbis were from the authorities of the Mishnah. For we have a Confession that incorporates the ideas of some of the rabbis before us but that also goes its own way. And that is the way of the Torah laid out by the rabbis of the Talmud. They read the written Torah and claim to provide yet another Torah—the Mishnah, the Oral Torah. But then later rabbis come along and treat the oral

Torah as a completion of the written Torah, not as an independent part of the Torah, which, for its part, it would seem to want to be. For what the Mishnah says on its own authority, the Talmud demands scriptural foundations, a verse in the written Torah.

The Talmud, too, would undergo in time the same experience. It would be received with care and reverence, but it would not prevent those who received it from responding, in their own fresh and interesting ways, to what it said. That is why at the outset we spoke not of asking for answers but of using our own minds to discover the answers. The experience of learning the Talmud teaches the lesson that we must always stand back and make up our own minds. We must always discover for ourselves those things that in the end, we shall affirm and believe. We do not merely ask other people to tell us what is so. We must find out for ourselves. And the only way in which we can find out for ourselves is by using our own minds and not by relying upon other people—however learned or holy, however much we admire and wish to follow them—to give us answers.

THE TALMUD ALL TOGETHER: BABYLONIAN TALMUD YOMA 87A–B (EXCERPT): For the last time, we look at the entire passage, Mishnah and Talmud, and ask how it has been put together. Since we deal with two distinct excerpts, we can not answer that question as it applies to the entire passage.

First, how does the Talmud treat the Mishnah-passage with which we started?

Second, how does the Talmud then expand on the topic of the Mishnah-passage?

We now know that the Talmud does two things. First, it most certainly does explain the Mishnah-passage, but in its own way. It answers questions the Mishnah-passage raises, but it does so in a fresh and subtle manner. Second, the Talmud will not stop within the boundaries of the Mishnah-passage. The editor of the pages of the Talmud under study here does not hesitate to use materials relevant to the Mishnah in only a general way.

Do we see any real relationship between the two operations:

explanation of the Mishnah, expansion of the explanation? Is the process of making peace with our friend, whom we have hurt, related to the confession that we say in our prayers? When we ask that question, we once more ask a basic question about the Talmud as well as a basic question about the contents of the Talmud. Is the Talmud more than an anthology? Is the lesson of the Talmud more than a sequence of unrelated thoughts? The answer is not difficult to see. In fact, once we have reread the two distinct passages, we should find the answer self-evident.

> He who says
> I shall sin and repent, sin and repent
> they do not give him sufficient power to make repentance
> [He who says], I shall sin, and the Day of Atonement will atone
> the Day of Atonement does not atone.
> 2 Sins which are between man and the Omnipresent
> the Day of Atonement atones for.
> Sins which are between man and his fellow
> the Day of Atonement does not atone for
> until one will win the good will of his fellow [once more].
> 3 This is what Rabbi Eleazar ben Azariah expounded:
> From all our sins shall we be clean before the Lord (Lev. 16:3)
> Sins which are between man and the Omnipresent
> the Day of Atonement atones for.
> Sins which are between man and his fellow
> the Day of Atonement does not atone for
> until one will win the good will of his fellow.
> 4 Said Rabbi 'Aqiba
> Happy are you, oh Israel!
> Before whom are your purified?
> Who purifies us?
> Your father who is in heaven.
> As it is said, And I will sprinkle clean water on us and we will
>   be clean (Ezek. 36:25).
> And it says, The hope of Israel is the Lord (Jer. 17:13).
> Just as the immersion-pool cleans the unclean people,
> So the Holy One, blessed be he, cleans Israel.

I. A. Said R. Isaac,
    B. Whoever offends his fellow,
    C. even [merely] through words,
    D. has to make peace with him,
    E. since it is said,
    F. My son, if you have become a surety for your neighbor, if you have struck our hands for a stranger, you are snared by the words of your mouth.
    Do this now, my son, and deliver yourself, since you have come into the hand of your neighbor. Go, humble yourself, and urge your neighbor (Prov. 6:1 3).
    G. If you are wealthy
    H. open the palm of your hand to him.
    I. And if not
    J. send many friends to him.
    K. Said R. Hisda,
    L. And he needs to make peace with him through three groups of three people,
    M. since it is said,
    N. He comes before men and says,
    O. I have sinned, and I have perverted that which was right, and it did me no profit (Job 33:27).
    P. Said R. Yosé b. R. Hanina,
    Q. Whoever seeks pardon of his fellow
    R. should not seek it from him more than three times,
    S. since it is said, Forgive, I pray you now, and now we pray you (Gen. 50:17).
    T. But if he dies,
    U. one brings ten men,
    V. and sets them up at his grave,
    W. and says,
    Y. I have sinned against the Lord, the God of Israel,
    Z. and against Mr. So and So, whom I have injured

II. A. R. Jeremiah had something against R. Abba.
    B. He went and sat down at the door of R. Abba.

   C. As the maid was throwing out water,

   D. a few drops of water touched his head.

   E. He said, They have made me into a dung-heap

   F. He cited the following verse about himself:

   G. He raises up the poor out of the dust (I Samuel 2:8).

   H. R. Abba heard.

   I. And he came to him.

   J. He said to him,

   K. Now I must make peace with you.

   L. For it is written,

   M. Go, humble yourself and urge your neighbor (Prov. 6:3).

III. A. R. Zeira, when he had something against someone,

   B. would go back and forth before him,

   C. and make himself available to the other,

   D. so that the other would come out

   E. and make peace with him.

IV. A. Rab [Rab Abba] had something against a certain butcher.

   B. He [the butcher] did not come to him [Rab].

   C. On the eve of the Day of Atonement, he [Rab] said, I shall go to make peace with him.

   D. R. Huna met him.

   E. He said to him, Where is the master going?

   F. He said to him, To make peace with so-and-so.

   G. He said, "Abba is going to kill someone."

   H. He [Rab] went and stood before him.

   I. He [the butcher] was sitting and chopping an [animal's] head.

   J. He [the butcher] raised his eyes and saw him.

   K. He said to him, You are Abba! Get out. I have nothing to do with you.

   L. While he was chopping the head,

   M. a bone flew off,

   N. and stuck his throat,

   O. and killed him.

V. A. Our rabbis have taught:

B. The religious duty [to say] the confession [applies] on the eve of the Day of Atonement, at dusk.

C. But said sages:

D. Let one say the confession before he eats and drinks,

E. Lest one be upset during the meal.

F. And even though he said the confession before he ate and drank,

G. he should say the confession after he eats and drinks,

H. lest some mishap took place during the meal.

I. And even though he said the confession in the evening service,

J. Let him say the confession in the morning service.

K. In the morning service, let him say the confession in the additional service;

L. in the additional service, let him say the confession in the afternoon service;

M. in the afternoon service, let him say it in the closing service.

N. And where [in the service] does he say it?

O. An individual [praying by himself or herself] says it after the [silent] Prayer.

P. And the agent of the congregation says it in the middle [of the Prayer].

Q. What does one say?

R. Said Rab, "We know the secrets of eternity."

S. And Samuel said, "From the depths of the heart."

T. And Levi said, "In our Torah, it is said . . ."

U. R. Yohanan said, "Lord of all worlds."

V. R. Judah said, "Our iniquities are too many to count, and our sins too numerous to be counted."

W. Rab Hamnuna said, "My God, before I was formed, I was of no worth. And now that I have been formed, it is as if I have not been formed. I am dust in my own life, how much more in my death. Behold, I am before you, like a dish full of shame and reproach. May it be your will that I sin no more, and what I have sinned, wipe away in your mercy, but not through suffering."

X. And this is the confession of Rabbah during the entire year,

Y. and of Rab Hamnuna the Lesser on the Day of Atonement.

We expand the Mishnah-passage by explaining how we appease someone we have harmed. The story concludes with Rab's actions on the eve of the Day of Atonement. The Mishnah-passage would be happy at this point. Then, we proceed and confess our sins. This, of course, is much more relevant to the Day of Atonement. We refer directly and explicitly to the prayers we say in the synagogue on that awesome day. So what has the Talmud told us? First, prepare for worship on the Day of Atonement. This we do by our behavior towards our friends. Second, worship on the Day of Atonement, say prayers that refer to our behavior both to our friends and to God. It would be difficult to imagine a more complete account of our theme. First, prepare ourselves to do. Second, while doing, refer back to our preparation. Correct our sins as much as possible, then confess our sins so God can do the rest.

The basic idea would not have surprised the rabbis who told us what blessings we say when we enjoy benefits of the world, and how God blesses us for doing God's will—studying Torah. The main point is before us, spread out in a different field, but familiar. It is that the will of God is to love God's creation and respect God's creatures, who are our fellow human beings. God's will is revealed to us in the Torah, which, therefore, we must study. The Confessions of the several rabbis should strike us in one more way; they stress the humility that characterizes the rabbis who are the greatest masters of Torah. These are not proud, but humble men. Their Torah study and their practice of the teachings of Torah—the commandments—result not in a sense of knowing and doing just what they should know and do. There is not much talk about how grand we are. Rabbis do not congratulate themselves for what they know and do. They underline their own failures; they are aware of their sins and transgressions. Rabbis humbly seek forgiveness of ordinary folk who have been hurt by them. When the butcher acts in a mean way, it *is* Heaven who punishes him.

These are some of the things that a reading of the entire passage calls to our minds. Let us now, for the last time, read the passage as it appears in the Talmud. We should be able to supply the needed periods and commas and be able to recognize the points at which one unit of thought—one paragraph—comes to an end and another begins. We now ask for the fourth time, "Has the Talmud said important things about the Mishnah? Or has the Talmud said essentially trivial and unimportant things?"

The Talmud has done two things. First, it has said important things about the Mishnah. Second, it has made the Mishnah still more important than it was. The Talmud has not left up in the air the matter of seeking forgiveness on the Day of Atonement. The Talmud has brought things down to earth by providing us with prayers we ourselves may, and do, say. So the Talmud makes concrete and everyday what, in the present instance, the Mishnah passage has left somewhere between heaven and earth. The adjective that applies to Judaism is "sublime," for here we have the religion of sublimity.

We conclude with the point at which we started—the relationship, in the Mishnah and the Talmud, between believing and behaving, between *aggadah* and *halakhah*. The Mishnah speaks about the meaning of the Day of Atonement and what it can and cannot do for us. The Talmud spells out *that* meaning in terms of everyday actions. But the Talmud does not leave things in the world of rules and laws, of *halakhah*. That is what it adds to the *aggadah* of the Mishnah. When the Talmud gives us rules, it also gives us *aggadah* of its own—a repertoire of prayers that we say.

These prayers are deep and penetrate to the foundations Of our inner life. Are they *halakhah* or are they *aggadah*? They obviously are both, for in the end our sages did not treat the one differently from the other. They are words we are supposed to say. The prayers, as prayers, are a part of *halakhah*. But the prayers, as expressions of beliefs, are an account of what is in our hearts. They evoke a certain response from us, and by saying them, we hope to call a certain response from Heaven as well. We wisely conclude with what we said before. The deeds express our faith. The faith gives meaning to the deeds. There is no Mishnah without Talmud, no *halakhah* without *aggadah*, no *aggadah* without *halakhah*. For our final exercise, we move beyond the limits of the Talmud and ask how the great philosopher of the West, Aristotle, and the great sages of the Talmud come together to present, each side in its own idiom and manner, the same idea. This exercise allows us to see what is quite unique to the sages of the Talmud, which, until now, we have not articulated.

VIII

Why the Talmud Works

Necessity, Cause, and Blame in Greek Philosophy and Talmudic Jurisprudence

ARISTOTLE'S MODE OF CLASSIFICATION, PLATO'S MODE OF DIALECTICAL ARGUMENT

Now that we have surveyed a number of passages of the Mishnah and followed the Talmud's amplification of them, we stand back and ask the basic question: Why has the Talmud enjoyed the success that has marked its long and influential career in the history of Judaism? For, as I said at the outset, the Talmud ranks among the most successful documents in the history of human civilization, influential, enduring, formative, from the time of its closure to this very morning.

The Talmud of Babylonia from the moment of its closure at about 600 C.E. [= A.D.] served as the textbook of Judaism and for Judaism today continues to provide the final and authoritative statement of the Torah revealed by God to Moses at Sinai. Why did the Talmud work so well as to constitute one of history's most influential documents in the formation of that social order its writers wished to define? For few writings out of any age command a hearing later on, and fewer still define the curriculum of a culture the way the Talmud does. As I said in the beginning, the sayings

164

of Confucius, the Gita, the Dialogues of Plato and the writings of Aristotle, the Bible and the Qur' an, the Mahabharata, the great traditions of mathematics and philosophy—these counterpart formations of intellect (human or divine, as the case may be) form the counterparts. And, among them, the Talmud is the least appreciated for the remarkable success attained by its writers. Why then does it work?

If we take as our sole undemonstrated premise the principle that ideas bear social consequences, so that we may explain the culture of a group by appeal to formative modes of thought and authoritative propositions of unquestioned validity and truth, then we may ask: What intellectual qualities of the Talmud account for its power? And, it will follow, we may also raise the question, how does the Talmud, by reason of its distinctive program of thought—medium and message alike—bear relevance to the formation of culture even now?

A brief sketch of the answer that I shall illustrate in this chapter suffices. The power of the Talmud lies in its translation into concrete and everyday matters of the two most powerful intellectual components of Western civilization from its roots to our own time, science and philosophy, specifically,

[1] Aristotle's principles of knowledge and
[2] Socrates' (Plato's) principles of rational inquiry and argument.

The modes of scientific inquiry of the one and of reasoned analysis of the other are translated by the Talmud into everyday terms, so that the experience of the everyday is turned into the academy for reasoned explanation of how things are: a book that turns concrete facts of the home and street into propositions of scientific interest and problems of philosophical inquiry. The Talmud turns the world into a class room, people into disciples, and culture into a concrete exemplification of abstract and reliable truth. Specifically: As we have seen, the Talmud is made up of two components, a philosophical law code, the Mishnah, which, in concrete ways, inculcates the principles of rational classification that Aristotle stated in abstract form; and a commentary to the Mishnah, called the Gemara (or simply, the Talmud proper), which, through the utilization of applied reason and practical logic, forms a moving ("dialectical") and analytical argument about the working of those principles in concrete cases. The importance of the moving argument lies in its open-endedness, so that successive generations found themselves not merely invited, but empowered to join in the argument and so assume the disciplines of rational argument that the Talmud exemplifies. In both aspects, therefore, the document serves as the medium of inductive instruction into the principles of science and philosophy that define the structure of the well-ordered society. I propose a single example of how Aristotle's principles of natural history—the correct classification of the like, the differentiation among cases that are not entirely alike, the formation of governing principles to govern the like—and Plato's (and Socrates') modes of dialectical argument come together in the Talmud.

What is the issue we shall pursue? A particular issue of both philosophical theory and jurisprudential concern deals with how a person becomes responsible for what he or she does. This will show us how the law of the Mishnah corresponds to a consequential theory of Graeco-Roman philosophy at a particular point. Specifically, we shall see how the same important distinctions that Aristotle makes as to causes are made also by the Mishnah. The correspondence concerns the structure of the same idea in the two distinct formulations, the Mishnaic and Talmudic, and the Graeco-Roman philosophical. In this specific case we shall see how the categorical structure of Graeco-Roman thought and that of the Mishnah correspond, point by point, the one saying abstractly what the other expresses only in humble, workaday words. That clear categorical correspondence will justify classifying the law of the Mishnah as a philosophical law, meaning, a law that states in jurisprudential cases the philosophical principles and distinctions that govern and come to realization in said cases. So the philosophy, concerning metaphysics, will have to form a tight fit with the law of the Mishnah.

When we turn to the Talmud of Babylonia's reading of the Mishnah-passage, we shall uncover in the unfolding, meandering, dialectical argument, a theological proposition deeply embedded in the exposition of that passage. The steps in the argument to follow are these:

[1] a Mishnaic rule is philosophical in its categorical structure;
[2] the Talmud examines that rule within the received Mishnaic categories;
[3] but there is a point at which the connection between one thing and something else requires elucidation, and that is the point at which, the Talmud (by definition) having fallen silent, we intervene.
[4] That is the point at which hermeneutics comes into play, requiring us to explain the connections and draw the conclusions. And these conclusions represent fundamental theological assertions.

NECESSITY, CAUSE, AND BLAME

The task, now fully set forth, carries a further requirement. I propose to show that the Mishnah and Aristotle treat the same problem in the same way. That will serve to demonstrate that the Mishnah's mode of formulating its principles corresponds in this case to that of Aristotle—and both reach the same conclusion as well. I have therefore to point to a topic that is not only philosophical in the Graeco-Roman canon, but also prominent in the Judaic canon of the dual Torah. Not only so, but we require a topic critical in both parts of the Torah, written and oral. For a topic important to the Talmud but not to Scripture, which in the theological language at hand means, to one part of the Torah but not another, will not serve for the large-scale dimensions of this argument. Since Judaism insists the two Torahs form a singular union (Scripture and the Mishnah, the written Torah and the oral), the topic of this exemplary exercise must be one that is prominent in both components of the Torah as well as in philosophical metaphysics and ethics.

The matter of responsibility meets that criterion. We are responsible for what we do, but how do we assess responsibility? We have forthwith to introduce the issue of causation: how does your action or lack of action relate to the consequence of what we do or not do? The written Torah introduces that issue when dealing with the goring ox, on the one side, and the difference between murder and manslaughter, on the other. The Mishnah knows that distinction, as we shall see, in rich detail, expounding as it does the written Torah's rules and its own problems as well. And for the Aristotelian tradition, on which we have concentrated, the issue finds its place at the very center of matters: the issue of causation.

That brings us to how we assess responsibility (as we saw in the opening Mishnah-paragraphs we treated, "liable," "exempt"). The issue concerns necessity, cause, and blame—abstractions of metaphysics, with concrete extension into ethics and jurisprudence, in philosophy, but also active ingredients in the detailed laws of the Torah, written and oral. In the context of the Torah, the counterpart to necessity, cause, and blame, is represented by the word "responsibility": What do people owe one another in a well-ordered society, how are people assigned the blame for what they do to others, the way in which we translate cause into blame in the setting of the variable defined by responsibility? Everyone understands we are responsible for what we do, but how do we know what we *do:* What is the nature of causation? These three then hold together in an uneasy, unstable balance, and it is the task of metaphysics, thinking about causation in physics for instance, and ethics, concerned with assessing blame and assigning guilt, to hold the whole together.

Now to the specifics of how the two parts of the Torah address the issue at hand, which is to say, how theology finds its voice in Judaism. The written Torah regards transactions between people— matters of injury and negligence, damages they or their chattels do to one another—as subject to divine concern; God wants Israel to treat one another in a fair manner, deeming justice the definitive trait of elect Israel's life together. And the oral Torah concurs, with the Mishnah devoting its best efforts to its part of the entire statement of the Torah's rules. So the topic we take up—responsibility, with special attention to damage one does to other persons or their property—forms a principal chapter in the religious system, inclusive of theology, of the Judaism of the dual Torah. The importance of the matter of responsibility to theology finds its match in its critical interest to philosophy. There, the importance of responsibility lies in making the necessary distinctions that are required among levels of responsibility to fix blame and the consequent penalties associated with them.

The theological question is just what must one do to restore the stasis of the holy community when he has wronged another member of Israel? The philosophical question asks, Where does one's personal responsibility begin, and to what degree and in what way do I bear culpability and therefore, the obligation of restoring the condition of another party, diminished in an event to which someone is party? The answers to these questions—which represent the theologization of the categories and distinctions of philosophy— form a chapter in the essay on the realization of justice in the shared life of Israel, the holy community formed by the Torah. Prominent in law, critical in ethics, the issue of responsibility indeed forms a central part of the theological message of the Judaism of the dual Torah.

Necessity, cause, and blame, the categories provided by the great Aristotle scholar, Richard Sorabji, form the grid that serves philosophy in its sorting out of questions of responsibility, a subdivision of the theory of causation.[1] A review of Aristotle's doctrine on this matter set side by side with the Mishnah's presentation of the same issues in its own idiom and for its own purpose defines the next stage in my argument. The category-formation governing

---

1. See Richard Sorabji, *Necessity, Cause and Blame: Perspectives on Aristotle's Theory* (London, 1980: Duckworth); this work is extensively cited presently.

responsibility and culpability put forth by Aristotle in a metaphysical setting, shown by Sorabji to spill over into jurisprudence, corresponds to the category-formation put forth by the Mishnah. That demonstrated, we shall have established as fact the philosophical character of the Mishnah's statement of matters.

Then, as is clear, the second step is to examine how the Talmud sustains the Mishnah's categories when it re-presents the Mishnah's philosophical statement. This will then lead us to that moment of puzzlement, that point of curiosity, in which we ourselves may join in the conversation: the point at which we have to figure out how one thing has something to do with another, and what consequence we are to draw from the connection.

PHILOSOPHY'S CATEGORICAL STRUCTURE

A brief account of the matter of responsibility as set forth by Aristotle suffices to make the point that the Mishnah's category-formation governing necessity, cause, and blame conforms to the lines of structure, with special attention to the governing distinctions, set forth by Aristotle. The issue of responsibility has to be set forth in two parts, first, in the context of Aristotle's general theory of causation—if we don't know that an act has caused a result, we cannot hold responsible the person who has done the act for the consequences the act has brought about—and only then, second, in the setting of the specific, juridical position set forth by Aristotle. We have for our purpose to pay close attention to the distinctions that he makes, for it is by showing that the Mishnah's law makes exactly the same distinctions that we may make the case: We may describe the Mishnah as philosophical in the Graeco-Roman meaning of philosophy.

First, as to causation in general: Aristotle discusses causation in the context of physics, not relationships or events in the social order. He finds, in accounting for changes in nature, four causes: [1] form, [2] matter, [3] moving cause, and [4] final cause. These are explained by G. E. R. Lloyd as follows:

Take first an example of artificial production, the making of a table. To give an account of this four factors must be mentioned. First matter, for the table is made out of something, usually wood. Secondly form, for the table is not just any lump of wood, but wood with a certain shape. Thirdly, moving cause, for the table must be made by someone, the carpenter. Fourthly, the final cause, for when the carpenter made the table, he made it for a purpose.[2]

These same factors are taken into account in describing change from potentiality to actuality:

The seed of a tree is potentially the mature tree; it is potentially what the mature tree is actually. This doctrine draws attention to the continuity of natural change. The goals towards which natural changes are directed are the ends of continuous processes. But while the ideas of potentiality and actuality are obviously relevant in this way to natural growth, Aristotle generalizes the doctrine and applies it to other types of change as well. A hunk of wood in a carpenter's shop is potentially a table or a chair or a desk. . . .

Therefore, Aristotle's interest in the four "causes" asks about "reason why," "through what," or "cause," in four senses:

He lists the From What, the Form, the Whence of the beginning of Change, and the End or For What.[3]

In analyzing the "why" of a thing or person or event, we have to take account of the material cause, the formal cause, the efficient cause, and the final cause.

Now to what is to us the important classification of cause, the efficient cause, the point at which culpability will enter in when transactions of the social order come under consideration. The efficient cause is the "whence the beings change," and the final

---

2. G. E. R. Lloyd, *Aristotle: The Growth and Structure of His Thought* (Cambridge, 1968: Cambridge University Press), pp. 58–9.

3. John Herman Randall, Jr., *Aristotle* (New York, 1960: Columbia University Press), p. 181.

cause is the "for-the-sake-of which, or the goal."[4] In natural processes, Edel says,

> the final cause is the mature development of the form itself in the particular materials: the acorn grows into an oak tree whose end is simply to express in its career what it is to be an oak tree. . . .

The efficient cause is "always some activity of the same type that the developed form exhibits." At the same time, in the consideration of causation, we take up the matter of chance, when something happens "by accident." Randall explains, "Chance is the name given to all events caused by factors that are not relevant to the ends of natural processes, by all the non-teleological factors, the brute events interfering with the natural working out of a process, or achieving a quite different end incidentally. . . ."[5] Chance will take its place in the grid to be placed over an event so as to affix responsibility. Any account of responsibility will have chance on the one side, total responsibility, based on volition expressed in wholly successful intention, on the other; but then, responsibility also will be modulated, with gradations from the one pole to the other.

Of the four causes, the one of greatest interest to us is efficient cause. From this point forward, Sorabji provides the account upon which we shall rely; everything that follows concerning category-formation depends upon his exposition. As to the definition of efficient cause, Sorabji explains: "The efficient cause is defined by reference to change; it is that whence comes the origin of change."[6] And—to state with heavy emphasis—*that is the point of intersection between the treatment of the matter by the Mishnah and Aristotle.*

Sorabji categorizes the treatment of efficient cause as the real

---

4. Abraham Edel, *Aristotle and His Philosophy* (Chapel Hill, 1982: University of North Carolina Press), pp. 61–2.

5. op. cit., p. 183.

6. Richard Sorabji, *Necessity, Cause and Blame: Perspectives on Aristotle's Theory* (London, 1980: Duckworth), p. 42.

point of Aristotle's contribution to legal theory. Concerning Aristotle's contribution as a whole, he states:[7]

> It lies in his whole enterprise of trying to classify the different kinds of excuse and of culpability. This important step drew attention to whole classes of cases, not only to the general categories of voluntary and involuntary, but also to overwhelming external force, fear of a greater evil, non-culpable ignorance of what one is doing, culpable ignorance, negligence, acts due to natural passion or to unnatural passion, acts due to deliberate choice. . . .[8]

Sorabji further comments:

> [Aristotle] introduces the criterion of what is not contrary to reasonable expectation, and so he turns the category of mistakes into a category of negligence. . . .
> Aristotle further divides injustices into those that are merely voluntary, and ones that are in addition inflicted because of a deliberate choice.[9]

Aristotle's treatment of negligence is set forth by Sorabji in these terms, which at last lead us from the territory of metaphysical theory to incorporated society: issues of the social order, such as those with which the Mishnah is concerned:

> Aristotle starts by distinguishing two kinds of injury inflicted in ignorance (and therefore involuntarily). The first is a mere mishap; the second is called a mistake . . . a culpable mistake. It is distinguished by reference to two ideas. First, the injurious outcome is not contrary to reasonable expectation, as it would have been in a mere mishap. Second, the origin of the cause . . . lies within the agent, not outside, as it would in a mere mishap. Aristotle's remaining categories of injury are two kinds of injustice. They are distinguished from the first two categories by the fact that the agent acts knowingly.[10]

---

7. Sorabji, pp. 291ff.
8. Sorabji, p. 291.
9. Sorabji, p. 293.
10. op. cit., pp. 278 ff.

What makes important Aristotle's conception of responsibility as Sorabji spells it out is his attention to the classification of different kinds of "excuse and culpability," which corresponds to the matter of responsibility.

What this set of distinctions yields are these gradations between total culpability or blame, by reason of one's forming the efficient cause without mitigating considerations, and total absolution from culpability and blame, by reason of one's bearing no responsibility whatsoever for what has happened:

[1] responsibility for all damages done, because the event that has caused loss and damage is voluntary and foreseeable, not the result of overwhelming external force; preventable; brought about by willful action; the result of culpable knowledge; deliberate choice, not mere negligence;

[2] responsibility for the greater part of the damages that are done, because the damage is foreseeable; not the result of overwhelming external force; preventable; thus in the event of ignorance is classified as culpable; but not voluntary;

[3] responsibility for the lesser part of the damages that are done, because the damage is foreseeable; but the result of overwhelming external force and not preventable, thus: involuntary, but the result of culpable ignorance and negligence;

[4] no responsibility at all, the event being involuntary, the result of overwhelming external force, not foreseeable, hence, inculpable ignorance; e.g., pure chance.

We, therefore, identify three oeprative criteria—points of differentiation in the analysis of events and the actions that produce them,[11] which form a cubic grid, with, in theory, nine gradations of blame and responsibility and consequent culpability:

---

11. That is in the assumption that the action is commensurate to the event, a problem that can be addressed but will be sidestepped to keep the matter economical. Commensurability is certainly a serious concern of the philosophers of the Mishnah, as their reading of the written Torah's law of the manslayer shows.

[1] an event produced by an action that is *voluntary vs. involuntary*;

[2] an event that is *foreseeable vs. not foreseeable*, or an action the consequences of which are foreseeable vs. not;

[3] an event that is *preventable vs. not preventable*; or an action that is necessary and therefore blameless, or one that is not.

Thus, we may construct a grid of three layers or dimensions, one grid formed of considerations of what is voluntary vs. involuntary, the second, of what is foreseeable vs. not foreseeable, the third, of what is preventable vs. not preventable, lines: a cube, with lines at each of the three intersecting levels drawn by the vertical of voluntary and the horizontal of involuntary, so, too, at the other layers, the whole then corresponding to the three categories just now given. One such mixed grid then will permit us to adjudicate complex cases of culpability and therefore compensation along lines projected at each of the layers. That permits us to identify an efficient cause that is voluntary, foreseeable, and preventable; voluntary, foreseeable, and not preventable; involuntary, foreseeable, and preventable; involuntary, not foreseeable, and not preventable; and so on for the rest. The nine possible combinations then allow us to sort out all situations which can arise; that is the compelling claim of philosophy that is "generalizable" or "universalizable."

The cubic grid will yield a set of consequences, each made up of its variables. These different classifications will contain their own calculations of culpability, on the one side, and their own corresponding levels of compensation, on the other; these range from total compensation for what is the result of voluntary action, the results of which are foreseeable, and in no way the result of overwhelming external force but preventable; to no liability at all for an event that is pure chance and not foreseeable, still the result of overwhelming external force, in no way intended. One need not elaborate to make the simple point that the lines of structure flow from the three categories enumerated just now. A treatment of the matter of cause and blame will then qualify as philosophical if it makes the same generalizing distinctions.

Now, to point to the philosophical character of the Mishnah's statement on responsibility, we ask how the Mishnah's law classifies responsibility and sorts out questions of negligence. At issue is the categorical structure yielded by the Mishnah's several rules: explaining the distinctions made by those rules by reference to the structure of differentiations implicit in them. We are interested in differentiation at levels of compensation, corresponding to differentiation at layers of responsibility, the whole an exercise in the applied reason and practical logic made possible by the distinctions yielding the category-formation just now outlined. Then, we shall return to the Talmud's treatment of part of the Mishnah-statement, stipulating that the treatment of the rest is uniform. What we want to identify are the generative variables, to find out whether they correspond to the set of three that yields the mixed grid described just now.

What we shall now see is that the same points of distinction operate; the same variables function to create, in very concrete terms, a grid of cause and blame and responsibility. When these are fully exposed, they produce the same process of sorting out as do Aristotle's distinctions as laid out by Sorabji; and they therefore are to be classified as philosophical in character: abstract, generalizing, extending to all possible cases, subject to criticism in abstract terms as well—not limited to cases, not qualified by episodic considerations, not a matter of anecdotal or casuistic formulation or conception. The negatives are important in differentiating the Mishnah's formulation from that of the Scripture, classifying the former's as philosophical, the latter's not. The Mishnah's formulations on the subject of responsibility yield in terms of blame and culpability precisely the categorical results to be anticipated from a recapitulation of Aristotle's variables in a jurisprudential formulation.

The Philosophical Character of the Mishnah's Categorical Structure of Responsibility

Of the Mishnah-chapters that pertain—Mishnah-tractate Baba Qamma, Chapters One through Four—we take up only part of the pertinent chapters, so as to outline what is essential for our inquiry. That is merely formal proof that the same pattern of distinctions that Aristotle portrays in his philosophy also operates in the Mishnah's presentation of the matter of cause and blame: culpability and compensation, in juridical terms. The first deals with what is logically critical: the matter of responsibility, its levels or degrees:

A. [There are] four generative classifications of causes of damages: (1) ox [Ex. 21;35–36], (2) pit [Ex. 21:33], (3) crop-destroying beast [Ex. 22:4], and (4) conflagration [Ex. 22:5].
B. [The indicative characteristic] of the ox is not equivalent to that of the crop-destroying beast;
C. nor is that of the crop-destroying beast equivalent to that of the ox;
D. nor are this one and that one, which are animate, equivalent to fire, which is not animate;
E. nor are this one and that one, which usually [get up and] go and do damage, equivalent to a pit, which does not usually [get up and] go and do damage.
F. What they have in common is that they customarily do damage and taking care of them is your responsibility.
G. And when one [of them] has caused damage, the [owner] of that which causes the damage is liable to pay compensation for damage out of the best of his land [Ex. 22:4].
                              Mishnah-tractate Baba Qamma 1:1

The important point comes at G: establishing responsibility for four damages done by four distinctive types of causes of damage. Then we shall have to know the traits of each, before we can assess responsibility and consequent compensation: what is each likely to do, for which I bear full responsibility, as against what each is unlikely to do, which I, therefore, cannot foresee and prevent. First comes the governing rule, stating the definition and consequence of responsibility:

A. In the case of anything of which I am liable to take care, I am deemed to render possible whatever damage it may do.

B. [If] I am deemed to have rendered possible part of the damage it may do,

C. I am liable for compensation as if [I have] made possible all of the damage it may do.

MISHNAH-TRACTATE BABA QAMMA 1:2

Now comes the distinction that is critical to the Mishnaic system, deriving as fact from the written Torah but formulated by the Mishnah as a general rule.

What is assumed to be harmless but does damage produces culpability different from what is assumed to be an attested danger; the difference then is in the compensation. So here comes the issue of whether or not an outcome is foreseeable. And, intrinsic to foresight is the possibility of preventing the damage. So the two form a single case, though the principles are distinct in theory. If a person could have foreseen the damage and did not prevent it, he is responsible for full damages; if he cannot, he pays only half of the total damages. In what follows we carefully delineate the specific aspects in which a danger from a given classification of danger, in fact, produces damage; damage produced in some other than the foreseeable manner is null:

A. [There are] five [deemed] harmless, and five [deemed] attested dangers.

B. A domesticated beast is not regarded as an attested danger in regard to butting, (2) pushing, (3) biting, (4) lying down, or (5) kicking.

C. (1) A tooth is deemed an attested danger in regard to eating what is suitable for [eating].

D. (2) The leg is deemed an attested danger in regard to breaking something as it walks along.

E. (3) And an ox that is an attested danger [so far as goring is concerned];

F. (4) and an ox that causes damage in the domain of the one who is injured;

G. and (5) man.

H. (1) A wolf, (2) lion, (3) bear, (4) leopard, (5) panther, and (6) a serpent—lo, these are attested dangers.

I. R. Eliezer says, "When they are trained, they are not attested dangers. But the serpent is always an attested danger."

J. What is the difference between what is deemed harmless and an attested danger?

K. But if that which is deemed harmless [causes damage], [the owner] pays half of the value of the damage which has been caused,

L. [with liability limited to the value of the] carcass [of the beast which has caused the damage].

M. But [if that which is] an attested danger [causes damage], [the owner] pays the whole of the value of the damage which has been caused from the best property

N. [he may own, and his liability is by no means limited to the value of the animal which has done the damage].

MISHNAH-TRACTATE BABA QAMMA 1:4

So much for the systematic presentation of the matter of foresight in interplay with responsibility. Let me give a single example of how the distinction between the damage that can be foreseen and the damage that cannot be foreseen is worked out for a single classification:

A. How is the leg deemed an attested danger in regard to breaking something as it walks along [M. 1:4D]?

B. A beast is an attested danger to go along in the normal way and to break [something].

C. [But if] it was kicking,

D. or if pebbles were scattered from under its feet and it [thereby] broke utensils—

E. [the owner] pays half of the value of the damages [caused by his ox].

F. [If] it stepped on a utensil and broke it,

G. and [the utensil] fell on another utensil and broke it,

H. for the first [the owner] pays the full value of the damage.

MISHNAH-TRACTATE BABA QAMMA 2:1

We have not covered distinctions of Aristotle between responsibility for all damages done, because the damage is [1] foreseeable and [2] preventable; responsibility for the greater part of the damages that are done, because the damage is not the result of overwhelming external force but preventable. The distinctions that flow then depend on the distinction between what is foreseeable—damage done by an attested danger in the ordinary course of events—therefore, preventable, and what is not foreseeable—damage done by an attested danger but not in the ordinary way in which that source of danger produces damage—but what is still preventable, for which partial compensation is paid.

Now, in light of the foregoing, we revert to the conception of efficient cause. In what follows, we have an attested danger; full compensation is then required. Why? Because the accident is subject to foresight, it could have been prevented, and one is, therefore, fully responsible. But there is the matter of efficient cause that now intervenes: direct vs. indirect causation has to be worked out. That is to say, a cause that is necessary but not sufficient and a cause that is necessary and sufficient produce different assessments of responsibility. One is responsible for the damages that a dog directly does in the normal manner; one bears less responsibility for damage that is the result of overwhelming external force and not preventable, but still derives from culpable ignorance, my class three above.

A. The dog or the goat which jumped from the top of the roof and broke utensils—

B. [the owner] pays the full value of the damage [they have caused],

C. because they are attested dangers.

D. The dog which took a cake [to which a cinder adhered] and went to standing grain, ate the cake, and set the stack on fire—

E. for the cake the owner pays full damages,

F. but for the standing grain he pays only for half of the damages [his dog has caused].

MISHNAH-TRACTATE BABA QAMMA 2:3

Here we see a fine example of the difference between Aristotle's classification [1] and Aristotle's classification [3]. Now the cause is necessary but not sufficient; the damage done to the standing grain is not preventable, in the way in which the danger done to the utensils is. The dog should have been tied up. Once the dog was not tied up and did the foreseeable damage, the owner is culpable for full responsibility. But if the dog has gone on and done damage that cannot have been foreseen, that is, to the standing grain, and that was not preventable, the owner is culpable only for half-damages.

The Mishnah is not a philosophical work, only a work that expresses philosophical concerns by building upon philosophical distinctions. An important jurisprudential distinction now intervenes, particular to the Mishnah but relevant to assessing responsibility. This distinction addresses the location at which the damage takes place. We distinguish damage [1] done in the domain of the injured party, for which full damages are paid, and that [2] done in the public domain, where the ox had every right to walk, where only half-damages are done. Here we have damage that is not the result of overwhelming external force—no one pushed the ox into the domain of the injured party—but chance; but culpability is incurred, since the mitigating power of chance (what is totally unforeseeable) is weighed against the incriminating power of foreknowledge: the attested danger. Still, there are diverse dimensions of responsibility that are defined by circumstance: Someone is responsible for what happens in the public domain, where I have to take extra precautions, but not for what happens in one's own property, where I have to take only normal precautions.

2:5 A. An ox that causes damage in the domain of the one who is injured [M. 1:4F]—how so?

B. [If] it gored, pushed, bit, lay down, or kicked [M. 1:4B],

C. in the public domain,

D. [the owner] pays half of the value of the damages [the ox has caused].

MISHNAH-TRACTATE BABA QAMMA 2:5

Now we come to the human being. Here we deal with a judgment of theological anthropology, expressed in a simple way: human beings are always, everywhere, under all circumstances, fully responsible for what they do. What they do is voluntary and foreseeable, preventable, willful, the result of deliberate choice. Chance is then to be held in the balance against total responsibility, and that forms the basis for the following:

A. Man is perpetually an attested danger [cf. M. 1:4G]—
B. whether [what is done is done] inadvertently or deliberately,
C. whether man is awake or asleep.
D. [If] he blinded the eye of his fellow or broke his utensils, he pays the full value of the damage he has caused.

MISHNAH-TRACTATE BABA QAMMA 2:5

So much for the basic fact. Now to the sorting out of the relationship between chance and willful action, the point where the Mishnah becomes very specific in its assessment of responsibility—and here we come back to familiar territory.

A. He who leaves a jug in the public domain,
B. and someone else came along and stumbled on it and broke it—
C. [the one who broke it] is exempt,
D. And if [the one who broke it] was injured by it, the owner of the jug is liable [to pay damages for] his injury.
E. [If] his jug was broken in the public domain,
F. and someone slipped on the water,
G. or was hurt by the sherds,
H. he is liable.

MISHNAH-TRACTATE BABA QAMMA 3:1

The owner of the jug bears full responsibility for whatever the jug has caused; we make no distinction between direct and indirect causation (an efficient cause that is necessary but not sufficient, in my language earlier). Here is where the Mishnah's formulation expresses in its familiar, concrete idiom—the category-formation that Aristotle (as read by Sorabji) sets forth in entirely abstract ways.

What about damages done by accident? We have to assess the liabilities, which means, assign responsibility: the one party is negligible, therefore culpable; but the other has not taken adequate precautions, therefore, also culpable—showing how, in my terms, the mixed grid helps to sort things out:

3:4 A. Two pot sellers who were going along, one after another,
    B. and the first of them stumbled and fell down,
    C. and the second stumbled over the first—
    D. the first one is liable [to pay compensation for] the injuries of the second.

3:5 A. This one comes along with his jar, and that one comes along with his beam—
    B. [if] the jar of this one was broken by the beam of that one,
    C. [the owner of the beam] is exempt,
    D. for this one has every right to walk along [in the street], and that one has every right to walk along [in the same street].
    E. [If] the one carrying the beam was coming first, and the one carrying the jar was following behind,
    E. [if] the jar was broken on the beam,
    G. (1) the one carrying the beam is exempt.
    H. (2) But if the one carrying the beam stopped short, he is liable.
    I. (3) And if he said to the one carrying the jar, "Wait up!" he is exempt.

3:6 A. Two who were going along in the public domain,
    B. one was running, the other ambling,
    C. or both of them running,
    D. and they injured one another—
    E. both of them are exempt.

MISHNAH-TRACTATE BABA QAMMA 3:4–6

Enough has been set forth to validate the claim that the category-formation set forth by Sorabji in behalf of Aristotle corresponds to the category-formation set forth by the Mishnah. For we distinguish in both structures between entire responsibility, therefore blame and obligation to pay total damages, and partial responsibility; we distinguish between damage that is voluntary and foreseeable and damage that is involuntary but foreseeable, damage that is the result of overwhelming external force and damage that is preventable; so producing two intermediate categories; and onward to the end. So the Mishnah and Aristotle explore the domain of the efficient cause, finding appropriate charts to divide the territory. The lines of structure and order are then the same: [1] voluntary; [2] foreseeable; [3] preventable as against [1] involuntary; [2] not foreseeable; [3] not preventable. In the several combinations of those three distinct but intersecting categories, we form the grid that yields the generalizations of Sorabji's picture of Aristotle—mishap as against mistake; cause by the agent or cause not solely by the agent; knowing versus inadvertence.

THE TALMUD EXAMINES THAT RULE WITHIN THE RECEIVED MISHNAIC CATEGORIES

What makes the Talmud philosophical is simply that it carries forward the Mishnah and analyzes its results. So far as the category-formation that the Mishnah lays out governs the analytical work of the Talmud, the entire result—that is, the Mishnah as the Talmud wants it read—is to be classified as philosophy in the precise sense at hand. The Talmud's re-presentation of the Mishnah's philosophical laws, preserves the received category-formation of the Mishnah. To address the Talmud's treatment of the topic at hand, we turn to Bavli Baba Qamma, Chapter Three. We take up the reading of Mishnah-paragraph 3:1 and give the larger part of the Talmud's treatment of that pericope.

A. He who leaves a jug in the public domain,
B. and someone else came along and stumbled on it and broke it—

C. [the one who broke it] is exempt.

D. And if [the one who broke it] was injured by it, the owner of the jug is liable [to pay damages for] his injury.

BAVLI BABA QAMMA 3:1 [27A] 3:1A–D

The Talmud has identified a few sentences for analysis, and it begins with a pre-theological study of the language at hand, showing by consequence the fundamental theological dogma, the perfection of the Mishnah, as evidenced by the absence of flaws of formulation. But we turn directly to the matter of substance: whether the victim has exercised the necessary precautions. If he has not, then the person who broke the jug, not the one who put it in the public domain, should be liable. The event is preventable and foreseeable—and borders on the willful.

II.1 A. and someone else came along and stumbled on it and broke it—[the one who broke it] is exempt:

    B. *Why should he be exempt? He should have opened his eyes as he walked along!*

    C. *They said in the household of Rab in the name of Rab,* "We deal with a case in which the whole of the public domain was filled with jugs."

    D. Samuel said, "We deal with a case in which the jugs were in a dark place."

    E. R. Yohanan said, "We deal with a case in which the jug was in a corner."

The question is answered in terms characteristic of the Mishnah: concrete and immediate; but the upshot is an abstract amplification of the law. The one who broke the jug would be exempt because the event of which one who placed the jug in the street was the cause was by him rendered unavoidable (C), or preventable through the taking of proper precautions (D, E). It was not the result of overwhelming external force, and it also is not the consequence of anything the person who broke the jug has done or his failure to do something to prevent what was foreseeable to him. So the one who placed the jug is the necessarily efficient cause (absent the jug, no breakage!), and also the sufficient cause, there being no other participant to the incident, even though the one who broke the jug is the actual cause. That is the point at which responsibility parts company from the (mere) facts of the case. The hermeneutics of the Talmud requires dispute concerning the reading of the Mishnah; the result is clarification of the operation of the principles of the Mishnah. The theology that emerges once more affirms the flawless character of the Mishnah: its conformity to the abstract principle of justice, worked out through the concrete application of fair and reasonable rules.

A further characteristic of the Talmud's hermeneutics, and the dynamic of its thought, is the spinning out of a dialectic argument. We shall now pursue the argument wherever it leads, and the close reading of the Mishnah's language vastly expands our understanding of the principles and how they apply:

F. *Said R. Pappa, "A close reading of our Mishnah-rule can accord only with the view of Samuel or R. Yohanan. For if it were in accord with the position of Rab, then what difference does it make that exemption is accorded only if the man stumbled over the pitcher? Why not rule in the same way even if he deliberately broke the pitcher?"*

G. *Said R. Zebid in the name of Raba, "In point of fact, the same rule really does apply even if the defendant deliberately broke the jug. And the reason that the language,* **and stumbled on it,** *is used, is that the latter clause goes on to say,* **And if [the one who broke it] was injured by it, the owner of the jug is liable [to pay damages for] his injury.** *But that would be the case only* **if he stumbled on it,** *but not if he deliberately broke the jug. How come? The man has deliberately injured himself. So that is why, to begin with, the word-choice was* **and stumbled on it.**

2. A. Said R. Abba to R. Ashi, "This is what they say in the West in the name of R. Ulla: 'The reason is that people do not ordinarily look out when they walk along the way.'"

Now we have a considerable extension of the Mishnah's rule, effected through clarification. The one who broke the jug bears no responsibility whatsoever, even though he did so deliberately. The action of the one who put the jug in the street forms the entire, sufficient, efficient cause; nothing that happens by consequence of that action is assigned to any other party. No. 2 then explains why: The ordinary rule is that people amble along without looking; they are not expected to watch their step, taking account of irregular actions; hence, the placing of the jug by the jug-owner accounts for everything that follows.

That lays the stress upon what is voluntary, as against what is foreseeable and preventable. Once an action is voluntary, we take account of several further matters. First comes the consideration of foresight—the one who broke the jug should have watched his step. Second is preventability (a variation of the foregoing). So as against a repertoire of considerations, the Talmud has identified only one that governs.

How has the Talmud continued the Mishnah's philosophical analysis of the issue of responsibility? It has not only amplified the sense and identified the operative considerations of the Mishnah's rendition of the category-formation comprising voluntarism, foresight, and preventability and their varying combinations; the author of the composition has selected one for a position of priority. Here the hermeneutics of the dispute and the dialectic have led to a concrete position at the outer limit of the Mishnah's case. Once we challenge the rule of the Mishnah, we are led by degrees to a reformulation of matters.

The next entry simply provides illustrative cases, a commonplace part of the hermeneutics of the Talmud, yielding the familiar conception that the conduct of the everyday is organized along the rational lines of the Torah:

3. A. *There was a case in Nehardea, and Samuel imposed liability [for the broken utensil]. In Pumbedita, and Rabbah imposed liability as well.*

   B. *Now there is no problem in understanding Samuel's ruling, since he acted in accord with his own tradition [if the pitcher was visible, there would be liability]. But shall we then say that Rabbah concurred with Samuel?*

C. *Said R. Pappa, "The damage was done at the corner of an oil factory, and, since it is entirely permitted to store jugs there, the defendant [who broke the jugs] should have walked along with his eyes wide open."*

So much for the exposition of the Mishnah and its rule. We now identify an initiative that goes its own way, connected to the Mishnah-rule only because at issue is damage done by an object, for example, the blade of a hoe or the handle of a hoe, rather than by a person's own hand. At 4.R, our own case is introduced in one of its formulations, and—superficially—that accounts for the introduction of the entire composite, formulated on its own terms.

And yet, if we take a deeper look, we see that the issue is entirely relevant to the large question of responsibility. Indeed, whether or not one has the right to take the law into his own hands introduces a fundamental variable into the issue of responsibility. For if one has a right to take the law into his own hands, then damage done to another party, while voluntary, foreseeable, and preventable, still is not culpable. Responsibility ends where just cause intervenes. If one has just cause, then the other considerations of responsibility—foreseeability, preventability—fall away; a voluntary action that is right bears no consequences, just as one that is wrong (putting a jug in the street) imposes all liability. Will in the end gives way before right (one way or the other). And that represents a profound statement that is far more than an amplification.

So what the Talmud now contributes through an initiative of redaction—the insertion of a set of compositions formed into a coherent composite—in fact constitutes a vast expansion on the principle of responsibility. The inquiry itself clearly links responsibility for damages done to another party and the reason for one's action:

4. A. R. Hisda sent word to R. Nahman, "Lo, they have said, 'For kicking with the knee, three selas; for kicking with the foot,

five; for a blow with the saddle of an ass, thirteen. *What is the penalty for wounding with the blade of a hoe or the handle of a hoe?"*

B. *He sent word, "Hisda! Hisda! Are you really imposing in Babylonia such extrajudicial fines as these [which you have no right to do over there]? Tell me the details of the case as it happened."*

C. *He sent word, "There was a well that belonged to two people, who used it on alternate days. One of them then went and drew water on a day that was not assigned to him. The other said, 'This is my day.' The latter ignored him. So the other took the blade of a hoe and struck him with it."*

D. *R. Nahman sent word, "Even if he hit him a hundred times with the blade of the hoe [it would not have mattered]. For even in the opinion of one who says, 'Someone may not take the law into his own hands,' where there will be a loss, he has every right to do so."*

Clearly, the composition, 4.A–D, is complete in itself; we require nothing more fully to understand all of its components. But in its own terms, the composition in no way accounts for its present location, in a way that Nos. 1–3 clearly do; they depend upon their position in context; No. 4 does not.

But the expansion shows how the issue of responsibility is profoundly restated by introduction of the principle that someone does (or does not) have the right to take the law into his or her own hands. What this has to do with causation and culpability has to be analyzed; the passage is the critical point in the entire analysis, and we read the whole of it:

E. *For it has been stated:*

F. *R. Judah said, "A man does not have the right to take the law into his own hands."*

G. *R. Nahman said, "A man does have the right to take the law into his own hands where there will be a loss."*

Now, the issue has been joined. But we are not told why the issue has to be raised at just this point. On the assumption that the document before us is purposive and not a mere scrapbook, however, we have to ask ourselves why this discussion is juxtaposed to the foregoing: what the issue of taking the law into one's own hands has to do with the matter of necessity, cause, and blame. When we ask that question, we move beyond the Talmud's boundaries; in the Talmud, what is juxtaposed is assumed to cohere, that is why the juxtaposition has taken place. But we are not bound to silence by the facts. The silence of the Talmud, on what its framers take for granted, invites our intervention; that is where we join the conversation. Let us see how the topic is explored in the dialectics:

H. *Now all parties concur that where there will be a loss, someone may take the law into his own hands. Where there is an argument, it concerns a case in which there will be a loss. R. Judah said, "A man does not have the right to take the law into his own hands." Since there will be no loss, he can go to court. But R. Nahman said, "A man does have the right to take the law into his own hands where there will be a loss." Since he is acting in accord with the law anyhow, why take the trouble to go to court?*

I. *Objected R. Kahana [to R. Judah's view],* **"Ben Bag Bag says, 'A person should not go and retrieve his own property from the household of someone else, lest he appear to be a thief. But he should be ready in public to break his teeth [answer back impudently] and you may say to him, "I am seizing what is my own from the thief's possession"'** [T. B.Q. 10:38.*" [This then would contradict Judah's position.]*

J. *[Judah] said to him,* **[28A]** *"True enough, Ben Bag Bag is on your side. But his is a dissenting view, differing from rabbis."*

K. *R. Yannai said, "What is the meaning, anyhow, of* **break his teeth**? *It is, he confronts him in court."*

L. *If so, the language,* **you may say to him,** *is inappropriate. Rather it should be,* **they [the court] may say to him**! *So, too, the language,* **I am seizing what is my own,** *is inappropriate, Rather, it should be,* **he is seizing what is his own**!

M. *So that's a problem.*

N. *Come and take note:* in the case of an ox that climbed up on another one to kill it, and the owner of the one on the bottom came along and pulled out his ox, so that the one on the top fell and was killed—the owner of the bottom ox is exempt from having to pay compensation. *Does this ruling not pertain to an ox that was an attested danger, in which case there is no loss to be expected?*

O. *No, it speaks of an ox that was deemed innocent, and there is a considerable loss to be expected.*

P. *If so, then look what's coming:* If he pulled off the ox on top and it died, he is liable to pay compensation. *But if the ox was deemed innocent, why should we have to pay compensation?*

Q. Because he should have pulled his ox out from underneath, and he did not do that.

We now come to our particular case. From here to the end, the Talmud speaks for itself, without my explanation, so that we may follow the twists and turns of what is an entirely continuous and cogent analytical argument: dialectics at its most compelling.

R. *Come and take note:* He who filled the courtyard of his fellow with jugs of wine and jugs of oil—the owner of the courtyard has every right to break the jugs in order to get out or break the jugs in order to get in.

S. Said R. Nahman bar Isaac, "He breaks the jugs to get out only if a court says he may do so, he may break the jugs to get in only to get whatever documents he needs to prove his case in court."

T. *Come and take note:* How on the basis of Scripture do we know that in the case of a slave whose ear had been bored [as an indication that he was in perpetual service, to the Jubilee year], the term of service of which has come to an end [with the Jubilee], the owner of which has been urging him to leave, and, in the process, injured him and done him damage, the owner is exempt from having to pay compensation? Scripture states, "You shall not take satisfaction for him who is . . . come again . . ." (Num. 35:12), meaning, for one who is determined to come again [as a slave, continuing his service], you will not take a ransom.

U. *Here with what sort of a case do we deal? It is a slave who was a thief* [Kirzner: so the owner is protecting himself from a genuine loss].

V. *Well, up to now he hasn't stolen anything, but now he's expected to go and steal?*

W. *Yes, that's quite plausible, since up to now he was afraid of his master, but now that he is about to go free, he isn't afraid of his master anymore.*

X. R. Nahman bar Isaac said, "At issue is a slave to whom his master gave a Canaanite serving-girl as a wife. *Up to this time it was a legitimate relationship, but once he is freed, it is not legitimate"* [Kirzner: so the master may use force to eject him].

Y. *Come and take note:* **He who leaves a jug in the public domain, and someone else came along and stumbled on it and broke it—[the one who broke it] is exempt.** *So the operative consideration is that he stumbled on it. Lo, if he had deliberately broken it, he would have been liable.* [This is contrary to Nahman's view.]

Z. *Said R. Zebid in the name of Raba, "In point of fact, the same rule really does apply even if the defendant deliberately broke the jug. And the reason that the language,* **and stumbled on it,** *is used, is that the latter clause goes on to say,* **And if [the one who broke it] was injured by it, the owner of the jug is liable [to pay damages for] his injury.** *But that would be the case only* **if he stumbled on it,** *but not if he deliberately broke the jug. How come? The man has deliberately injured himself. So that is why, to begin with, the word-choice was* **and stumbled on it.**

AA. *Come and take note:* "Then you shall cut off her hand" (Deut. 25:12)—that refers to a monetary fine equivalent in value to the hand. *Does this not speak of a case in which the woman has no other way of saving her husband but doing what she did [proving one may not take the law into one's own hands]?*

BB.   No, it involves a case in which she can save her husband in some other way.

CC.   Well, if she cannot save her husband in some other way, would she be free of all liability? *Then why go on to say,* "And puts forth her hand" (Deut. 25:11)—excluding an officer of the court [from liability for humiliation that he may cause when acting in behalf of the court] *Rather, why not recast matters by dealing with the case before us, thus:* Under what circumstances? When she can save her husband by some other means. But if she cannot save him by some other means, then she is exempt.

DD.   *This is the sense of the passage.* Under what circumstances? When she can save her husband by some other means. But if she cannot save him by some other means, then her hand serves as the agency of the court and she is indeed exempt.

EE.   *Come and take note:* **He who had a public way passing through his field, and who took it away and gave [the public another path] along the side, what he has given he has given. But what is his does not pass to him [revert to his ownership; the gift is irrevocable, but the land now in the public domain remains public property] [M. B.B. 6:7A–3].** *Now if you maintain that someone may take the law into his own hands, then let the man just take a whip and sit there [and keep people out of his property]!*

FF.   Said R. Zebid in the name of Raba, "It is a precautionary decree, lest he assign to the public a crooked path."

GG.   R. Mesharshayya said, "It is a case in which he gives them a crooked path."

HH.   R. Ashi said, "Any path that is off to the side is classified as a crooked path to begin with, since what is nearer for one party will be farther for another."

II.   *If that's so, then why specify,* **But what is his does not pass to him***? Why can't he just say to the public, "Take what is yours and give me what is mine?"*

JJ.   *That is because of what R. Judah said, for* said R. Judah, "A path that the public has taken over is not to be disrupted."

KK.   *Come and take note: a householder who designated* peah *at one corner of the field, and the poor come along and take the* peah *from another side of the field—both this and that are classified as* peah. *Now if you maintain that a person may take the law into his own hands, why should it be the fact that both this and that are so classified? Just let the man take a whip and sit there [and keep people out of his property]!*

LL.   *Said Raba, "What is the meaning of the phrase,* both this and that are so classified? *It is for the purpose of exempting the designated produce from the requirement of separating tithes. For so it has been taught on Tannaite authority:* He who declares his vineyard to be ownerless and then gets up early in the morning and harvests the grapes is liable to leave for the poor the grapes that fall to the ground, the puny bunches, the forgotten ones, and the corner of the field, but is exempt from having to designate tithes."

The dialectical argument runs its course; a clear picture of how the Talmud makes its statement is required, lest a précis deny the reader access to the notes in all their specificity. Now, to the heart of matters: At no point does the discussion say what the theory spelled out here claims that it says; the theological message is not expressed—except at the important turnings in the argument. But there, when we ask the right questions—questions of composition and context in particular—we see that someone has deliberately put together freestanding composites, themselves made up of sizable compositions, so as to yield a point that vastly recasts the original statement of the Mishnah.

Drawing Conclusions from the Talmud's Fabricated Connections

There is a point at which the connection between one thing and something else requires elucidation, and that is the point at which, the Talmud (by definition) having fallen silent, we intervene. The Mishnah, continued by the Talmud, has set forth a philosophical category-formation that held in the balance three equally pertinent criteria of responsibility: the intersection of lines covering what is voluntary, foreseeable, and preventable and the opposites. The Talmud has contributed two points.

First of all, the criterion of what is done voluntarily outweighs all else; but, second, and entirely new, the Talmud sets forth and elaborates the criterion not introduced in the Mishnah at all:

> *doing what one has the right to do sets aside even the criterion of deliberation.*

The law of the Torah is now recast; the oral Torah has announced three components to a decision on responsibility; the Talmudic representation has selected one of those components, then contrasted it with a consideration external to the initial program and subordinated it to that consideration. Now, in line with my insistence that when the Talmud arouses our curiosity, it also leaves space for our own inquiry, one may point out very simply that that new point is not continuous with the other. Indeed, the connection between the exposition of the received categories of the Mishnah and the introduction of an entirely new consideration has to be established, meaning rationally explained. If we can draw a rational conclusion, a theological conclusion, from that odd juxtaposition, the adventitious intersection of two distinct compositions—"can one take the law into one's own hands" standing separate from issues of cause, blame, and responsibility—becomes a deliberate statement, and imposes upon us the task of reasoned inquiry into the substance of that statement.

The substantive, theological statement (implicit as we should expect, by reason of the character of this writing) proclaims that what is right overrides considerations even of will. If (within one theory of matters) one maky take the law into his own hands, then even though the event is voluntary, foreseeable, and preventable, one still bears no responsibility for the resulting damage. If not, then the body that does have the right to enforce the law obviously bears no responsibility. The upshot is the same: We have now subordinated issues of causation—cause and blame, in Sorabji's terms—to another matter altogether. Since, we recognize, the category-formation that guides the analysis of responsibility treats responsibility as a consequence of causation, we find the theological re-presentation in fact stunningly fresh.

For the upshot of the juxtaposition of the several compositions and the two distinct composites and the sequence of their messages may be stated very simply:

[1]   responsibility is adjudicated not by causation in the philosophical reading of causation (such as the Mishnah has given us),

[2]   but by appeal to a higher criterion: what is right by the law of the Torah.

Exactly how does this work? It is at the specific point of discontinuity—the boundary marked by the conclusion of the Mishnah-exposition by the Talmud, followed by the turning toward what is jarring and discontinuous—that our particular entry-point opens up. Then, we ask, what has this got to do with that? *And we answer the question for ourselves.*

We have heard the Talmud's melody, identified a discordant note, and asked about it. And that is the particular point at which we join the conversation: we do so by making a connection, or, as here, by explaining the connection between what is merely juxtaposed but superficially discontinuous. Then, we draw a conclusion from the connection we have explained. The discord now has been resolved, harmony restored: a single message formed out of two discrete statements.

Let me spell this claim of mine out by specifying the completed compositions and the point at which they are merely juxtaposed but by no means continuous. An example of the completed composition is at II.1A–E, complete in itself; proved by the fact that, without anything added, read along with the Mishnah-paragraph, the passage is fully accessible. A composite is made up of II.1A–E joined by F–G, which make sense only when joined to the foregoing but which then richly amplify the prior passage; and No. 2. Another completed composition is No. 3.A, which provides us with everything we need to know to understand its point; but then 3.B, C join A to the larger, now established context.

My entire case consists of pointing to the jarring sequence at hand. We now ask how

[1] the Mishnah, then
[2] two massive composites

have been juxtaposed. This procedure called our attention to the Mishnah's presentation of issues of responsibility in terms of causation (the point at which we started). Then, the Talmud dealt with first, the sorting out, in priority, of the criteria of causation (Nos. 1–3), and second, the freestanding exposition of the matter of taking the law into one's own hands (No. 4). In context, in sequence, No. 4 imposes a judgment upon the results of the Mishnah and Nos. 1–3. On these simple, entirely literary facts—the discontinuity of No. 4 with Nos. 1–3—my entire case rests: someone put these distinct compositions into a single composite, in this order, not in some other composite, or in some other order. Why? My "because" is now fully exposed.

To proceed to the next step in my argument. It is by joining a freestanding composite, itself made up of composites that hold together compositions, that the Talmud sets forth the point that it makes concerning responsibility—all considerations of responsibility are subordinate to what is right; the issues of causation are declared instrumental and derivative; in this setting, then, right overrides even will. But how has that statement been made? The answer is negative and positive. The negative is, it has not been made in so many words or even by the formulation of a dispute, amplificatory composites, and a dialectrical argument.

What is the positive side? The premise of all that has been said is that the Talmud is the way its framers wanted it to be. The document conforms to its teleology; then we may seek out the connections between this and that and draw rational conclusions from those connections. *This we do by explaining how what is juxtaposed in fact interrelates.* So if the compilation of the Talmud is deliberate and not simply the juxtaposition without purpose of thematically congruent materials, then the Talmud makes a powerful statement not only through the contents of its compositions (which really form the nouns of its sentences) or the context defined by its composites (the verbs of the sentences), but through the selection, formulation, and presentation of the whole—which is what we mean by hermeneutics, the explication of received texts, and the rules thereof.

Explaining the Connections and Drawing the Conclusions

Read from start to finish, meaning from a Mishnah-paragraph to the conclusion of its Talmud, the Talmud turns out to make a well-considered statement, not merely to collect relevant composites of compositions. So the Talmud aims at showing the connections between things. And, it is self-evident, these things being left implicit in the text for us to discover, the hermeneutics dictates the asking of questions concerning what is not said or even suggested, meaning in this case, what one thing has to do with something else (Nos. 4 and 1–3). Everything depends on the rules for making connections, which also govern the drawing of conclusions. God lives in the connection between Nos. 1–3 and No. 4.

The work before us is clear; it is the task of continuing to study the Talmud. That is, specifically, because we have to examine the specificities of connections; where are the discontinuities, and how do our sages of blessed memory build bridges between them? Where do we discern the breaks in the tale, and how do our sages of blessed memory re-form the narrative? Knowing that the Talmud re-presents the Torah teaches us only how to ask the right questions. The answers all lie before us, in work not yet undertaken; the explication of the text always forces us into the future tense; making connections requires a perspective upon what is coming, drawing conclusions, upon the road now taken. That is where the formation of Judaism reached its fulfillment, and the Judaism of the dual Torah left history behind, to form the future.

IX

Into the Long Future: How the Talmud Works and Why the Talmud Won

HOW THE TALMUD WORKS

A single document, the Talmud of Babylonia—that is to say, the Mishnah, a philosophical law code that reached closure at ca. 200 C.E., as read by the Gemara, a commentary to thirty-seven of the sixty-three tractates of that code, compiled in Babylonia, reaching closure by ca. 600 C.E.,—from ancient times to the present day has served as the medium of instruction for all literate Jews, teaching, by example alone, the craft of clear thinking, compelling argument, correct rhetoric. That craft originated in Athens with Plato's Socrates for the medium of thought, and with Aristotle for the method of thought, and predominated in the intellectual life of Western civilization thereafter. When we correlate the modes of thought and analysis of the Talmud with the ones of classical philosophy, which pertain, we see how the Talmud works, by which I mean, how its framers made connections and drew conclusions, for the Mishnah and Gemara respectively. And when we can explain how the Talmud works, I claim, we may also understand why it exercised the remarkable power that it did for the entire history of Judaism from its closure in the seventh century to our own time. Those two questions—how it works, why it won—define the task of this conclusion.

Let me now summarize my argument, spelled out in detail. The Talmud makes connections in the manner of Western science as defined by Aristotle in his work of natural history, and it draws conclusions in the manner of Western philosophy as defined by Plato's Socrates and by Aristotle in their logic, specifically, their dialectical analysis and argument. To be concrete and claim no more than I mean: natural history, specifically, governs the composition of the Mishnah, and philosophical dialects, the Gemara. Modes of thought and analysis, media of the formulation of the same, and methods of explanation—these answer to the question of how one thing is deemed to connect to another but not to a third, and what conclusions we are to draw from the juxtapositions, connections, and intersections of things. And the answers to that question form the structure and system of thought that for a given society explain sense and also define nonsense. The modes of public thought of the Talmud that turned out to govern the affairs of an entire social order, the one that is portrayed by, and ultimately realized through, that Talmud, certainly, seen in its selected context, one of the most influential pieces of writing and public thought in the history of mankind.

From its closure to our own day, the Talmud of Babylonia (Mishnah and Gemara together) has formed the paramount authoritative writing of Judaism. It has served as the governing medium by which the revelation of Sinai, the Torah, oral and written, has reached age succeeding age. By reason of its unique character, the Talmud turned out not only to provide legal ruling and supporting opinion, but a model of how rulings and opinions were to be reached—and, more important still, a paradigm for the education of successive generations in the method of right thought. When faithful Israelites undertook to "study Torah," they opened the Talmud, and, when they did, they learned—entirely inductively—how to turn themselves into scientists and philosophers, that is to say, natural historians working with the data of the everyday and disciples capable of joining in a dialectical analysis through argument. I so allege that [1] the basic structural document of the Talmud, the Mishnah, makes connections in the manner of classical natural history, and [2] the exegesis and amplification of that document, the Gemara, conducts its analysis through the dialectical method of classical philosophy. The Talmud and its Judaism (or, Judaic religious system) then emerge from this account as distinctive but native chapters in the intellectual history of Western civilization, as much in their point of origin, in late antiquity, as was later the case in medieval times among Judaic philosophers in the Aristotelian tradition.

In particular, the Talmud's modes of organizing data into intelligible patterns ("rules") follow the rules of natural history common to Western science from Aristotle onward, and its media for the conduct of analytical argument and construction of compelling arguments and reliable judgments prove congruent to those of Western philosophy. I refer, specifically, both to those of Socrates as Plato presents him and of Aristotle in his lectures on how to frame arguments, his *Topics*. So the Talmud imposes rationality upon, or explains, diverse and discrete data by modes of Western science, specifically natural history set forth by Aristotle, and transforms those organizations of data into encompassing, well-tested generalizations capable of encompassing fresh data, doing so in the way in which that principal labor is carried out by Western philosophy, tests of generalizations conducted in accord with the method of analytical argument (not merely static demonstration) laid out by Socrates' Plato and utilized also by Aristotle.

That the whole forms an exercise, the analysis of the everyday through applied logic and practical reason, is clear from the topics that are treated by the Talmud. Classical science dealt with the natural world, biology and zoology and physics, for example; dialectics investigated the definition of abstract categories of virtue. Not so in the Talmud. While possibilities for abstract inquiry presented themselves, for example, in topical tractates concerning matters of no immediate practical fact, the Talmud in the main bypasses those tractates in favor of those deemed practical. That is to say, while the Mishnah's law covers a wide variety of practical and theoretical subjects, the Gemara deals, in the main, with those tractates of the Mishnah that concern everyday life (specifically, the divisions of the Mishnah presenting laws on the festivals and holy days, laws of home and family, and the corpus of civil law, court procedure, and governance). The Talmud—Mishnah and Gemara together—works by bringing to bear upon the workaday world principal modes of scientific and philosophical thought[1] characteristic of Western civilization.

Before I proceed, let me give a simple, concrete example of what I mean by making connections and drawing conclusions, that is, the method of classification of data in a process of comparison and contrast. The method involves taking facts concerning a given matter and comparing those facts with the ones concerning a kindred matter, so as to lend context and meaning to both sets of facts. My concrete instance concerns the relative status of the two sources of authority, the king and the high priest, in the theoretical Israelite politics put forth by the Mishnah. In the briefest of examples, we see that the facts concerning the one are collected and set forth in comparison and contrast with the facts concerning the other:

> A high priest (1) judges, and [others] judge him; (2) gives testimony, and [others] give testimony about him;
> The king (1) does not judge, and [others] do not judge him; (2) does not give testimony, and [others] do not give testimony about him;
> MISHNAH-TRACTATE SANHEDRIN 2:1–2

What we see is that four facts are collected and joined in a common classification, high priest, then king; and when we contrast the one set of well-organized facts with the other, we further hierarchize what has been classified, showing that the king enjoys higher status than the high priest. That demonstration turns facts into a generalization, the whole forming a syllogism. The work of natural history proceeds in just this way, through comparing like to like, and differentiating like from like, and producing new knowledge.

To give an example of a dialectical argument proves somewhat

---

1. The terms "science" and "philosophy" serve contemporary sensibility, to be sure, since in ancient times no one made the distinction important to us now.

more difficult in the nature of things. A simple example shows how the dispute about a ruling shades over into a debate about the principles operative in making the ruling. Then each party to the dispute gives his reasons and challenges the premises of the other. In the end, the two positions are balanced and yield a clearcut choice, and those assembled vote.

In the case at hand, what we want to know is how to resolve a matter of doubt, whether by appeal to the status quo or the status quo ante. That is, do we confirm the status quo retroactively, and say an invalid situation has been invalid for so long as we do not know that it was valid? Or do we determine that the situation has changed only when we have discovered the change, so that the discovery of the invalidity marks the beginning of the period of invalidity.

The case involves an immersion pool, used for purifying unclean objects. We have this morning discovered that the pool was invalid, by reason of an insufficient volume of water. Two weeks ago, we examined the pool and found that it was valid, with a sufficient volume of water. What is the status of the objects immersed over the past two weeks? Do we assume they were cleaned until the pool was proven invalid? Or do we declare them unclean by reason of the newly discovered invalid status of the pool? What is important to us is the unfolding of the argument. Each party invokes a governing analogy, one which declares invalidity to be retroactive, the other not. Then each challenges the validity of the other's analogy. Finally, the issues and arguments and facts are fully exposed. People have to vote:

> The water-reservoir of Disqus in Yavneh was measured and found lacking. And R. Tarfon did declare clean all the objects immersed in the pool unit until it was found to be invalid, and R. 'Aqiva unclean all the objects immersed in the pool from the last occasion on which it had been measured and found valid.
>
> Said R. Tarfon, "Since this immersion-pool is in the assumption of being clean, it remains perpetually in this presumption of cleanness until it will be known for sure that it is made unclean."

Said R. 'Aqiva, "Since this immersion-pool is in the assumption of being unclean, it perpetually remains in the presumption of uncleanness until it will be known for sure that it is clean."

Said R. Tarfon, "To what is the matter to be likened? To one who was standing and offering [a sacrifice] at the altar, and it became known that he is not a valid priest. *His* act of service is valid."

Said R. 'Aqiva, "To what is the matter to be likened? To one who was standing and offering [a sacrifice] at the altar, and it became known that he is disqualified by reason of a blemish—for his service is invalid."

Said R. Tarfon to him, "You draw an analogy to one who is blemished. I draw an analogy to one who is invalid to begin with. Let us now see to what the matter is appropriately likened. If it is analogous to a blemished priest, let us learn the law from the case of the blemished priest. If it is analogous to one who is invalid to begin with."

R. 'Aqiva says, "The unfitness affecting an immersion-pool affects the immersion-pool itself, and the unfit aspect of the blemished priest affects the blemished priest himself.

"But let not the case of the one who is invalid to begin prove matters, for his matter of unfitness depends upon others.

"A ritual pool's unfitness [depends] on one only, and the unfitness of a blemished priest [depends] on an individual only, but let not the case of the one who is invalid to begin with prove the matter, for the unfitness of this one depends upon ancestry."

They took a vote concerning the case and declared it unclean.

Said R. Tarfon to R. 'Aqiva, "He who departs from you is like one who perishes."

TOSEFTA MIQVAOT 1:17–20

These two concrete cases are meant to illustrate what I mean by natural history, on the one side, and dialectical, or moving, argument, on the other.

When I speak of philosophy, inclusive of natural history, I do so within a very limited framework. Classical philosophy encompasses a broad range of modes of thought and analysis. But here only a single, principal mode in each instance comes under consideration. For modes of thought, I speak only of science in the form of natural history, which explains the rationality[2] of nature by showing the connections between diverse data and by classifying them. That is why we turn to the methods of hierarchical classification set forth by Aristotle in his study of natural history. For modes of analysis, I point to philosophy, which draws conclusions through the testifying of hypotheses in analytical argument. I refer specifically to the methods of dialectical argument—challenge and response, rigorous questioning and well-articulated answering of questions—the mode of dialectical analysis defined by Plato's presentation of Socrates. That is why the names of Aristotle, for natural history, and Socrates as read by Plato, and Aristotle in his *Topics*, for dialectics, make their appearance as we find our way toward the right reading of the Talmud's writing.

What, specifically, do I mean by applied reason and practical logic? Immediately upon entering any passage, whether legal, for the Mishnah, or analytical, for the Gemara, the Talmud focuses upon humble affairs of the here and now. Among these it makes its connections by a process of comparison and contrast, linking like to like, unlike to unlike. It then derives its comprehensive truths from received formulations of practical rules, for its problematic commonly finds definition in conflicts among received formulations of petty rules about inconsequential matters, that is to say, from the issue of generalization from cases to rules, from rules to principles, from principles to fresh cases of a different kind all together. The Gemara then proposes generalizations, hypotheses governing many and diverse cases from the conclusions drawn in a few, uniform ones. But herein lies the Talmud's remarkable accomplishment, one of intellect: the everyday was subjected to the dictates of rationality: [1] hierarchical classification, as in Aristotle's natural history, making sense of diversity; [2] argument through challenge and response, as in Socrates' and Plato's and Aristotle's dialectical argument. In the great tradition, then, our

---

2. Perhaps in its own (Aristotelian) context, "teleology" would have provided a better word than "rationality," but in the end we are constrained to use the language of our world, even when transmitting the intellect of another one, however influential that other is upon our own.

sages of blessed memory explored the path that leads in a straight line from what is virtuous to what is kosher.

The dialectical argument of the Gemara conforms to philosophical dialectics not only in logic, but also in rhetoric. Just as a fair part of Plato's Socratic dialogues is made up of scripts to be acted out, and most of Aristotle's writings are composed of lecture notes, so the authors of the dialectical analytical arguments that are set forth in the Talmud of Babylonia supply only notes toward the reconstitution of an argument and a purposive inquiry. Of those notes of what can be said, we are able to recapitulate the oral exchange, the public argument, that exposes right and worthwhile thought. While the Mishnah is fully articulated only to whom it may concern, the Gemara is made up of notes, not fully spelled out sentences, paragraphs, arguments, propositions meant to affect the judgment of all who are concerned enough to join in the debate.

Much as scholarship understands, we receive Aristotle's writings in the form of extended lecture notes but no finished compositions, so we have to view the Talmud's main type of writing, the protracted, analytical argument, as a set of notes that permits us to join in the thought processes of the framers. We then construct logical argument out of the notes the Talmud provides as guidance on the recovery of reasoned thought concerning right and wrong in practice. Accordingly, when we speak of how the Talmud works, the message is not only general—the intellectual context of the document, in classical philosophy—but quite particular to the very distinctive characteristics of the writing itself: why in this form rather than in some other? The form—question-answer, in scarcely-articulated wording—proves to make sense in that very same context of philosophical analysis inaugurated by Socrates-Plato and Aristotle. So my claim concerning the Classical character of the Talmud concerns not only the generalities of rules of rationality, but the specificities or rhetoric.

To take a step further, I refer in particular to the rhetoric of dialectical argument, not only its inner logic. Specifically, the Gemara, in particular, is to be seen not as a piece of writing, but only as notes on the reconstruction of thought leading to the recapitulation of the logic of what was originally thought, rather than what was originally said in just these words. This is a process of reconstruction requiring also fresh articulation in age succeeding age. Everyone understands that the Talmud is not a document to be read. Rather, we see it as a script for a conversation to be reenacted. That is why in the classical yeshivas, where the Talmud is not read but correctly studied through ritualized debate reminiscent of that of the Tibetan schools, all study takes place orally,[3] and, ordinarily, in the context of pairs of debaters, students who work together to recapitulate thought by reading and explaining what is before them. Properly prepared in language and information, Plato's Socrates and Aristotle would find themselves quite at home in the authentic yeshivas. Even the echoes of music in the argument, the song propositions, might reach deep into their intellectual consciousness. Or, to put it differently, because of their preference for oral representation of thought and argument, they will have shared my view that in our hands we hold the best of all possible Talmuds. To do the work properly, it must be done in this manner and in no other, in this kind of writing and not in any other mode of writing (e.g., essays, commentaries, codes, exegesis of a prior document, and on and on through the entire repertoire of types of writing among ancient Judaisms). So much for what is at stake here for the reading of the Talmud.

---

3. That emphasis upon a completely oral process of formulation and transmission yields a powerful taboo against writing and publishing more than brief notes or episodic observations. To take a contemporary example, J. B. Soloveitchik, principal voice of integrationist-Orthodoxy ("Torah uMada," joining Talmud study and contemporary academic sciences), published very little but left a huge corpus of tape-recorded lectures and sermons. When these are transcribed, they show what is lost by a purely oral medium of thought and expression: coherence, proportion, balance, clarity, discipline of thought, precision of expression. A further taboo functions in the same context against *reading* books as against *learning* texts. That is more difficult to document, but a bias against actually engaging with the thesis of a systematic exposition and following it through to the end prevents intellects shaped in Yeshiva-learning from mastering coherent and fully articulated bodies of learning. Then, everything depends on ad hoc expositions of this and that, and the opinion of authorities dictates the reception of reasoned and systematic thought—opinion, not analysis, argument, rational encounter. So, the oral process exacts a heavy charge against intellect and culture.

But the issue of a context in which the Talmud is to be read does not exhaust matters. For, second, beyond the limits of the document and its formal protocol in rhetoric, we have still to ask a further question. It is, for the history of Judaism and the analysis of its cultural context, what is at stake in this approach to the philosophical and rhetorical character of the Talmud? It is to place that authoritative writing, and the religious system that it represents, squarely in the center of the intellectual heritage of Western civilization. The reason is simple. The upshot of this reading of mine is that the document of Judaism that is both most influential and also most particular and distinctive—I should say, unique—is shown also to bear traits of logic and intellect that mark that same writing as an integral, formidable part of the common heritage of Western scientific and philosophical endeavor. When we read and reconstruct the Talmud rightly, we therefore find ourselves at the center and soul of the intellectual tradition of the West. And to grasp the full implications for enduring culture of the Graeco-Roman philosophical heritage, we have to pay attention, also, to the distinctive (I think, unique) realization of those implications in the Talmud, too.

Accordingly, the Torah (a.k.a. "Judaism"), as the Talmud, set forth the Torah as a profoundly Western statement, an expression of the West as characteristic as is Christianity in its theological and philosophical form. And that is for a reason that all acknowledge: Christianity determined the intellectual foundations of Western civilization. It hardly suffices to say, as just now noted, that science (natural history) and philosophy together form the foundations of the intellectual life of the West. It is necessary, by way of explanation, to add, and that is because the principal religion of the West, Christianity, along with its competition, Islam, and, we now shall see, in addition also to Judaism in its Talmudic statement, all made their own the Graeco-Roman heritage of mind.

The proximate reason is that Christianity, which defined Western civilization, identified theology, conducted along philosophical lines, as its principal medium of expression. For everyone knows that Christian theologians and philosophers recast the Gospels into a philosophical statement of theology, calling upon the voice of Athens to deliver the word of Jerusalem. In due course, Islam would do the same. What has not been recognized until now is that at the same time that Christianity would speak through theology, conducted along the lines of philosophical argument, so Judaism[4] would speak through norms of law, also set forth along the lines of philosophical argument—and, within broad limits, the same philosophical argument.[5] Christianity and that minority component of Western, Christian civilization, which is Judaism in its Rabbinic formulation, meet in philosophy, which is why, at some specific points in their intersecting histories, they were able to conduct civil and rational debate. As much as Catholic Christianity—the Christianity of philosophy, theology, and intellect—defined the Western formulation of the Gospel,[6] so Talmudic Judaism—the Judaism of hierarchical classification and dialectical argument—defined in the Christian[7] West the Judaic re-presentation of Sinai.

Judaic jurisprudents—who also accomplished the work of theology and philosophy, but in a distinctive and unfamiliar idiom, namely, saying abstract things in concrete ways—accomplished a counterpart feat. And in its own terms it was equally remarkable. To turn Christian faith into the language and logic of classical philosophy and philology required solving intractable problems, bridging from heaven to earth, so to speak. The theologians solved them. For Judaism, others had already set forth the Torah in the language of Graeco-Roman civilization. But to turn the details of

---

4. And Islam, with both theology and law at stake in philosophy. In that context, I need only point out how the great Judaic Aristotelian, Maimonides, produced not only an Aristotelian account of philosophical theology, but also an Aristotelian representation of the law. But the way in which these matters come to realization in Islam lies beyond my horizon.

5. That proposition forms the generative thesis of Harry Wolfson's account of Western philosophy from Philo to Spinoza, encompassing the Church Fathers and Muslim philosophy as well.

6. So, too, the Islam of philosophy and theology. But these matters become important in the study of Rabbinic Judaism in medieval times, in the context of which Talmud-exegesis in that same context has to be addressed as well.

7. And Muslim, with the same qualification as in the preceding note. That explains why, in the present formulation, Islam is bypassed for the moment.

the Torah's laws, theology, and exegesis into data for Graeco-Roman scientific and philosophical inquiry and yet to preserve all the specificity of those details—that involved far more than a labor of mediation through translation. It was a task of not philology, but philosophy. Our sages, of blessed memory, had to throw a bridge across the abyss between the here and now of marketplace and alley and the rationalities of a well-ordered social world of proportion and abstract theory.

For our sages of blessed memory confronted a problem still more challenging than the one worked out by the Christian philosophers and theologians. The latter could find in philosophy the abstract, philosophical language and categories for issues of intangible faith, for example, from ontology to Christology. But where could the sages discover appropriate scientific and philosophical categories for the material and tangible relationships of home and family, kitchen and bed room, marketplace and synagogue and study house, that the Torah set forth as the loci of the authentically sacred life? The fact is that our sages dealt not with abstract theological formulations of the faith, but with concrete rules. Rather than reflecting on the spiritual and angelic and sublime, they thought about the worldly and human and ordinary and secular. And in doing so, what they accomplished was to turn everyday life and its accidents into the medium of instruction on right thinking, sound argument, and compelling, affecting rhetoric. That is why the Talmud's writers' and compilers' achievement compares in grandeur and wit to the one of the Greek- and Syriac-writing theologians of Christianity of their own time and place.

Their success in the Talmud and its well-analyzed, rigorously considered law (as much as the success of Christianity in theology) forms eloquent tribute to the power of classical philosophy to accomplish the goals of rationality whatever the arena. The Greek philosophers aimed at finding universal truths through universally valid methods. That they accomplished that goal is shown by Christianity's philosophical theologians. But I should maintain that still more compelling evidence of their success comes to us in the pages of the Talmud. That is because the two philosophical modes of thought and analysis that would govern Aristotle's natural history and Plato's Socrates' dialectics proved sufficiently abstract and general as to serve quite nicely in the analysis of matters that fall between the acute particularity of Aristotle's zoology, on the one side, and the abstract grandeur of Plato's metaphysics, on the other. In many ways, then, the true vindication of science and philosophy in their shared claim to deal with all things in a single way comes in the middle passage taken by our sages. It emerges with the success of the Talmud in doing its work of workaday, concrete, and practical character through the universals of thought that philosophy (including science) put forth.[8]

---

8. In this context it is worth addressing the question I am asked from time to time: If you are right about the Aristotelian character of the Mishnah, then why did Maimonides not notice it? He was (I am instructed) an Aristotelian and would love to have found out precisely what I maintain. I regret that I cannot envisage an explanation of why even the greatest intellect in the history of Judaism (excluding only Moses, and he had help) did not happen to notice what he did not notice. I surely do not doubt that he was looking carefully at the document, for among his greatest gifts to posterity was the best commentary to the Mishnah written until the nineteenth century. But it should be said that Maimonides was not supposed to present philosophy outside of the framework of law, and law without sustained and specific engagement with philosophy. This came about because he did not realize the full extent to which the Mishnah, Maimonides' correct choice of the foundation-document of Judaism after Scripture, stood squarely within the Aristotelian philosophical tradition. Specifically, when Maimonides systematized philosophy in his original *Guide to the Perplexed* and law in his imitative *Mishneh Torah*, he misunderstood the fact that the law, for the Judaism of the Dual Torah, constitutes the medium for theological and philosophical reflection and expression. And that is the fact, even though at numerous specific examples, he introduced into the explanation or elucidation of the law philosophical considerations. All of these preliminary impressions await sustained clarification, but they do serve to place this project into perspective. In his separation of the presentation of law from philosophy, he tore apart what in the Mishnah had been inextricably joined in a lasting union, which was (and is) the law of that Judaism and both its theology and also its philosophy. Seeing the law in *Mishneh Torah* as a problem merely of organization and rationalization, Maimonides did not perceive that that same law contained within itself, and fully expressed, the very same principles of theology and philosophy that in the *Guide to the Perplexed* are invoked to define what we should call Judaism. Maimonides therefore did not grasp that the law in the very document that, in his (correct) judgment contained its classic formulation, that is, the Mishnah, also set forth precisely those principles of philosophy that, in Aristotle's system as Maimonides adapted it, would frame the proposed

How did this take place? Through the method of hierarchical classification, bits and pieces of data—undifferentiated, discrete facts without regard to the status or character or context of those facts—would gain sense and meaning. That same method then could and would determine the Mishnah's presentation of the facts of the law. This would take the form of a topical schematization of laws in such a way that coherent formations of data, in the form of well-composed lists, would impart the order of laws to the chaos of rules.[9] Lists by themselves order data in intelligible patterns, but, on their own, do not generate laws beyond themselves. Only analysis of the consequences of list-making does; that is the point at which the labor of generalization takes over from the work of systematization, and lists are transformed into the beginnings of series.

Dialectical analysis, for its part, served equally well in the quest for correct definitions (that is, governing principles or generalizations) of the virtuous and of the kosher.[10] Talmudic analysis of Mishnaic lists aims at the labor of systematization and generalization. And that analysis, when effective, takes the form of the dialectical, or moving, argument, a matter defined in philosophical terms in due course. That argument comes at the end of a long period of prior, critical thought of a philosophical character. Specifically, in

---

philosophy and theology of Judaism of *The Guide to the Perplexed*. Then, in the *Guide*, Maimonides (mis)represented philosophy and theology by divorcing them from their legal media of articulation, as though these could come to expression entirely outside the framework of the legal sources of Judaism. So the greatest scholar of the Mishnah of all time and the greatest Aristotelian Judaism has ever known misperceived the profound intellectual structure of the Mishnah. The reason for this error, in my view, is that Maimonides did not understand the deeply Aristotelian character of the Mishnah, which is the initial and definitive statement of the law of Judaism.

9. That is the argument of my *Judaism as Philosophy: The Method and Message of the Mishnah*.

10. Dialectics was the necessary choice for our sages, of blessed memory, considering the enormous heritage of contention and conflict and disharmony that the Mishnah and compilations of rules as well as free-floating statements of its period left them. How better receive these inconsistent norms than a mode of thought aiming at identifying inconsistency and defining with precision the encompassing categories and rules of a coherent order.

documents that reached closure long before the Talmud of Babylonia and that were utilized in the composition of that Talmud, arguments constructed along fairly commonplace philosophical principles made their way. For instance, moving from the known to the unknown by identifying the governing analogy—X is like Y, therefore, follows the rule of Y, X is unlike Y in the following aspect, so does not follow the rule of Y, the analogy falling away—represented a common mode of analytical argument. So, too, sorting out contradiction through the making of distinctions to explain difference will not have surprised participants in Rabbinic argument long before the Bavli came on the scene.

But the writers of those compositions and composites in the Bavli that go beyond the received modes of thought and argument and venture into dialectics of a very particular order—these are the ones who took over and recast the entire antecedent heritage of thought and the rules governing argument. Specifically, they took the static, systematic exchange of proposition and counter-proposition, argument and refutation, and turned it into a dynamic, sometimes meandering sequence of propositions, lacking the neatness of the received, neat exchange of positions and reasons for those provisions. For what marks the Bavli's mode of dialectics is the power of an argument to change course, the possibility of re-framing a position altogether in direct response to a powerful counter-argument.

Here we find not only the reasoned exchange of proposition, evidence, and argument, but the equally rational response to a good argument through a revision of the original, contrary position. When a player listens to what the other says and responds not by repeating, with better arguments and more compelling evidence, his original position, but by recasting his position all together, then we have that moving argument that stands for dialectics in its purest sense. For there we address the possibility of not merely refuting the position of the other, but even changing his mind. In other words, at its best,[11] the Talmud replicates in writing the actualities

---

11. The authentic dialectical argument in the Bavli is by no means the principal or even the predominant mode of composition; many of the compositions and

of real, everyday arguments, not merely the acting out, in rhetorical form of questions and answers, of set-piece positions. And that observation returns us to our interest in rhetoric, not only logic. For we see that approaching the replication of authentic, living argument, the Bavli's writers did well to hand on not the script for set-piece recitation of still-life positions—the fully articulated set-piece positions of the one side and the other, as in a philosophical dialogue—but notes for the reconstruction of the real-life conversation between—and among!—real people, actually listening to one another and taking account of what they were hearing on the spot.

Once we admit to the possibility that the players may change positions, the course of argument, not only its issues, takes over. Then (as Plato thought, and in the manner of Aristotle's main writings), the right rhetoric is required. Notes for the reconstruction of an argument prove the ideal medium of preserving thought—that is, notes in writing. There is no other way. If I had to choose an analogy out of the arts, I would compare the prior modes of writing—spelling it all out—to the notes by which music is preserved for replication.

I would further compare the Talmud's mode of writing—annotations that would guide the reconstruction of the action of thought—to the symbols by which the dance is preserved for re-enactment and renewal. The one is exact, the other approximate; both leave space for the performer's participation, but with an important difference. The composer writes down the notes out of what he hears in his head. In recording the ballet, the choreographer (counterpart to the composer) is the one who dances the dance, and then the recorder writes down the symbols that preserve on paper what the choreographer has already done. If we can imagine an orchestra playing music and only then writing it down, or a soloist-composer performing the music as he made it up (and there have been such, though not many), we can see the difficulty facing those who would write down, in advance, the *oeuvre* of

---

most of the composites of the Bavli undertake other tasks all together, as I have shown in *Talmudic Dialectics: Types and Forms.*

thought. And that act of imagination helps us account for the character of the Talmud's writing, a post-facto recording of the processes of thought to make possible others' progression through those same processes: not performance, but intellectual recapitulation, not replication, but reconstruction and renewal. The Talmud lives because it opens to us the intellectual life of those who lived it first, then wrote it down for us.

Accordingly, when we understand, in particular, the Talmud's dialectical argument, the rhetoric that encapsulates it, the analytical initiatives that drive it, the purposive program that sustains it, then we realize how our sages, of blessed memory, would frame the intellect of Israel in accord with the intellectual model of philosophy (including science) that through theological Christianity also was to define the West. Here then is how our sages of blessed memory would determine the necessary and sufficient way of making connections (natural history) and drawing conclusions (dialectics).

Why the Talmud Won

We come now to the problem in the history of ideas in medieval times that deserves some thought: Why, exactly, did the Talmud make its way from its completion onward? How come the document took over Judaism? I propose to answer the question by appeal to the substance of ideas, rather than circumstances of society, culture, or even economy. My sole unproved premise, as I shall explain, is that, in a world such as the medieval one, in which ideas governed, appeal to the character of ideas ought also to explain their consequences for the social order: People really took seriously the furniture of their minds and its arrangement.

Let me now spell out the problem. Through the centuries from the formal closure of the Talmud, in about 600 C.E. [A.D.], the Talmud formed the single authoritative writing of Judaism, the source of the theology and the law that defined the faith and the community of holy Israel, wherever they might be located. Enriched by commentaries, responsa, and law codes over the centuries, the Talmud defined the practical affairs of the community of Judaism. But because of its particular character, as the script for a sustained analytical argument, the Talmud further shaped the minds of those who mastered its modes of thought and, because of its profound sensibility, the document further imparted to those who responded to its teachings a character of intellectual refinement and personal responsibility, an alertness to the meaning of word and deed alike. No wonder, then, that the master of Talmudic learning, the disciple of sages in its native category, has defined the virtuous life for Judaic faithful, down to our own time. Because of its power to impart form and structure to the mind of holy Israel, its capacity to define the good and holy way of life for those who wished to be Israel, God's people, the Talmud enjoyed complete success in that various world to which its compilers or authors entrusted their work. Not many books can compete.

WHAT THE TALMUD ACCOMPLISHED

How did a document turn out to impart structure and order to an entire social order, wherever that order replicated itself across time and change? The authors of the compositions and compilers of the composites of the Talmud of Babylonia accomplished a goal that surely transcended their ambition. They proposed to make sense of the law, to discover the correspondence between everyday life and the rationality of the Torah. But the document that they brought into being—the Mishnah and Gemara together—turned out to make the definitive statement of the Torah, oral and written, that the world calls "Judaism." From the closure of the Talmud to our own day, the sages of Judaism found in the Talmud the starting point for all inquiry, the court of appeal for all contended questions. The written part of the Torah that the world knows as the Hebrew Scriptures or "Old Testament" would reach holy Israel through the Talmud. The oral portion of the Torah, initially written down in the Mishnah, would enjoy no independent existence, but, like the written part, would find its authoritative reading and interpretation in the Talmud. Law, theology, and the exegesis of Scripture—all three constitutive components of the Torah—found their classical formulation in the Talmud.

How, then, are we to find an explanation for the amazing success of the Talmud, which is to say, for its intellectual power? What is needed is a guide to not only how the principal normative documents of Rabbinic Judaism are to be read and reconstructed, but why they gained the remarkable influence that they exercised through the subsequent history of Judaism. Specifically, why did the Talmud work so well as to constitute one of history's most influential documents in the formation of that social order its writers wished to define? For few writings out of any age command a hearing later on, and fewer still define the curriculum of a culture the way the Talmud does. The sayings of Confucius, the Gita, the Dialogues of Plato and the writings of Aristotle, the Bible and the Quran, the great traditions of mathematics and philosophy—these formations of intellect (human or divine, as the case may be) form the counterparts. And, among them, the Talmud is the least appreciated for the remarkable success attained by its writers.

Here I do not investigate the after-life of the Talmud but offer only a single proposition for further speculation and testing. It seems to me plausible to argue that, if ideas have power to perpetuate themselves and extend their own influence, then the recapitulation of principal ideas of science and philosophy within the setting of ordinary affairs ought to account for the enduring capacity of the Talmud to define the holy life of Israel, the people. The Talmud formed in concrete terms an infinitely detailed and concrete statement of the abstract rationality that the West in general deemed self-evident—that is, the matching rationalities of science and philosophy. So, the Talmud served as the medium of inductive instruction in the universal modes of right thinking about workaday matters.

Then, to practice Judaism one entered into the disciplines of rationality that define the very ground of being for the West—the science and philosophy of Western civilization, formulated in clas

sical Greece and transmitted in Christian Rome. It was in that very
same intellectual context that the Talmud shaped the intellection
and rational intuition of Israel and so made of Israel not only a
kingdom of priests and a holy people, but a nation of scientists and
philosophers of the everyday. That is what this further hypothesis,
demanding investigation in its own terms for medieval and modern times, would propose. Those historians of ideas in medieval
and modern times interested in the interplay between religion and
society, ideas and the people who hold them, may find that
hypothesis worth further consideration.

Let me spell out the hypothesis that I cannot here demonstrate.
Sound explanation derives, I maintain, from the character of consciousness and conscience, the shape and structure of well-considered ideas, the coercive power of rationality. Politics, rather than
intellectual power, accounts for only a brief moment of a document's privilege. For the institutions of political power come and
go, none of them lasting very long. Politics defines an accident in
the life of ideas, much as a university president marks an accident
(possibly even a happy one!) in the life of a university. Politics does
not constitute the essential of the explanation of the power of an
idea or a mode of thought. Politics may be claimed to be necessary
in the process of explanation, but, I would maintain, it never is sufficient. In the end, for a writing to enjoy long-term readership, long
after the original political power and sponsorship have passed
from the scene, the document's own resources, its power to
demand attention and compel assent, take over.

Take the Mishnah, for instance, which, people generally suppose, gained its privilege by reason of its sponsor (supposedly:
author), Judah the Patriarch. The Mishnah, however it originated,
is alleged to have enjoyed the sponsorship of the governor of the
Jews of the Land of Israel (a.k.a. Palestine) with Roman support.
The same document, it appears from the Talmud, likewise was
treated as authoritative by the governor of the Jews of the Babylonian satrapy of the Iranian empire, the exilarch. The Romans long
since have gone their way, and Iranian rule of Babylonia (now part
of Iraq) ended with the Muslim conquest of that region. But the

Mishnah, whether with new political support or none at all, would command attention for long centuries to come. Hence, when we know how a document works, we also approach the question of why, over time, that same document would continue to compel future generations to accept its authority. It is, then, an authority of sound thinking and persuasive argument, a power of intellect, that I propose to explain.[12]

I propose to explain that fact by appeal specifically to the intellectual power of the document, not its utter originality—the main outlines of the paramount modes of argument can be identified in the Tosefta and Sifra. Rather, I point to two considerations. The first is its fresh and strong utilization of available media of thought and argument. The second is its introduction of the power of balanced argument, the energy of well-regulated contention. The great achievements in the intellectual arts flow not from originality mainly, but from the power to put together in a compelling manner what others may well know in a random manner. What attests to the power of the document and makes us want to know how, within its framework, the document dictates that we read it, is what happened to the Talmud but no other writing that reaches us from Judaic antiquity, except for Scripture.

Specifically, as we now realize, the Talmud was, and remains,

---

12. Those familiar with my inquiries from the early 1970s forward will find familiar that point of insistence upon unpacking the inner logical coherence of documents, their philosophical cogency (or lack of the same, in some cases), their intregity as intelligible and compelling statements. That point of insistence comes to expression in the documentary reading of the components of the Rabbinic canon, which I have formulated. In many ways, the present work moves along lines set forth twenty-five years ago, when I began my commentary to the Mishnah that takes the form of my *History of the Mishnaic Law* in forty-three volumes. A very brief introduction to the documentary method in Rabbinics, together with a bibliography of my other works on the subject, is in the opening chapter of *The Documentary Foundation of Rabbinic Culture: Mopping Up After Debates with Gerald L. Bruns, S. J. D. Cohen, Arnold Maria Goldberg, Susan Handelman, Christine Hayes, James Kugel, Peter Schaefer, Eliezer Segal, E. P. Sanders, and Lawrence H. Schiffman* (Atlanta, 1995: Scholars Press for South Florida Studies in the History of Judaism). I summarize the main lines of the results in my *Introduction to Rabbinic Literature* (New York, 1994: Doubleday, The Doubleday Anchor Reference Library, Religious Book Club Selection).

the privileged document of Judaism, accorded the standing of the principal writing of the Torah (a.k.a. Judaism), beyond Scripture itself but governing the reading even of Scripture. The Talmud of Babylonia from the moment of its closure at about 600 C.E. [= A.D.] served as the textbook of Judaism. For Judaism today, that same protean writing continues to provide the final and authoritative statement of the Torah revealed by God to Moses at Sinai. From it, truth flows; to it, doubts and dilemmas are referred. Its modes of thought govern, commentaries on it precipitate intellectual activity, decisions based upon its law and reached through the analytical argument dictated by its model, provoke reflection. It is the textbook for the holy Israel for whom its framers legislated. I propose to find in the power of Western philosophy embodied in its founding figures, Socrates-Plato and Aristotle, the answer to the question, how come?

So should I like to move from how the Talmud works to why the Talmud matters. It is because I take for granted—as do intellectuals and scholars in general at the commencement of their work—the principle that ideas bear social consequences. The ideas people hold both shape and also express the attitudes that animate their mind. Specifically, the kind of arguments they find compelling, the sort of language they find affecting, the modes of presenting problems and solving them that they find self-evidently valid, and the ways in which they make connections and draw conclusions— these matters of theory shape the structure of common practice. Conviction, formed in the crucible of intellect and argument, governs. Accordingly—so I assume as primary to all else—we may explain the culture of a group by appeal to formative modes of thought and authoritative propositions of unquestioned validity and truth, then we may ask: What intellectual qualities of the Talmud account for its power? And, it will follow, we may also raise the question, how does the Talmud, by reason of its distinctive program of thought—medium and message alike—bear relevance to the formation of culture even now?

The Talmud works through modes of thought and argument that for the West in general form the foundations of science and philosophy, which are (in this context) natural history and analytical dialectics. What makes the Talmud special, the power of the Talmud in particular, lies in its translation into concrete and everyday matters of the two most powerful intellectual components of Western civilization from its roots to our own time, science and philosophy, to review: [1] Aristotle's principles of knowledge and [2] Socrates' (Plato's) principles of rational inquiry and argument. The modes of scientific inquiry of the one and of reasoned analysis of the other are translated by the Talmud into everyday terms, so that the experience of the everyday is turned in to the academy for reasoned explanation of how things are: a book that turns concrete facts of the home and street into propositions of scientific interest and problems of philosophical inquiry.

The Talmud turns the world into a classroom, the holy people into disciples, and culture into a concrete exemplification of abstract and reliable truth. Here is the source of the Talmud's power: its capacity to hold together its two components, a philosophical law code, the Mishnah, which, in concrete ways, inculcates the principles of natural history, those of rational classification that Aristotle stated in abstract form; and a commentary to the Mishnah, called the Gemara, which, through the utilization of applied reason and practical logic, forms a moving ("dialectical") and analytical argument about the working of those principles in concrete cases. Therein, we now see, lies the continuing importance of the moving argument. Its open-endedness made it possible for successive generations to find themselves not merely invited, but empowered to join in the argument. So from age to coming age, Israel was to assume the disciplines of rational argument that the Talmud exemplifies. And the elite did, and ordinary folk honored those who did and imitated them. Then for what did "Jerusalem" come to stand, if not for Temple and priesthood in long centuries of transcendental mourning? "Jerusalem," which would stand for the full realization of the Torah's ideals in some place or other, came to mean, a town crowded with academies and peopled by disciples of our sages of blessed memory. And so, to realize the Torah in that profoundly intellectual sense, towns had to imitate Athens in the name of Jerusalem. So Talmudic Israel made itself into an academy without walls, an Athens beyond all boundaries of time and place, a new Jerusalem of rationality.

In both aspects, therefore, the document serves as the medium of inductive instruction in the principles of science and philosophy, which define the structure of the well-ordered society, and that is precisely what the document's writers—authors of its compositions, compilers of its composites—proposed to accomplish. Their very style forms a testament to the substance of their intent: let the talk go forward, let the argument begin.

When people not only pronounce opinions, but exchange ideas, each empowers the other. The participants offer their own views for the criticism of the other. But they also implicitly accept the judgment of the other upon their original pronouncements. Dialectics constitutes a form of mutual empowerment effected through shared rationality. Communities of intellect take shape, imparting to the social order a component of thought and enriching it with the possibilities of change through persuasion, not the legitimate coercion, only, of politics. The Gemara put forth for holy Israel a source of reasoned community that for all time would make of holy Israel a preserve of contentious argument in a world of inarticulate force. Its dialectics civilized Israel, the holy community and, the theologians would add, Israel then conformed to the model and the image of the God who created all being through reasoned speech. And that is why the Talmud won.